D0872712

COMMUNICATING
Christ
IN THE BUDDHIST WORLD

PAUL DE NEUI AND DAVID LIM, EDS.

COMMUNICATING *Christ*
IN THE BUDDHIST WORLD

WILLIAM CAREY
LIBRARY

Communicating Christ in the Buddhist World
Copyright © 2006 by SEANET

All rights reserved.
No part of this work may be reproduced or transmitted in any form or by any means—for example, electronic or mechanical, including photocopying and recording—without prior written permission of the publisher.

All scripture quotations, unless otherwise indicated, are taken from the Holy Bible, New International Version. ©1973, 1978, 1984 by the International Bible Society. Used by permission of Zondervan Publishing House.

Cover Design: Amanda Valloza
Copyediting, Typesetting: Paul H. De Neui, E. Kirsten Kronberg, Daniel G. Larson

Published by William Carey Library
1605 E. Elizabeth Street, Pasadena, California 91104
www.WCLBooks.com
William Carey Library is a ministry of the U.S. Center for World Mission, Pasadena, California.

Printed in the United States of America

Library of Congress Cataloging-in-Publication Data

Communicating Christ in the Buddhist world / Paul H. De Neui and David S. Lim, eds.
    p. cm.
Includes bibliographical references and index.
ISBN-13: 978-0-87808-510-1
ISBN-10: 0-87808-510-6
1. Missions to Buddhists. 2. Christianity and other religions--Buddhism. 3. Buddhism--Relations--Christianity. I. Lim, David (David S.) II. De Neui, Paul H.
BV2618.C66 2007
266.0088'2943--dc22
                    2006038144

CONTENTS

INTRODUCTION

We issue this book amidst the challenges arising from the resurgence of religions in the various nations of the post-modern world. As Islamic fundamentalism grabs the headlines, Buddhist fundamentalism has also been on the rise, particularly in Southeast Asia, mainly in reaction to the conversionist incursions of Islam and Christianity among them. Over the last thirty years, Buddhism has also seen growth in the West as its non-dogmatic rationality, offer of spiritual mentoring, and opportunity for personal transformation have made it attractive to post-modern society.

Are there both theological approaches as well as practical strategies for Evangelical Christians to use in our evangelization efforts among Buddhists—without adding any unnecessary problems to the increasing conflicts in the encounter of religions? We believe there are.

This is the fourth volume in the series that have been produced from the papers presented at a Missiological Forum held annually by SEANET in Chiang Mai, Thailand. All the authors consider themselves to be writing as Evangelical mission theologians and practitioners. The first four chapters reflect on the theological framework by which Christians can fulfill the biblical mandate to evangelize and transform peoples. The next five chapters consider the significant sociological issues that have arisen in the Christian encounter with Buddhist peoples. And the last three suggest some strategic ways forward for effective evangelization in the Buddhist world.

This work follows three others, entitled *Sharing Jesus in the Buddhist World*, *Sharing Jesus Holistically with the Buddhist World*, and *Sharing Jesus Effectively in the Buddhist World*, all published by William Carey Library. All these books are good resources for those committed to the evangelization and transformation of peoples and nations in the Buddhist world. In an effort to make the information and resources in this newest volume more accessible to researchers and practitioners a topical index has been included.

We thank Paul H. De Neui and Kang-San Tan for facilitating the fourth forum. We thank Steve Spaulding, David Lim and Alex G. Smith who helped coordinate the SEANET conference. Special thanks to E. Kirsten Kronberg and Daniel G. Larson who helped untiringly with the details of editing, formatting, and indexing to produce the final camera ready copy. We also thank Suzanne Harlan of William Carey Library and the editorial staff for making this publication available in the most efficient way.

May this book challenge the international Christian community to better ways of relating with and approaching people of other faiths!

Paul H. De Neui, Ph.D.
Chicago, Illinois, U.S.A.

David S. Lim, Ph.D.
Quezon City, Philippines

CONTRIBUTORS

Bailey, Stephen K. Ph.D., Fuller Theological Seminary, Associate Professor of Missiology, Alliance Theological Seminary, Director of Alliance Graduate School of Mission, Nyack, New York, Senior Associate for the Institute for Global Engagement.

De Neui, Paul H. Ph.D., Fuller Theological Seminary, Visiting Assistant Professor of World Mission, North Park Theological Seminary, Chicago, IL, Missionary, Evangelical Covenant Church, Thailand.

Johnson, Alan R. Ph.D., Oxford Centre for Mission Studies/ University of Wales, Missionary Assembly of God, Thailand.

Lim, David S. Ph.D., Theology (NT), Fuller Theological Seminary, Executive Director of China Ministries International– Philippines; President of Asian School for Development, Director of Cross-cultural Studies, Manila, Philippines.

Mejudhon, Ubonwan. D.Miss., Asbury Theological Seminary. Co-pastor, Muang Thai Church, Bangkok, Co-director, Cross-Cultural Training Center, Bangkok, Thailand.

Minick, Russell. M.Div., M.A., Southeastern Baptist Theological Seminary. Strategy Coordinator, International Mission Board.

Somaratna, G.P.V. Ph.D., South Asian History, University of London; Senior Research Professor, Colombo Theological Seminary, Sri Lanka.

Smith, Alex G. D.Miss., Fuller Theological Seminary. Missionary, Overseas Missionary Fellowship, Thailand.

Tan, Kang-San. D.Min., Missiology, Trinity International University, USA. Head of Mission Studies, Redcliffe College, United Kingdom.

Vasanthakumar, Michael S. Th.M., British Open University. Director, Tamil Bible Research Centre, London.

Wagner, Paul. Missiologist practitioner living in Buddhist Southeast Asia.

.

PART I

THEOLOGICAL ISSUES

1

LIFE EXEGESIS

Ubolwan Mejudhon

This article is a product of a thirty-year quest for theories and methods of exegeting the Word of God in the Third World context. I remember learning the western ways of exegesis from a great teacher. I spent week after week digging through the gospel of John and the Minor Prophets. After putting forth my best effort in class, I was rewarded with an "A." But something was missing in my heart. My head was so big, yet my heart remained empty. As a result, I had constant headaches and my blood pressure shot up very high. I wondered if I had any hidden sins that prevented me from enjoying Jesus while performing the western ways of exegesis. I could not understand the feelings I was having. I was confused. I thought I should experience joy while exegeting the living Word of God. I longed to find my Lord and Savior in my exegesis.

Ten years ago I conducted research in order to understand how my people, the Thai, learn religion. The research showed that there is a great chasm between western ways of learning religion and ways of learning religion in the Third World context. This understanding helped shape my ideas, theories and methods into a life exegesis for the Third World context. Over the last two years I have extensively practiced life exegesis, both in my church as well as in many other churches. People have responded very positively.

Despite the positive response to my use of life exegesis, writing this article is a risky endeavor for me. I realize that some

2

fundamentalist Christians, as well as narrative theologians may be suspicious. "Can any good thing come from Thailand, especially from a female believer?" However, I know it is important for the whole world to hear a voice of a Third World believer about exegesis. I believe my Savior is leading me to write this article, and many Thai and western believers have encouraged me in this project. So with fear and trembling, and with a great conviction, I proceed.

In the following pages I will present both what life exegesis is and what it is not. The first part will provide an overview of life exegesis. In the second part I will present the theoretical framework of life exegesis in theology, anthropology, religious study, psychology, and communication. In the third part I will illustrate life exegesis by exegeting Acts 3:1-26 in the form of a sermon. I will then provide concluding thoughts.

LIFE EXEGESIS

It happened one Sunday after preaching at a Chinese Church in Bangkok, Thailand. An elder of the church graciously offered to drive me back to my church. I wondered why he was so kind to a female preacher like me. As soon as we settled into the car, he eagerly asked a question, "Did you really receive a doctoral degree?" I smiled and nodded my head and asked him what prompted him to ask such a question. I was stunned by his answer. "Most Ph.D. preachers preach above our heads. I wondered what made me understand your sermon." I laughed and told him that it certainly was not that I was smart. I wanted to tell him that I did life exegesis together with concept exegesis, followed by inductive preaching. However, that day I was too tired to talk about difficult things, so I kept quiet about the reasons he understood my sermon.

I developed life exegesis during my thirty years of ministry among the Thai people. I would like to explain what life exegesis is not. First, life exegesis is not against the traditional way of exegesis: concept exegesis, which leads to systematic theology. Robert J. Schreiter proposed mapping a local theology as an important guideline of contextual theology (1984:25). He emphasized the importance of church tradition. To some extent I agree with him. But I believe that people who live in the Third World context will best understand and experience Jesus through the Word of God if we exegete lives in the Bible before we exegete concepts. In short, I think Christians in the Third World should learn about life theology before they learn systematic theology. People in the Third World context believe strongly in oral tradition. They understand the dynamic God more than the mechanic God. Moreover the dynamic God also helps them understand the mechanic God of westerners. They want to know both ways.

Secondly, life exegesis is not narrative theology, though I elucidate an important role of narrativity in life exegesis. Eric Snow explained the concept of narrative theology, in *Religion Online*, as follows:

> Narrative theology is a system of interpreting the Bible subjectively, according to the perspective of any group of readers or particular reader. Hence, the scriptures will have different meanings manufactured by different readers according to their own individual perspectives and biases.

William C. Placher discussed Hans Frei, a renowned theologian at Yale who was sometimes credited with founding a school called narrative theology. Plachar pointed out that Frei always doubted that there was such a thing.

> He thought the narrative character of the biblical texts had some implications for how those texts ought to be interpreted. But to try to develop some general theory of the narrative shape of human experience as a foundation for Christian theology seemed to him "first to put the cart before the horse and then cut the lines and pretend the vehicle is self-propelled" (2002:8).

I agree with Frei. Narrativity seems to be a mode of communication more than a mode of theology. Narrativity helps people think and draw out some concepts by themselves. However, those concepts are still under the scope of systematic theology. Life exegesis allows people to do the application. In life exegesis I let people learn about life and concepts. They then make their own application within a framework.

I understand that systematic theology is the work of modernity. Modernity puts everything in order. It is the world of either/or. The world is now shifting towards post-modernity as a sort of rebellion against modernity. Knowledge is no longer for knowledge's sake. Rather, knowledge is for usage. Post-modern people prefer flexibility, unity out of disunity. Christians should be aware of this changing context. We should be willing to adapt to the world, yet be true to the world.

Life exegesis exegetes life in the biblical stories, laws, discourses and concepts. I use story exegesis and methodical Bible study as tools. I also use knowledge of Jewish culture and Christian psychology. Life exegesis draws together interpretation and preparation of sermons and lesson plans into one process. In addition, life exegesis is learner-centered. The learner does the application.

Theoretical Framework

The theoretical frameworks of life exegesis consist of the theory of contextualization of theology, the theory of the cultural context, an analysis of a story, inductive Bible studies, knowledge of the Jewish culture, discipline of psychology and a theory of inductive preaching and teaching. The framework at large of life exegesis is shown in the chart below.

Life exegesis =

Contextual theology
+
Cultural context
+
Analysis of stories
+
Inductive Bible studies
+
Jewish culture
+
Psychology
+
Inductive preaching and teaching

Placher stated in his book, *A History of Christian Theology*, that before modernity most Christian theologians had read the Bible as a kind of realistic narrative. Around the eighteenth century they began to read the Bible differently. He also pointed out how philosophies in each era affected the interpretation of the Bible.

Scholars who presented a report of a consultation on gospel and culture in The Willowbank Report suggested that there were three approaches to interpreting the Bible:

Traditional Approach

The most common way is to come straight to the words of the biblical text, and to study them without any awareness that the writer's cultural context differs from that of the reader. The reader interprets the text as if it had been written in his own language, culture, and time.

Historical Approach

The second approach takes with due seriousness the original historical and cultural context. It seeks also to discover what the text meant in its original language, and how it relates to the rest of scripture. The weakness of this historical approach, however, is that it fails to consider what scripture may be saying to the contemporary reader.

Contextual Approach

A third approach begins by combining the positive elements of both the popular and the historical approaches. It takes seriously the cultural context of the contemporary readers as well as of the biblical text, and recognizes that a dialogue must develop between the two (1978:6-7).

Life exegesis uses the contextual approach. The authors of The Willowbank Report also emphasized that the task of understanding the scriptures belongs not just to individuals but to the entire Christian community. I agree with the authors of The Willowbank Report. Through preaching in various local churches in Thailand, and through writing, I have tested my theoretical framework concerning an Asian way of biblical interpretation. Many Thai Christians agree that my sermons and writings present in an intelligible manner the words of God, and that my work is applicable to the Thai worldview. Also, since 1998 I have presented my ideas and examples of an Asian way of biblical interpretation to hundreds of missionaries throughout Thailand. They have responded positively to my presentations and have repeatedly asked me how I did it. Therefore this paper is a call for response and reaction, from the community of faith at large, to my Asian way of interaction.

I also use the exegesis of the Thai cultural context in forming my theoretical framework. I studied Thai personalities and values from Suntaree Komin's research, *Psychology of the Thai People: Values and Behavior Pattern*. Komin pointed out that the Thai are first and foremost ego-oriented. They are characterized by the highest ego value. Thai people use the Thai way of meekness to avoid confrontation in order to maintain smooth relationships and to protect their identity. As a result, in order to avoid confrontation the Thai individual uses indirect ways of communication to soften negative assertion. Thai people use a lot of folktales, proverbs, mottos and stories to communicate their ideas.

My research, *The Way of Meekness: Being Thai and Christian in the Thai Way*, yielded an important theory about the ways the Thai learn religion: (1) religion is affective; (2) religion is applicable to the present felt needs; (3) religion is practical, solving life's problems; (4) religion emphasizes rituals, ceremonies, and festival; (5) religion has integrative functions; (6) religion is concretely experiential; (7) religion is bonding; and (8) religion does not force faith.

Thai personality emphasizes the important role of narrativity in religious learning. Buddhism explains Buddhist theology through stories in *Kuttakanikai Jataka*. Narratives are the primary form of communicating the truth in Buddhism. I believe this is true in all cultural contexts that cherish relationships. Since the scripture was born in the womb of the Third World context, I tend to believe that God uses stories to convey his ideas to his people. Wesley A. Kort affirms this idea:

> Is narrative a derivative and secondary form of discourse, or is it primary and originating? Of course, no final answer can be given to such questions, but it is important to understand that we tend to assume that narrative is derivative and secondary. There are compelling epistemological reasons for this assumption. We should recognize them in order to entertain the notion that narrative may be the primary and originating form of discourse (1985:2).

Kort also suggested that narrativity always implies textuality. Textuality always implies narrativity.

In life exegesis, contextual theology and local cultural context are the conceptual frameworks of life exegesis shown in the figure below.

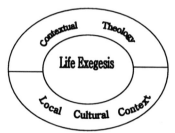

Figure 1: Conceptual Framework of Life Exegesis

Now I will explain the practical framework of life exegesis. How should we interpret a story? While there are many ideas from numerous writers, I use Warne's suggestion as my framework in interpreting a story. Clifford Warne was a renowned Christian writer and storyteller who visited Thailand many years ago. In addition to my learning much from him, through his teaching, my personal ministry was transformed in many ways. During his time in Thailand, Warne told me how to analyze a story. He pointed out that every plot in any story consists of the following important elements: context, conflict, climax and a turning point. In his book, *The 'Magic' of Story-Telling,* Warne explained that there are three types of stories: (a) the accomplishment story: a person struggles to solve a problem or achieve a purpose; (b) the decision story: a person struggles with forces for or against, which influence his decision; and (c) the theme story: a person struggles to realize a truth of vital importance of his living. He explains:

> David's struggle to bring down the Philistine giant is an accomplishment story…When the judge has to decide guilty or not guilty, when the girl must choose between the rich, old man and the poor young man, when the hero choose between liberty and death, there's a decision story…When a man realizes that you must look before you "elope"…When a young fellow finds out that beauty is only skin deep…When someone learns that he who hesitates gets bumped in the rear, there's a theme story (1971:14-16).

Warne also explains conflict in a story:

> Conflict is the heartbeat of a story. Stories just can't do without it. Conflict comes in many forms…The first basic conflict is man against man…The second basic conflict is between man and his conscience…The third basic conflict is man's struggle against the forces of nature…Often storytellers combine the conflict of man against nature with the conflict of man against man or man against his conscience…other forms of conflicts are man against

God, man against tradition, and man against beast.
There's also beast against beast (1971:24-28).

Warne proposed that there is suspense in every good story.
Suspense is the state of worry whether the main character will solve
the problem or not. Writers increase suspense until the story reaches
its climax. Writers create suspense when the main character meets
complications while trying to solve the problem. First there is the
time limit. Another limitation to add suspense is limited possible
solutions to the problem. Common fears can stimulate suspense.
Another suspense trick is to take something normally pleasant and
make it an unexpected menace.

Warne suggested that the best way to bring any characters to life
in a story is by using dialogue. Dialogue gives information about
plot and character. Warne suggested that motivation is the most
important part of characterization. We have to question why the
characters in a story act and react the way they do. He suggested,
"If you read and tell Bible stories, get into the habit of looking for
the reasons behind everything the characters say and do" (1971:45).

Warne also told us how to exegete a Bible story as follows:

> When you adapt a Bible story, take a separate sheet of
> paper for each character. On top of the page put the
> character's name. Then list everything he does, hears,
> sees, and feels. Put down every action and reaction.
> Then go back and note why he did all this. Find his
> motives. Write down the reasons for all his behaviors.
> Check when this happened and where this happened.
> Does this direct you to any other information about the
> characters or the plot? You should now have as many
> sheets of paper as there are characters in the story.
> Each page tells you who, what, where, when, and why
> about one character. Study these characters. Get to
> know them. See the story through their eyes. Is there

any other source of information about them? Check it. Does it help you see the character more clearly? Do you understand him? Decide from whose viewpoint it's best to tell the story. What does this character do at the moment of climax? Does he accomplish it? What's his problem? What must he have? Why can't he have it? Who or what stands in his way? Identify the conflict. What does he do about the opposition? What complications arise? What showdown does it lead to? Does he get what he wants? Make a story outline. Plan the scenes. Build each scene to a climax which makes the audience want to hear more. Plot the final scene and climax. Now go back and write the dialogue for each scene. Then fill in the narration.

The next set of questions show any weaknesses in your story. Use them as a checklist and you'll save much time and effort. What is the background of each character? What's his or her relationship to the other characters? Do any characters undergo changes towards other characters? What causes these changes? What causes the problem? Where and when does the conflict begin? Are each character's motives clear, strong, and convincing? What devices are used to get us to like the goodies and hate the baddies? Does the introduction capture immediate interest? Does it arouse curiosity? Is the information in the introduction clear? Who? When? Where? Does the opening promise conflict? How do you create and introduce suspense? How do you hold and increase suspense right up to the climax? Does the dialogue carry the story forward? Does it reveal information about plot and character? Is the dialogue alive with emotion? Does the dialogue have point and emotion? Is the story contrived or depending on circumstance? Have you appealed to the senses using sound, color and smell to picture a scene or create mood and atmosphere? And the all important questions: Who are the audience? Is the story for men, women or children? Or a general audience? If it's a children story, is it for seniors, juniors, or the kindergarten? What do you hope to do? Entertain? Teach? Persuade? Get action? Does the story make clear the message you want to communicate? (1971:47-50)

Warne mingled the process of exegesis with the process of delivering the message. He confirmed my theory that the process of interpretation should also include the process of delivering the message.

Life exegesis also utilizes methodical bible study by Robert A Triana, and David I. Thompson's *Bible Study that Works* as tools in interpreting the scripture. Triana's methodical bible study is the classic tool for inductive Bible study. Thompson studied under Triana and I studied under Thompson. I struggled to observe the content and the structure in each individual's work. After twenty years, however, it dawned on me that structures hint at important themes in each passage. I think both of my professors were wonderful scholars. They were ahead of their time. Triana emphasized the psychological factor in interpretation. He elucidated his idea as follows:

> Since human experience transcends its literary expression, the true exposition of the scriptures will search for more than their linguistic phenomena. He will look for emotions, desires, hopes, motives, thoughts, attitudes. He will make the object of his quest the disclosure of the self-consciousness of Biblical authors and characters. He will see beyond the symbols to the reality, namely, the experience of which Scriptural literature is but the product and the means of conveyance (1981:154).

Thomson emphasized the role of culture in interpreting the scripture. He elicited interpretation according to the deep meaning so that Christians can learn from the past and apply the thematic concepts to the present situation. While I agree with him, I also allow my audience to do the applications within the framework of life exegesis. Preachers and teachers become learners in the application of life exegesis. Application becomes two-way communication.

The knowledge of Jewish culture and the discipline of psychology also help the interpretation of the Bible to the postmodern world. Since scripture was written in the Jewish context, when exegeting a biblical story I also research the Jewish cultural context. Studying the Jewish context helps me understand the worldview, values, behavior patterns and expressions of the Jewish. In addition it helps me understand Jewish family concepts.

I utilize some excellent books which discuss Jewish culture such as *Understanding the Difficult World of Jesus: New Insight From a Hebraic Perspective* by David Blain and Roy Blizzard, *Jesus the Jewish Theologian* by Brad H. Young, *Joshua: A Guide to Real Jesus and the Original Church* by Ron Moseley and *Our Father Abraham: Jewish Roots of the Christian Faith* by Marvin R. Wilson. Some insights from these books will help one understand the benefits gained from the study. Some extracts are quoted below. Wilson wrote:

> To the Hebrew mind, everything is theological. That is, the Hebrew makes no distinction between the sacred and the secular areas of life. They see all of life as a unity. It is all God's domain. He has a stake in all that comes to pass whether trials or joys (1985:156).

Wilson pointed out that Jews were energetic people and their language was descriptive. Moseley explained many Hebrew expressions in the New Testament. One example is shown below:

> The final concept is contained within the terms "good eye" and "bad eye," which Jesus used in Matthew 6:22-23. These were popular terms in ancient Judaism, but are often misunderstood by modern readers. In first century Judaism the term "good" or "single eye" (*ayin tovah*) meant that a person was generous. The "bad" or "evil eye" (*aiyin ra'ah*) meant he was stingy (1996:28-29).

Blain and Blizzard argued that the Synoptic Gospels were of Hebrew origin. They explained:

> One of the best indications of the Hebrew origin of the Synoptic Gospels is to be found within the texts of the Gospels themselves. The Hebraic undertext is revealed not only in sentence structure but in the many literalisms and idioms present, which are peculiar to the Hebrew language. An inability to recognize these Hebraisms has caused much difficulty in the interpretation and understanding of many of the saying of Jesus (1994:53).

Young explained that understanding of Hebrew expressions would help Christians understand Hebrew origin of many expressions in the New Testament. He used "suffers violence" as an example:

> The prophets functioned until John, but now God's kingdom "suffers violence." As we will see, instead of "suffers violence," the action words "the kingdom of heaven breaks forth" are much closer to the original meaning of the text (1995:48).

The knowledge of Hebrew culture will help us understand the ideas, feeling, attitude and belief systems of Jewish people during the Old Testament and the New Testament.

I also use the discipline of psychology to help dig into the personalities of biblical characters. It helps one understand, for example, why Abraham was a man of action but Isaac was rather passive. This discipline helps us understand human reactions to crisis and the uses of symbols in the human belief system.

David Keirsey and Marilyn Bates, who wrote *Please Understand Me: Character and Temperament Types,* help me understand sixty character and temperament types. Biblical characters had lived long before their life stories were recorded. Each character must own one of these character and temperament types. *Honoring the Self: Self Esteem and Personal Transformation* by Nathanial Branden helps me understand more about human identity. Roberta M. Bilbert's *Extraordinary Relationships: a New Way of Thinking about Human Interactions* expands my understanding of various perspectives of relationships. *Death and Dying,* by Elisabeth Kubler-Ross, explains the five progressive stages people go through when facing traumatic crises: denial, anger, bargaining, depression, and acceptance.

In *Jung and the Bible,* Wayne G. Rollins gives various Jungian ideas: Jungian Approach to Biblical Interpretation, God, the Bible, and the Self in Jungian Perspective. I like what Rollins quoted in his book about Jung's idea of spiritual renewal:

> The psychopathology of the masses is rooted in the psychology of the individual, Jung was convinced, and "if the individual is not truly regenerated in spirit, society cannot be either, for society is the sum total of individuals in need of redemption." What is required is "a complete spiritual renewal" (1981:40).

The final piece of the theoretical framework of life exegesis relates to the preparation and delivery of sermons. In my article, *Evangelism in the New Millennium: An Integrated Model of Theology, Anthropology and Religious Studies* (2002), I elicited that Thai Buddhist religious learning is progressive. Therefore, in life exegesis I also include the process of preparing and delivering sermons related to biblical exegesis. Walter C. Kaiser, Jr. had voiced his concern in this area as quoted below:

> I feel there is one place where I have a special debt to the Church which I must discharge. I have been aware for some time now of a gap that has existed in academic preparation for the ministry. It's the gap that exists between the study of the Biblical text (most frequently in the original languages of Hebrew, Aramaic, and Greek) and the actual delivery of messages to God's people (1981:8).

I use *Inductive Preaching* by Ralph L. Lewis and Gregg Lewis as my main theoretical framework for the delivery of sermons. I studied under Lewis from 1983-1984. I have never forgotten his teaching about inductive preaching. He pointed out that Jesus preached inductively:

> Jesus doesn't start the Sermon on the Mount with a declaration of the importance of listening to his words or with a threat for those who don't listen. He doesn't start with his declared conclusion, but leads his hearers with the reasonableness of his beatitudes and analogies, his comparisons and contrasts to a place of choice. At the end of the sermon he offers them a decision, to heed and be wise or to ignore his words and be foolish. And once that point of decision is reached, Jesus allows the people to draw their own conclusions. Jesus, here on the Mount and in other

teachings, begins with the known, the concrete, the personal to guide hearers to the unknown, the abstract and the universal (1985:70-71).

Lewis also suggested a strategy for making traditional sermon structures inductive. It is a must for every serious preacher to read pages 218-220 in his book.

Now I have demonstrated to you that story exegesis, inductive Bible studies, Jewish culture, discipline of psychology and inductive preaching (teaching) are practical frameworks of life exegesis (see figure 2). Figure 3 explains the theories of detail processes involved in doing life exegesis.

Figure 2: Practical Framework of Life Exegesis

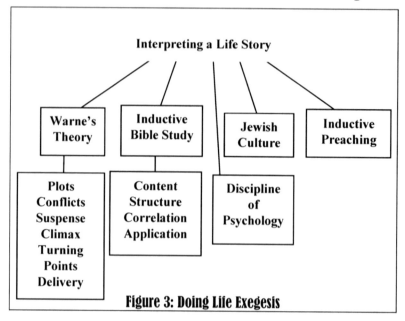

Interpreting a Life Story

| Warne's Theory | Inductive Bible Study | Jewish Culture | Inductive Preaching |

| Plots Conflicts Suspense Climax Turning Points Delivery | Content Structure Correlation Application | Discipline of Psychology |

Figure 3: Doing Life Exegesis

An Illustration

I will now demonstrate how to do a life exegesis and sermon from Acts 3:1-26. I will begin with an analysis of the structure and the main content of the passage, followed by a brief inductive sermon of Acts 3:1-26.

As I study Acts 3:1-26, I see the structure of cause and effect. The healing of the lame man leads Peter to preach the gospel. The miracle at the Beautiful Gate is a means to an end. The miracle is an excellent combination of the Great Commission and the commandment to love. It is an important theology of evangelism for the post-modern world. As for a structure that applies to one's daily living, I find that, as believers of our Lord Jesus, our lives are surely means to an end. The end of our lives is to glorify him in all situations. Lives emit bitterness, frustration, resentment and anger if we look at life as an end in itself.

As for the content, Acts 3:1-26 indicates many kinds of conflicts involving the lame man. He probably has conflicts with himself, and with Peter and Jesus because of his handicap. The passage also alludes to an obscure person who kindly carries the lame man to the Beautiful Gate everyday. The passage also illustrates a transformed Peter and the lame man. The story flows through conflict after conflict to reach the climax of the situation when Peter refuses to give the man any money. The turning point comes in the second part of Peter's sentence, after which the sad atmosphere turns to joy. Following the lame man's healing, Peter takes the opportunity to preach the gospel of Jesus.

The details of the life exegesis of Acts 3:1-26 will now be presented in the form of an inductive sermon.

Life as a Means to an End

I once heard about an interesting missionary to Africa. He was about to leave from his hometown to board a ship at Liverpool. He happened to fall off the train while he waved to his parents. Tragically, the train cut off his right leg. He was frustrated by this event but remained faithful to his calling. He did go to Africa with one artificial leg that he could take off and put on as he liked. As he left his station to travel deep into a jungle, he was caught by a group of cannibals. They were very happy that they had a special dinner. The whole tribe tied the missionary to a big totem. They danced with great joy around the missionary and the waiting gigantic pot of boiling water. The missionary could not take it any more! God had failed him and had taken away his right leg! And now, as the cannibals were about to take his life, God did not even help him! In great distress the missionary used one of his free hands to screw off his artificial leg. He then threw the leg at the chieftain's head, hitting it very hard. The chieftain's pain and surprise quickly turned to reverence, and he suddenly knelt down. He cried, "God has visited us. Only God can take off his leg. Untie the God." The whole tribe worshiped the missionary. However, the missionary told them to worship the only God, Jesus Christ. Later on, the whole tribe knew Jesus and the missionary knew that his life was a means to an end.

The lame man at the Beautiful Gate knew the same thing at long last. At first he probably had problems with his Creator who allowed him to be lame from his birth. He became a living dead man in his neighbors' sight. We do not know his name. Perhaps he was not important because he was very poor. He probably had conflicts with Jesus. A kind person carried him to sit at the Beautiful Gate where Jesus passed in and out. The lame man and that anonymous person knew that Jesus healed many lame people. Perhaps one day it would be his turn. That day never came. Both of them heard that Jesus was crucified. The hope of the lame man had come to an end. Still those kind hands carried him to the Beautiful Gate so that he could beg. His life had to go on though he could not understand why Jesus did not care about him. He perhaps heard the rumor that Jesus was raised from death. But Jesus had not revisited the temple. But his disciples did. Scripture records the event as follows:

> And when he saw Peter and John about to go into the temple, he began asking to receive alms. And, Peter along with John, fixed his gaze upon him and said, "Look at us!" And he began to give them his attention,

expecting to receive something from them. But Peter said, "I do not possess silver and gold" (Acts 3:3-6a).

What a disaster for the lame man! He might expect that Jesus' disciples would compensate his master's unkindness toward him with some alms. Listening to half of the sentence the lame man might say to himself, "Peter, you don't need to say that. I know you have nothing, just nothing indeed for me…" Then Peter continued to speak, saying:

> "But what I do have I give to you: In the name of Jesus Christ the Nazarene—walk!" And seizing him by the right hand, he raised him up; and immediately his feet and his ankles were strengthened. And with a leap, he stood upright and began to walk; and he entered the temple with them, walking and leaping and praising God (Acts 3:6b-8).

Many times Christians listen to only half of sentences. Some walk only half of the way. Quite a few Christians finish just half of the jobs they undertake. A lot of Christians have this kind of perspective towards life, a halfway perspective, and their lives become the ends in themselves.

That day the lame man reconciled with his God and Savior. He understood now the reason behind his lameness. He was lame so that he could give glory to his Creator. He knew now that Jesus cared and Jesus was raised from the dead. Jesus lived in his believers' lives. That day Peter learned that he cared less for what he did not have but he was so proud of what he had, Jesus Christ, his Lord and Savior.

It is interesting to think about the obscure person who faithfully carried the lame man to the Beautiful Gate. Without him the miracle couldn't take place by Jesus' disciples and Peter couldn't preach the powerful gospel to the masses. I cannot be Peter, but I can, like the lame man's helper, easily be kind hands which reach out to the needy and the marginal. I want to shake hands with that person when I meet him or her in the future. I also learn that the commandment to love must go with the great commission in evangelism. People no longer care how much I know about Jesus but they want to know how much I care like Jesus.

What did you learn from this story? Please kindly share it. I can apply the story from my perspective and personal experiences. But if all of you share from your own perspectives and experiences your application of the passage, we can see a more holistic picture of the passage. (I let the listeners share for five minutes. After that I conclude the story with a story).

Readers' Digest (2004) reported about Betty Ferguson who found out that her life was a means to an end after her beloved daughter Debbie was killed. Debbie was murdered by her English teacher in 1975 without a clear reason or motive. Betty said her life was overwhelmed with hatred. She suffered severe aches and became addicted to alcohol. Betty also ignored her other four children. In 1981, a verse in a prayer book spoke to her. "Please forgive those who have wronged me."

Betty began reading many books about forgiving. She felt that forgiving might solve her personal problems. She visited Debbie's grave. The wording on the tombstone repeatedly spoke to her heart, "What the world needs is love and sweetness." Soon Betty kept speaking, "I am willing to forgive Ray," many times a day. Less than one year later she wrote to Ray, "I give up hating you. I will go to see you and tell you about my journey."

In 1986, Betty visited Ray in the prison. She told him her love for Debbie. She shared her broken heart and the greatest loss she had ever had. They wept together. When Betty came back she experienced transformation within. She was a new person with a gentle heart and loving-kindness. Most importantly, she felt a great liberty. Now she is a government official who works with victims of severe crimes. Betty said, "My healing is so powerful and it saved my life." If Betty's suffering was an end in itself, Betty's life would have ended differently. Betty had found out that life was a means to an end. That end is glorifying Him in all situations. When we do this, we will find that His will is our greatest joy. Betty found it. The lame man experienced it and we can learn from them too.

Conclusion

I have explained in this article that life exegesis is not opposed to the classical method of exegesis. However, it also cannot be classified as narrative theology. Rather, life exegesis enhances the classical methods of exegesis by adding to them the theories and methods of exegeting lives in scripture. Also, life exegesis includes the theories and methods of preparing inductive sermons. Life exegesis derives from the Asian context which elucidates oral tradition, narration, and lives rather than concepts. I believe that Christians in the Third World context should learn to exegete lives and stories before they learn to perform western methods of exegesis because this more appropriately fits their worldviews, values and ways of learning about Jesus. Life exegesis will help people in the Third World context easily understand Jesus, who was also born in the Third World context. Perhaps life exegesis will also help western believers to appreciate Jesus, as He is known in the Asian context. As a result of utilizing these theories and methods, scripture will become life experiences instead of a mere academic search for truth.

2

GENESIS 1-11 AND BUDDHIST SCRIPTURES: HOW THE GOSPEL CAN TRANSFORM BUDDHIST WORLDVIEWS

Kang-San Tan

Serving and living among Buddhists in Asia, I became aware that Christian mission has had little success (qualitatively as well as quantitatively) in developing indigenous communities in countries such as Thailand, Laos, Vietnam, and Japan. After two centuries of Protestant missionary work, Christian populations remain only one or two percent in most major Buddhist countries such as Thailand, Japan and Sri Lanka. Some writers have argued against past evangelical's tendencies to misrepresent Buddhism through caricatures and negative attacks (for example Paul J. Griffiths 1994, Harold Netland 1994). On the other hand, pluralistic western approaches tend to discuss Buddhism as a theory that is alien to the heartlands of practicing Buddhists in Asia. Efforts by Christian pluralists to merge Buddhism with Christianity were happily matched by Buddhist writers such as Thich Nhat Hanh and Dalai Lama.

I define interfaith encounter as an inter-religious conversation whereby both Christians and Buddhists desire to witness to their faiths as well as listen and learn from the neighbor's faith. Worldview can be said to be "a set of shared framework of ideas of a particular society concerning how they perceive the world" (Burnett 1990:13). In focusing on worldview transformation,

Christian mission is concern with neither conversion nor the formation of indigenous Christian communities in Buddhist lands but rather that the gospel truly transform society through new ways of being human. The new humanity ("third race") bears witness through willingness to suffer for Christ and reaching out in loving service for those in need. Within the limits of this paper, I will use the biblical themes in Genesis 1-11 to engage with dominant Buddhist beliefs as presented in specific Buddhist writings and doctrines. Similarities and differences will be discussed and evaluative criteria proposed. Based on these discussions, I will offer key programmatic agendas for evangelical missions interested in deeper worldview encounters with Buddhist beliefs.

Buddhism: A Global Religion?

Buddhism is never as weak as it appears, and never as strong as it appears
(adapted Russian adage).

Before we look at the creation account in Genesis, we need to briefly locate the world of Buddhism today. There is no country in Asia which has not been influenced at one time or another by Buddhism. It can be said that Buddhism has been the prime inspiration behind many Asian civilizations. With regional economic cooperation and migration trends in Asia, mutual cooperation and intra-dialogues within various Buddhist traditions will increase. At the Third Global Congress on Buddhism held in Singapore in June 2004 almost all major Buddhist traditions were represented.

Buddhism is a missionary religion that traces its missionary spirit to the Buddha's earliest instructions to his disciples:

I am delivered, monks, from all fetters, human and divine. You, monks, are also delivered from all fetters, human and divine. Go ye now, monks, and wander for the gain of the many, for the happiness of the many, out of compassion for the world, for the good, for the gain, and for the welfare of gods and man. Let not two of you go the same way. Preach, monks, the *Dharma*, which is lovely in the beginning, lovely in the middle, lovely in the end, in the spirit and in the letter; proclaim a consummate, perfect, and pure life of holiness. There are beings whose mental eyes are covered by scarcely any dust, but if the *Dharma* is not preached to them they cannot attain salvation.

The spread of Buddhism beyond Asia, beginning in the 1960s, through Buddhist missionary activities, Asian migrations and the decline of Christianity in the West is now an accepted reality. Buddhism is the fastest growing religion in Australia, United States, and France, largely due to Asian migrations. Each year, one hundred times as many Britons became Buddhists as became Muslims. Whether the popularity of Buddhism in the West will grow is uncertain. Currently, the directing of the Buddhist Society Directory in the United Kingdom lists over 250 Buddhist temples. There is now a European Buddhist Union to provide a forum for the discussion of Buddhist activities. According to David Burnett, author of "The Spirit of Buddhism," in 1990 there were 5000 Buddhists in Britain. According to 2001 census, there are 151,816 Buddhists in Britain.[1]   Much scholarly work has been done in universities in France and Germany. France has an estimated 600,000 Buddhist practitioners (http://www.gospelcom.net/ apologeticsindex/rnb/archives/00001079.html).   The   largest

---

[1]This figure does not include many westerners who become Buddhists without undergoing official change of religious status.

Buddhist meditation center in Europe is based in the region of Touraine, France. In Italy, Buddhism is taught in universities including the famous Roman Catholic Gregorian University. Buddhist temples are now established in Leningrad and the Buddhist Religious Board, recognized officially in Russia, coordinates Buddhist activities in that country.

Interest in Buddhism in the United States, made popular since the World's Parliament of Religions in 1893, continues to grow unabated through Tibetan and Zen Buddhism. Religious study faculties in Yale and Harvard contributed to the development of Buddhism through publications and scholarships. Charles Prebish, Professor of Religious Studies at Pennsylvania State University, places an estimate of three to four million Buddhists in America, with about 800,000 American converts (www.urbandharma.org /udharma5/tension2.html). With Asian migrations to Latin America (for example, Japanese in Brazil) and Africa (especially South Africa), Buddhism will find its place in the marketplace of religions in these two continents.[2] This brief survey seeks to paint Buddhism as not only a global religion but points firstly to its philosophical strengths in encountering traditional western worldviews, and secondly, its accompanied mushrooming of religious studies in funding Buddhism as a missionary religion.

Apology for Cross-textual Studies

What should the Christian attitude be toward Buddhist scriptures? Many evangelical churches forbid their new converts from reading

---

[2] See Wratten, Darrel, *Buddhism in South Africa: From Textual Imagination to Contexual Innovation*, Ph.D. thesis, Department of Religious Studies, University of Cape Town, 441 pp.

any Buddhist scriptures for a variety of reasons ranging from the fear of brainwashing to demonic possession. When I became a Christian as a teenager, I was strongly commanded by my church leaders to burn those Buddhist scriptures in my possession. I was not encouraged to touch these scriptures, certainly not to learn from them. Likewise, many Asian pastors or missionaries coming to Asia are hardly acquainted with these key texts of Buddhist scriptures. With the growth of Buddhism in the West, and serving in a shrinking marketplace of religions, what changes are needed in Christian training institutions as we seek to train leaders to serve in multi-faith contexts? Unfortunately, evangelicals today continue to view Buddhist scriptures as demonic, subversive texts and something to be avoided at all costs. While I am sympathetic to some of the rationales offered such as to protect young believers from false teachings, potential doctrinal confusions, and spiritual influences associated with Buddhist scriptures, I do not think that these are strong grounds for prohibiting the study of Buddhist scriptures. Such views are based on fear rather than strong beliefs in the truth and veracity of the Christian Bible. They commonly generate ignorance of non-Christian beliefs on the part of Christian witnesses and prevent Christians from genuinely addressing those deep seated religious beliefs located in the minds of Buddhist background believers.

Tripolar View of Religions

One of the factors generating evangelical suspicions toward Christian-Buddhist textual studies is that these studies were dominated by pluralist academicians in secular institutions of higher learning. Another underlying barrier is evangelicalism's lack of a valid theology of non-Christian religions. Christian conception of non-Christian religions were developed within Christendom in the West rather than a contextual struggle of being a convert in the midst of other religions and the struggles of making sense of one's own past religious beliefs and practices. In the former articulation of intra-Christian projections of non-Christian religions, one can dissect and neatly separate non-Christian religions as evil and demonic and categorize them into pigeonhole schemes, away from daily faith. However, for converts who become Christians from a Buddhist family, past social values and previous worldviews cannot be so easily compartmentalized. Buddhist thoughts and practices are something I need to engage with as a Christian coming from a non-Christian Buddhist family. Previous Buddhist worldviews as well as family identities and contexts (mental maps and societal obligations) remain deeply entrenched and are in need of biblical redemption. Rendering them evil or dismissing them without accompanied biblical analysis will only force these Buddhist worldviews underground where these belief systems are located in the subconscious realms and recesses of Buddhist converts. There these worldviews remain deeply entrenched in the minds and thinking of Buddhist converts, and remain unchallenged only to resurface in times of crisis and critical choices in life.

Peter Beyerhaus, in a lecture given at a Colloquium at Trinity Evangelical Divinity School entitled, "The Authority of the Gospel and Interreligious Dialogue," proposed a tripolar view of religions. I find this model of thinking about non-Christian religions a promising framework for cross-cultural textual studies and for engaging in inter-religious dialogue. A monopolar view of religion assumes that religions are projections of the human mind. It has only one source of origin: the human mind. A bipolar view of religion suggests that religion not only arises from human quest for the transcendent but is also the result of God's seeking after man universally through general revelation. It has two sources: the human quest and the divine call. Many who hold to a bipolar view assume, for example, that it is the same God who revealed himself to Buddha and granted him enlightenment. All religions are good because they are the result of God's work. The truth is, as Beyerhaus proposed, the biblical authors hold a tripolar view of religions. Namely, there are three constitutive elements or sources of origin: the human, the divine and the demonic. All religions, Christianity included, contain elements of humanity's yearning for God, but also intimately connected with humanity's distortion of God. Beyerhaus asserts:

> Man's genuine longing for his Divine Maker is met by the mercy of God who preserves our earthly life in view of His offer of salvation in Christ. The self-asserting attempt of the sinner to work out his own redemption and perfection is met by the treacherous offer of Satan which leads to demonic activity. This complex entanglement of conflicting transcendental relations is essential for the biblical view of pre-Christian religions (1996:15).

Scriptures in Buddhist Traditions

Although we do not have good historical evidence on the life of Buddha, Christians must be willing to engage with the Buddhist scriptures because these scripture are the sources of religious beliefs for the Buddhists. While it is true that the extant versions of Buddha's life were created long after his death by his followers, our purpose in religious encounters is to understand what Buddhist believe and how the Christian gospel addresses those belief systems.

The words of the Buddha, which became the Buddhist scriptures, were stories of how he sought after truth and finally achieve Nirvana. The words he spoke were intended to exhort others to enter into the same experience of release. These words were new and different from the handed down Hindu Vedas:

> That this was the noble truth concerning sorrow, was not, O Bhikkhus, among the doctrines handed down (ie., the Vedas), but there arose within me the eye (to perceive it), there arose the knowledge (of its nature), there arose the understanding (of its cause), there arose wisdom (to guide in the path of tranquility), there arose the light (to dispel darkness from it) (Coward 2000:140).

Buddhists held that the authority of Buddhist scriptures arose out of Buddha's enlightenment experience. Unlike the Christian position on the Bible as divinely revealed and inspired, Buddhists are open to subsequent scriptures from other Buddhas. Tradition records that within the year that Buddha died (c483 BC), 500 monks gathered and agreed to codify the Rule of the Monastic Order. Ananda, Buddha's closest follower and relative, were reported to recite all the "remembered words" which were then approved by the world community (Sangha). Ananda is said to have recited the original five *Nikayas* (also called Agama) in the *Sutra Pitaka*, or the "Basket of Discourses." Centuries later, these were compiled into Sutras (Buddha's teachings) as part of the Buddhist canon. In addition, the School of Elders (Theravada) expanded texts (*Abhidharma*) were judged necessary part of the Dharma. Consequently, we have the *tripitaka* or "three baskets of scripture": *sutra* (Buddha's teachings), *vinaya* (monastic rules) and

Abhidharma (philosophic treatise). Many Theravada Buddhists felt that only these transmitted sayings of the Buddha could be part of the scriptures while others take a more open view of the Buddhist canon. These more open groups accepted the same general sutras and *vinayas* but developed their own *Abhidharma* or *sastra* (philosophic literatures). The Mahayanas also add many new sutras such as *Prajnaparamita* Sutras and the Lotus Sutras. Later, other devotional texts such as Tantras (inspired words of Buddhas) and Jatakas (popular stories or fables about Buddha) were developed. Although folk Buddhists may not be literate in Buddhist scriptures, the teachings of Buddha shape the worldviews of Asian societies. There is certainly more to Buddhist religious life than their doctrines, but with revivals of Buddhist intellectualism and complexities of various streams of Buddhism, it will be very difficult for the Christian missionary to gain an appreciation of what Buddhists really believe without a good grounding of Buddhist doctrines as found in these scriptures.

Significance of Genesis Creation Account for Buddhist Religiosity

In the creation account of Genesis 1-3, Israel's Elohim is presented as the universal, transcendent Creator who is distinct from creation. "God is the subject of the first sentence of the Bible" (Kidner 1967:43). God speaks, and his words give shape to creation:

> And God said, "Let there be light," and there was light. God saw that the light was good, and he separated the light from darkness. God called the light "day," and the darkness he called "night." And there was evening and there was morning—the first day (Genesis 1:3-5).

The account is set in contrast to other Ancient Near Eastern gods such as Baal or Marduk, who are united with nature. In Genesis, we are introduced to an Absolute Other, a Supreme Creator God who is above creation. The existence of God may be the most fundamental difference between Christianity and Buddhism, as described by Paul Williams, President of the UK Association for Buddhist studies and Professor of Indian and Tibetan Philosophy at University of Bristol:

> Buddhists do not believe in the existence of God. There need be no debating about this. In practicing Buddhism one never finds talk of God, there is no role for God and it is not difficult to find in Buddhist texts attacks on the existence of an omniscient, omnipotent, all-good Creator of the universe (2002:25).

In Mahayana Buddhism, there is a belief in a *bodhisattva*, one who takes the vow to delay his enlightenment, in order to help sentient beings find liberation. However, the Buddhist gods (*deva*) are part of the cycle of death and rebirth, more akin to Greek and Roman mythologies. In folk Buddhism, adherents do worship Buddhist deities. But none of these is seen as the Supreme Being, the Creator God, as presented in the biblical revelation. In a genuine Christian-Buddhist encounter, sooner or later, both parties will discover that central to their different system of beliefs is the polarity between theism and atheism.

Understanding Buddhist Critiques on Christian Theism

Paul J. Griffiths, in his book, *Christianity Through Non-Christian Eyes*, quoted a famous story by Buddha about a monk who used a raft to cross the river. Having crossed the river, the monk said:

Now, this raft has been useful to me. Depending on this raft, and striving with my hands and feet, crossed safely over to the beyond. Supposed now, that I, having put this raft on my head, or having lifted it up on my shoulder, should proceed as I desire? What do you think about this, monks? If that man does this, is he doing what should be done with that raft?

The expected answer, of course, is no. Rafts are for crossing rivers. If you continue to carry them on dry land your progress will be slow. Similarly, with Buddhist doctrines, when their use is fully utilized, they should be discarded. This is in contrast to Christian views of doctrines as unchanging and timeless truths to be held on to as life guides. We can then understand that Buddhists assess the truthfulness of Christian doctrines by their effects on self, society and peace of community.

One raft which eventually must be discarded, for the Buddhist, is the Christian doctrine of theism. Theism is useful up to a certain extent. Even in Mahayana Buddhism, theism is tolerated as something necessary for some people at certain stages of their lives. God is needed as a psychological crutch for the weak, but God is a stumbling block to achieve *nirvana* where attachments hinder full liberation.

Christian attempts to present the existence of God have often been grounded in doctrines about God. However, at ground level, such arguments often fail to convince the Buddhist, irrespective of whether he is a philosophical or folk Buddhist. For the Buddhist, religious doctrines have utility rather than truth. As conditions of believers vary widely, similar doctrines will have different effects on each believer. Buddhists are less concerned with doctrinal fidelity because identical doctrines will not have identical effects on all believers. Therefore, Buddhist philosophy often deals with incompatible truth claims without needing to reconcile all doctrines into one comprehensive, compatible truth system. It is perfectly acceptable for different individuals to assent to incompatible truth claims (between Theravada and Mahayana sects) and to engage in incompatible religious practices such as atheistic self-dependence and idol worship.

It is said that Buddha himself taught different incompatible doctrines to different hearers to help them advance along the path of *nirvana*. The Buddha's perfect skill in doing this is called, *upayakaushalya*, translated "skill in means." This capability is recommended to all Buddhists, as told in the beautiful story of a compassionate father who discovers that his sons are caught in a burning house, but not realizing that the house is burning, refuse to listen to his pleas to leave the house. In order to get them out of the house, the father induced them with different promises of gifts: one is offered a goat-drawn carriage, another a deer-drawn carriage and the third, an ox-drawn carriage. When they get outside, each child is presented with a single magnificent ox-drawn carriage. The moral of the story is each child was given a different promise that had the desired effect, so also with the Buddha's preaching of religious doctrines. The Buddhist view of religious doctrines is that they are instruments for transformation rather than descriptions of reality.

Buddhist Cosmology and the New Creation

What is the Buddhist answer to the origins of humanity and the creation of the universe? Buddha refused to give categorical answers but indicated that the universe began eons ago.[3] The universe comprises not only humanity and animals but also various gods (*devas*) as part of "world systems" (*cakra-vada*). The early Nikaya-Agama texts talk in terms of "the thrice-thousand fold world systems." One's *karma* determines in which realm a being is born. One's intentional actions of body, speech and mind (psychological states) are intimately related to the realms of existences. When one experiences unhappy mental states, then there is a sense that one makes a brief visit to lower realms of existence. When these unpleasant mental states passed, one returns to human existence. But when such unhappy mental states such as greed, hatred become a habitual part of one's character, then there is a danger that one dies and experiences rebirth into a lower level of existence altogether.

In order to avoid such unhappy states, both Christian and Buddhist traditions agree that we must renounce self. The way to renounce self in Buddhism is not to become attached to things. Buddhists teach emptiness *(syunyata)* where the ego is dissolved. Many of the causes of suffering are avoided when the ego is not controlling the life and values of the person. "I have been crucified with Christ and I no longer live, but Christ who lives in me." (Gal. 2:20). Although both Buddhist and Christians agreed on the futility of selves, the negation of self in Christian teaching is centred on Christ taking over the throne of self. Instead of merely no-self, the Christian vision is for a new self, which is a Christ-filled life. The vision for a new self, for the Christian, must not be divorced, from the vision for the new world. Romans 8:17-27 is a good illustration that the church must not withdraw from the problems of the

---

[3] For a good summary of Buddhist cosmos, see Gethin, *The Foundations of Buddhism*, 112-132

groaning creation. For the Buddhist, the vision of a better world, for social justice and alleviation of poverty, is one form of attachment to this world. How will a Buddhist identify and empathizes with the sufferings of the world if he or she can only achieve salvation through non-attachment?

According to Masao Abe, the Buddhist doctrines of *nirvana* and the transcendence of all distinctions caused Buddhists to detach from concrete historical concern in the sense of involvement with social injustices and historical evils (Vroom 1996:40). It is not possible to remove sufferings in the world if we do not become attached to the sufferings of the poor and marginalized. For the Buddhist, such attachment will hinder the path toward enlightenment.

The causes of suffering are desire, attachment, and ignorance. The Christian view is suffering resulted from man's desire to be like God— "knowing good and evil." Adam desires to achieve autonomy from God and live without law. Buddhism promotes self-effort in seeking *nirvana* through the observance of the eightfold noble path. On the surface, it seems like Jesus' ethical teachings on the Sermon of the Mount. The apostle Paul says, the "very commandment that was intended to bring life actually brought death" (Romans 7:10). "We know that the law is spiritual, but I am unspiritual, sold as a slave to sin… For what I want to do I do not do but what I hate I do." (Romans 7:14-15) Religious laws, whether Jewish, Buddhist or Christian, or the best of human ideals, cannot bring true enlightenment. I can never make myself into a good person.

What is so amazing about grace is that one does not need to make merit but one needs to entrust oneself to a loving God, without fearing that such attachments are soteriological impediments. The gospel is a message for sinners, and for failures who can find forgiveness in the grace of Jesus Christ. The burden of being engulfed in endless cycles of reincarnation over centuries and eons of years can be freed through acceptance of God's grace in Christ. Knowing the assurance of salvation is one thing, communicating it to the Buddhist requires more than words but a radical witness of a life fully abandoned to God's providence and loving care.

Christian and Buddhist Ethics

The pagans of ANE societies believe that only the gods enjoy eternal life. Adam naturally longed for divine knowledge. Instead of enjoying God's banqueting table of life as creature, Adam sought to become like God. From this desire for autonomy, self-rule and life without God, Adam and Eve rebelled against God's rule. In Genesis 1-11, sin develops and escalates into societal proportions with chaotic consequences. Sin is more than personal alienation from God, but is comprehensive: humanity's sense of moral, social and political justice is perverted without God's law. God's world is fully dependent on the Creator for sustenance, in contrast with *Gaia* hypothesis, that the universe is self-regulating. The creation is not entirely evil, therefore, it should not to be simplistically renounced or rejected (Romans 8:17-27). The basis for Christian ethics is due to humanity's relationship with and accountability to God, for Yahweh is the God of ethics.

The term Buddha is derived from *budh*, to be awakened. The aim of Buddhists in Theravada is to become an *Arahat*, a being who has attained enlightenment and not being reborn.

> For him who has completed the journey (*Samsara*, the cycle of life), for him who is sorrowless (completely

eradicated ill will and attachment to sense desires) for
him who from everything is wholly free, for him who
has destroyed all ties, the fever of passion exists not
(The Dhammapada, v. 90).

The ethical focus in Mahayana Buddhism is on the idea that a
Buddhist should aspire to become a Buddha and an essential goal
along this path is to help others on the same path. The first step is to
generate *Boddhichitta* (Buddha mind). This mental attitude cannot
come naturally but has to be achieved through ethical practice,
meditation and compassion for all beings. Having achieved this, as
Buddha did, the Buddhist then resolves to practice the six
perfections which form the path to Buddhahood. These are:

1. Generosity (*Dana*) – giving material things, money, service of
all kinds, teaching of *Dhamma*, helping others;
2. Moral discipline (*Sila*) – living according to the ethical rules,
restraining one's senses and evil passions;
3. Patience (*Kshanti*) – overcoming anger, ill-will, and hatred,
maintaining an inner peace and tranquility, not retaliating;
4. Energy (*Viriya*) – abandoning laziness and postponement,
being energetic, not being weak or discouraged;
5. Meditation *(Dhyana)* – developing mindfulness, concentration
and insight;
6. Wisdom (*Prajna*) – understanding what is virtuous, and
realizing emptiness and the truth (Goonewarde 1996:109).

Four perfections were added later, namely skilful means (*upaya*),
resolution (*pranidhana*), strength (*bala*), and knowledge (*jnana*).
Through these good practices, one makes merit and obtain good
karma. Central to Buddhist thought is the idea of moral order: good
deeds produce happiness and bad deeds produce suffering. This

basic belief can be challenged as we know from experience and social reality that good deeds do not always produce happiness and may indeed be the "cross" for sufferings. Christian ethics is anchored instead on the character of a holy and loving God who enters into covenantal relationship with humanity.

Christian witness among Buddhists must move beyond truth-validation. Sometimes theoretical truth-validations can be problematic due to the nature of Buddhist thought that allows incompatible and paradoxical statements. The truthfulness of Buddhist (as well as Christian) doctrines is best tested in the crucible of life's trials and ethics. Principally, it can be tested in life's realities but it can also be validated through case studies of how both traditions will respond to specific ethical problems.[4]

From Lotus Sutra to the Cross

I come from a Chinese Buddhist family, which is not common as most Chinese practice a mixture of Buddhism with Confucianism, Taoism and folk belief systems. As my dad passed away when I was ten years old, my eldest brother took over the position as head of the family. He became a devout Buddhist and took us for *dharma* classes every Friday. The Buddhist Temple was exquisitely designed, coated with gold, and full of incense and worshippers at all time. During *Wesak Day,* which is a public holiday nationally (in a Muslim country!), we gathered for teaching, for meditation and chanting, and fasting. Eldest brother eventually became a monk and

---

[4] One example of exploring world religion through ethical studies is Regina W. Wolfe and Christine E. Gudorf., eds. *Ethics and World Religions: Cross Cultural Case Studies* (Maryknoll: Orbis Books, 2001).

today he travels to propagate Mahayana Buddhism, not only within Malaysia but also to Europe.

In folk Buddhism, pragmatic charms, amulets, specific prayers for specific needs helped to connect the earthly needs with heavenly powers. Before we sat for exams, we would go to Buddhist temples to seek some help from the gods to bless our efforts. When children are sick, parents seek healing water to protect their children from the evil spirits. In my teenage rebellion years, I rebelled against such beliefs, which seemed superstitious and required "faith without scientific evidences."

Merits and demerits are easy to understand. Buddhists believe that good deeds earn merit and bad deeds earn demerits. When one earns sufficient merits, it improves one's chances for a better rebirth. Demerits cancel good merit and disturb the process toward enlightenment and could cause a lower rebirth. Gradually, I experienced a crisis of faith when I became aware that I can never earn enough points to achieve *nirvana*. I think the majority of Buddhists know that it will take many rebirths to be delivered from the sufferings of this world.

In Buddhism, salvation is dependent on self-effort; without having to rely on others to decide my destiny. Many Buddhists find it difficult to surrender their future salvation to a gospel of free grace. Self-reliance has always been part of human attraction but it is increasingly appealing to a generation without God.

Being Chinese is to be identified with Buddhism. Because of personal family identity, kinship networks among a wide web of relatives, social networks among Chinese business contacts, the temple serves as more than a place for religious worship but also as a symbol of racial identity. Buddhism is not just a religious term. It is a whole way of life. But genuine love and friendship can enter into these social support structures if it proves to be part of the community. Most people come to Christ because of someone who consistently and genuinely cared. In my case, it was my biology teacher, a Chinese gentleman who patiently nurtured me from unbelief to belief. When I was kicked out of my home for becoming a Christian, another teacher friend welcomed me to stay with him.

Buddhist philosophy which dates centuries before the Christian Era, and the recent resurgence of Buddhist literature gave a sense of intellectual superiority for Buddhists. However, as more rigorous interactions take place, such comfortable assertions will be tested.

For Buddhists to convert to Christianity, there must be a realization that self-effort cannot bring about happiness, certainly not achieving salvation (or *nirvana*). The Holy Spirit must bring convictions that one must be reborn through Christ into a new creation (John 3:3,5; 2 Cor. 5:17). The Christian must be willing to develop long term relationships with Buddhist friends, follow through their human efforts to become good and to fulfill all religious laws and ideals. After a period of relationship and law fulfilling, the honest Buddhist may come to terms with his or her inability to fulfill religious ideals.

In *The Unexpected Ways,* Paul Williams wrote an intellectually stimulating and emotionally moving testimony on his conversion from Buddhism to Catholicism. Williams concluded in his closing chapter that:

> The orthodox Christian position, and that of the Buddhist are exact opposites on many fundamental issues. The Christian orients him- or herself towards God, the absolutely Other....The Christian sees everything in terms of God and the grace of God. The Christian is aware of his or her own spiritual incapacity. Everything flows from God who is quite

Other than his creation even if He is a God who has in Christ entered into creation and become part of it. The Buddhist thinks in terms of mental transformation, a transformation of the mind from greed, hatred and delusion to the opposites. With the exception of someone like Shinran, in the last analysis the Buddhist brings about his or her own mental transformation. "Buddha but points the way" (2002:197).

Agendas for Christian-Buddhist Worldview Encounters

The use of cross-textual studies between Christianity and Buddhism is a growing discipline in academic and regional study centers but shunned by evangelicals due to fear of syncretism and lack of training in Buddhist philosophies among Christians. In Malaysia and Singapore, where lay Buddhist movements are strong, Buddhist intellectualism is growing steadily as evidenced by the growth of academic studies in Buddhist philosophy and scriptural studies. For example, the Singapore Buddhist Association runs a post-graduate diploma in Buddhist studies, specializing in Buddhist philosophy and Pali textual criticism. Although ritualism and folks Buddhism will continue to be prevalent among the masses, Buddhist communities in urban and middle class Asia will increasingly be led and sustained by rigorous intellectualism. However, the predominant characteristic in Asian Christianity is marked by a move toward anti-intellectualism. Mega-churches in Bangkok, Singapore and Taipei are generally not interested in Buddhist studies. This is a cause for concern with regards to capabilities of Christians to engage effective in Christian-Buddhist encounter in coming decades.

This paper seeks to demonstrate the need to engage with Buddhism on its own terms. Widespread ignorance among Christians and caricatures of Buddhist beliefs are no longer tenable in multi-faith contexts where Buddhists are increasing informed and instructed of their religious teachings. Today, Christians can learn about Buddhism from the streets, study centers and hundreds of Buddhist websites. Sociological, phenomenological and educational studies that relate to cross-cultural and interreligious communication are partners to biblical hermeneutics. Cross-textual studies is not a dilution of Christian commitment to the Bible as authoritative text. Rather, it demands a deeper commitment to our biblical scripture as something we need to master and be mastered by; for without such mastery of Biblical scriptures, how can we engage with Buddhist scriptures?

Key theological and biblical themes such as creation and salvation need to be explored through careful translations and dynamic equivalent of biblical meanings to Buddhist hearers. Talks about dynamic equivalence will not be undertaken theoretically but worked out in the rigorous disciplines of handling representative religious texts. Cultural, anthropological and worldview analysis on people groups vis-à-vis dominant Buddhist worldviews (Theravada, Zen or Tibetan?) will foster more specific communication of the gospel message. What are their views on God, on Christianity, on the role of religion in society, and the impact of secularization? In particular, Christians need to interact with the numerous publications by members of Buddhist community in Asia.

Lastly, what should be the shape of Christian community in the midst of Buddhist temples? How will they worship and fellowship? How can the church disciple believers in Buddhist societies in such a manner that they remain in their social contexts? What is their contribution to the social networks outside the church? What is the quality and credibility of national believers and communities in traditional Buddhist societies? The above questions are important because hindrances to gospel receptivity in Asia are closely connected with socialization processes and community beliefs. Many Japanese and Thais are attracted to Christianity but refrained of faith commitments due to family ancestral obligations, community loyalty, fear of shaming the good name of the family, and perception of Christianity as foreign and anti-national. Christianity's search for indigenous and authentic communities that are truly at home in ancient Asian civilizations cannot be built without engaging with these religious texts.

3

APPROACHING BUDDHISTS ACCORDING TO ACTS CHAPTER SEVENTEEN

Michael S. Vasanthakumar

The book of Acts, which depicts some of the early Christian attempts and approaches to reach non-Christians with the good news of Jesus Christ, still serves as a guiding light to evangelize the globe. Even though some of the activities of the early Christians were conditioned by first century Jewish as well as Greco-Roman cultures, they contain significant principles and practical advice which could be applied in reaching the people of other faiths in any age and place. As D. Wilkinson has pointed out:

> The sermons in Acts have been selected by Luke not only to give an account of how the church preached the gospel, but also to give us an understanding of why they preached the gospel. The contents of the sermons both explain the gospel to the unbeliever and is an account of the emerging missiology that was developing as God led them by his Holy Spirit (2002:206).

This paper concentrates on the seventeenth chapter of the Books of Acts, especially the ministry of Paul to the people of Athens, in order draw some principles which could enable the Christians to reach the Buddhists. Hence Paul's attitude towards the Athenians and his address to the Areopagus are analyzed in this essay.

Paul's Attitude Towards The Athenians

In Christian mission, the minister's attitude towards people plays a vital role, for it determines how he or she functions in the mission field. For instance, during the time of European colonial expansion, the Christian missionaries had a lower view of non-European cultures and manners which compelled them not only to Christianize but also to Europeanize the conquered countries (Dharmaraj 1993). Converts discarded their native language and culture and became very proud of their newly adapted European lifestyle which they perceived as the true Christian conduct. This attitude still prevails among Christians and has become a major obstacle for the people of other faiths to appreciate Christianity and accept Jesus Christ as their Lord. Therefore, it is necessary for contemporary Christians to have the right kind of attitudes toward non-Christians, which would enable them to relate the Christian message to the people of other faiths in an appropriate manner. In Acts seventeen, Paul's attitude towards the Athenians is different to that of his disposition concerning the Jews and Christians. In fact, his attitude towards the Athenian is a good example for Christians to have towards Buddhists, who think of themselves as people who have the highest form of philosophically oriented doctrines. Even though Paul was emotionally exasperated (Acts 17:16) when he saw the idolatry of the Athenians (Acts 17:16), his evangelistic engagement in that city was conducted in a manner which is appropriate in encountering educationalists (Acts 18-22), such as philosophers and Buddhists

Emotional Exasperation
The book of Acts says that Paul *was greatly distressed to see that the city was full of idols* (17:16). Historically, when Paul arrived in

Athens, the city had lost its pre-eminence. It had been one of the greatest cities of the world in the fourth and fifth centuries BC. In the fifth century, Athens achieved a series of military victories which had brought it to the height of world power. Then the Greeks rebuilt their city with houses, grand temples, topped by the magnificent Parthenon. More significantly Athens advanced in civilization by becoming the first example of a democracy in human history. Greek literature, art and philosophy flourished during this period. Classical Greek plays, philosophies of Socrates and Plato as well as classical forms of human sculpture emerged in that golden era. But in latter days, the Athenians were involved in a disastrous war with Sparta that dragged on for twenty-seven years and resulted in the destruction of Greek power and much of Greek civilization. During Paul's time it was in the "late afternoon of her glory" (Blaiklock 1959:132). Nevertheless, it was "still a strikingly beautiful city as well as the intellectual capital of the ancient world," (Boice 1998:294) and "lived on its great past" (Haenchen 1971:517). During Paul's time "there were more gods in Athens than in all the rest of the country… It was easier to find a god there than a man" (Conybeare and Howson 1949:280). According to reasonable estimates there were 30,000 idols in Athens at that time, (Clark and Winter 1991:138) while the population of the city was less than 10,000 (Larkin 1995:251). In fact, Paul "found himself confronted by a veritable forest of idols" (Wycherley 1968:619-21).[1] It is extremely strange to note that the intellectual capital of

---

[1] In the Parthenon stood a huge gold and ivory statue of Athena, "whose gleaming spear-point was visible forty miles away (E.M.Blaiklock, p. 137). Elsewhere there were images of Apollo, the city's patron, of Jupiter, Venus, Mercury, Bacchus, Neptune, Diana, and Aesculapius. In fact, the whole Greek pantheon was in Athens. Further, each houses and shrines had a square pillar with the head of Hermes, the god of roads, gateways

the ancient world was filled with idols. Instead of producing more wise people it was "producing idolatry" (Toussaint 1983:402). The idols of gods were elegantly fashioned and beautifully made of stone, brass, gold, silver, ivory and marble. But, the beauty and elegance did not fascinate the mind of Paul. He was "infuriated at the sight"(Polhill 1992:366).

The word which depicts Paul's emotional exasperation (NIV uses the word distress) over the idolatry had medical associations in the original language and was generally used of a seizure or epileptic fit. The English word "paroxysm" has derived from this Greek verb *paroxyno*. Hence it could be said that Paul "experiences a paroxysm in his spirit" (Larkin 1995:251-252). The Greek verb also has the meaning of stimulation, especially to irritate, provoke, and rouse to anger (Grimm and Thayer). Its only other occurrence in the New Testament is in Paul's first letter to the Corinthian church, where he describes love as "not easily angered." Some translations use either "irritated" (Moffatt) or "exasperated" (NEB and JBP) to express Paul's response to idolatry of Athens. As the Jerusalem Bible has stated, Paul's "whole soul was revolted at the sight of a city given over to idolatry."

Paul's emotional exasperation, however, was not an uncontrolled outburst of anger, for the verb is in the imperfect tense, which "expresses not a sudden loss of temper but rather a continuous, settled reaction to what Paul saw" (Stott 1994:278). In fact, this is the word used in the LXX for God's displeasure or anger towards idolatry.[2] Hence Paul's feeling or reaction was similar to that of

---

and the marketplace. For more detailed description of the Athenian idols and temples see O.Broneer, "Athens City of Idol Worship" in *Biblical Archaeologist*. 21 (1958), pp. 2-28; G.T.Montague, "Paul and Athens" in *The Bible Today*. 49 (1970), pp. 14-23.

[2] Cf. Is. 63:2-3, Dt. 9:7, 9:18, 9:22, Ps. 106:28-29, Ho. 8:5

God and it was not a sinful attitude in anyway. His spirit was provoked, "because the glory due to God alone was being given to idols"(Larkin 1995:252). In Buddhist countries, idols of the Buddha and other deities flourish. Even though the Buddhists claim that their religion has a higher degree of philosophical orientation, they go behind various gods which are in the forms of idols. The idols are kept, not only in the temples, but also in other places as well, as gods and guardians of the people and places. People not only venerate them, they also worship them. Hence the fact remains that these idols too take the honor and glory due only to God. Hence, the sight of the idols should bring this truth to the minds of the Christians, who wish to bring the world to worship the true God.

Evangelistic Engagement

Even though Paul was emotionally exasperated, he did not express his anger towards the idols or those who venerated and worshipped them. On the contrary he began to speak to the idolaters about Jesus Christ. "The stirrings of his spirit with righteous indignation opened his mouth in testimony" (Stott 1994:280). Acts 17:17 says, "So he reasoned in the synagogue with the Jews and the God-fearing Greeks, as well as in the marketplace day by day with those who happened to be there." Even though Buddhism theoretically denies the existence of God, Buddhists generally stand behind various gods for practical needs and their temples are filled with numerous idols.[3] The missionaries of the colonial era who ministered among the Buddhists were accustomed to condemning them for worshipping idols. According to the missionaries who served in Sri

---

[3] In Sri Lanka all the Hindu deities dwell in Buddhist temples. For some case studies see R.Gombrich and G.Obeyesekere, *Buddhism Transformed: Religious Change in Sri Lanka*, pp. 67-199.

Lanka, Buddhism was a "wretched system... [and] a stronghold of Satan" (Gogerly 1831). They condemned Buddhism as "false, absurd, blasphemous, dangerous... [and a] gigantic system of error" (Small 1971:74). Buddhist worship and temple ceremonies were all horrifying and appalling, abominable and wicked in the eyes of the missionaries. Even today, the Christian ministers who follow the footsteps of the colonial missionaries openly ridicule idolatry and criticize Buddhist practices as well. Such behaviors of Christians often prevent Buddhists from appreciating the message of Jesus Christ. Further, it has provoked Buddhists to react against the activities of Christians. But Paul, instead of condemning idolatry, conveyed the message of Jesus Christ to idolaters in a conclusive manner. Likewise, Christians should avoid negative and provocative criticism of Buddhism and Buddhist practices. They need to share the love of Christ and proclaim his salvation to them, who try to attain *nibbana* by their own efforts.

When Paul made a formal address to the Athenians, he did not scold them as "you foolish idolaters." On the contrary, he commended their religiosity, even though their religion was filled with idols, and he was emotionally exasperated by them. Paul was of course, not endorsing or sanctioning idolatry. On the contrary, he approached them with a positive attitude. Therefore, without condemning their idolatry, he appreciated their religiosity. The Greek word translated as "religious" in verse twenty-two could be used either in good or bad sense. The KJV rendering, "You are superstitious" implies criticism. But, "it is an unlikely way to start an evangelistic speech" (Fernando 1998:475). Some, however, citing an ancient writer Lucian, say that it cannot be a complimentary expression, for "it was forbidden to use complimentary exordia in addressing Areopagus court, with the hope of securing its goodwill."(Bruce 1997:355). But such a conclusion does not consider the fact, whether or not Paul was abiding by this prohibition and the NIV rendering is more positive. Further, as some have assumed Paul was not tried before a formal Athenian court named Areopagus (Longenecker :474). Some think that Paul was taken before the "education commission" of the court (Gartner 1955:52-65). The RSV translates the phrase in verse nineteen as 'they took hold of him' in the sense of arresting him. He delivered a public address "to satisfy the curiosity of the philosophers who led them there" (Polhill 1992:368). There is no suggestion that he was in any sense on trial (Neil 1973:190). "The context is without a vestige of judicial process" (Alexander 1963:149). "He was not formally charged. Once finished he made an easy exit—there were no deliberations" (Polhill 1992:368). Since the Athenian's reputation for religious piety is well attested (Larkin 1995:255), Paul was undoubtedly expressing commendation in his speech, "to provide a way into his address that would engage the attention of the audience" (Grayston 1966:285). In this approach, "we have a respectful recognition of religious endeavors," (Larkin 1995:255) for it was "a cultured compliment to the distinguished audience" (Dunn 1996:234). In fact, such a positive attitude and broadmindedness are vital when encountering Buddhists with the message of Christ.

Encountering Educationalists

In the Athenian marketplace Paul encountered some representatives of two kinds of philosophies of that era, namely Epicureans and Stoics. According to the Epicureans the world was due to chance, a mere random concourse. There would be no survival of death, and no judgment. The chief end of human life was condemned to be pleasure which was described as freedom from pain, passions (for the body) and disturbances (for the mind) especially the fear of death. Epicureans though did not deny the existence of gods, did not consider them to be involved in human affairs at all. Epicureans, however, were influential among the educated upper class people only (Keener 1993:372). Stoics, on the other hand were more popular philosophers, opposed pleasure and were critical about the Epicureans. They had a pantheistic theology, which regarded God as the world-soul. The Stoics aimed at living consistently with nature, and in practice they laid great emphasis on the primacy of the rational faculty in humanity, and on individual self-sufficiency (Bruce 1997:330). Since Buddhist doctrines are philosophical in nature, Paul's approach to the philosophers is relevant to reach the Buddhists to a great extent. It is true that most of the tenets of Epicureans and Stoics are not in harmony with the teachings of the Buddha, however, Paul's approach provides some guidelines to present the gospel message to Buddhists in a meaningful way.

The Greek word used for "reasoned" in verse seventeen (*dialegomai*) suggests that Paul had "adopted the famous Socratic method dialogue, involving questions and answers" (Stott 1994:280) in his attempt to communicate the Christian message to the Athenians. Evangelical Christians sometimes think that direct preaching is the one and only method to evangelize Buddhists. But, past experiences had shown that direct preaching which did not give sufficient time for the listeners to raise their questions and doubts did not draw many people to Jesus Christ. In Sri Lanka it had a counterproductive result. Christian evangelistic preaching during the colonial era inspired a Buddhist revival which influences the contemporary Buddhists as well. In fact, direct preaching is unable to satisfactorily answer the questions people have on religious issues. In recent times the churches have grown through personal evangelism and not via crusades. Christians need to be involved in personal dialogue with Buddhists to reach them with the message of Jesus Christ. Paul used this method in Athens when he met people at the marketplace. Since Buddhists have various questions concerning Christianity and its association with the western countries, it is necessary for Christians to clarify the doubts Buddhists have on a personal level, instead of engaging in a typical evangelistic preaching ministry. Buddhists can learn much about Christianity by engaging in a dialogue with Christians rather than listening to typical evangelistic messages.

Paul's Address to the Areopagus

Subsequent to the encounter with the philosophers at the marketplace, Paul was given an opportunity to present his teachings in a formal way to the Athenian intellectuals. Paul's address to the Areopagus was, however, different to that of his usual gospel message. Earlier commentators, who were greatly influenced by W. Ramsay thought that in Athens Paul's novel approach encountered much opposition and it was to be considered as a failure in his mission. Consequently it has been argued that this unsuccessful method should not be followed when evangelizing the people of other faiths. It is true that Paul's address to the Areopagus lacks some of the usual and even essential elements of Christian gospel. But, it should not be forgotten that Paul's address was the reply to the issues raised by the philosophers at the market place. J.D.G. Dunn correctly points out that Paul's ministry at the market place is the context for his speech to the Areopagus. Hence the speech addresses the concerns raised in the market place (1996:230). As his fundamental missionary policy (1 Cor.1:23), Paul would have discussed the crucifixion of Jesus Christ with these philosophers when he met them at the market place. Otherwise it would have been meaningless to tell them about Jesus' resurrection in the Areopagus address. Ajith Fernando says, "though the cross is missing in this summary report of his talk, the death of Christ must have been mentioned for him to mention the resurrection, and there is nothing to say that this was not clearly presented during his reasoning with the people of Athens prior to this event. It could be also be that Paul was hoping to talk about the cross (which was "foolishness to Gentiles" 1 Cor.1:23) after presenting the victory of the resurrection, but he could not get to that point because of the response of his audience" (1998:477).

It should not be forgotten that in his Areopagus address, Paul approached his audience in their own philosophical and religious spheres. Hence he could not in his usual way prove from the Old Testament scriptures that Jesus was the messiah to them for the simple reason that they did not possess knowledge concerning the Jewish messianic expectations Paul "knew it would be futile to refer to a history no one knew or argue from fulfillment of prophecy no one was interested in or quote from a book no one read or accepted as authoritative"(Longenecker 1992:475). Therefore, in Athens, "a philosophical approach was demanded" (Williams 1985:301). Hence, like the apostle John, who employed a Greek philosophical concept, *logos,* to Jesus in his Gospel, Paul used some of the Greek philosophical ideas and concepts to relate his message to the philosophically oriented people of Athens. It is important to note that Christian mission needs to come down from its traditional western theological towers, and meet people in their own cultural and religious territories. In contemporary missiological terms Paul had contextualized his message in order to make it comprehensible and intelligent to his audience. Hence, it "provides us with a paradigm of his preaching to pagans" (Williams 1985:301) and "remains a model of sensitive but forthright confrontation of an intellectual audience with the claims of the gospel" (Fernando 1998:475).

Paul's Areopagus address is filled with several Greek philosophical concepts and phraseologies. Therefore, some have concluded that Paul's speech was totally influenced by Greek philosophy and he had even compromised the gospel without presenting a clear-cut Christian message (Dibelius 1956:57-63; Conzelmann 1966). Others, however, argue that Paul's speech was influenced by the Old Testament (Gartner: 369-370). Nevertheless it cannot be denied that his speech contains several Greek philosophical phraseologies and concepts. Paul employs Greek concepts to build bridges to reach the Athenian intellectuals. Hence Paul's speech gives not only some guidelines but also an authority for Christians to find concepts, phrases, and even doctrines from other religions, which could become a link or bridge to reach the people of other faiths. Yet, in this method Christians needs to have some guidelines which Paul had provided in his Areopagus address. Paul adopted an Athenian concept as a point of contact. He also acknowledged Athenian concepts as a process of communication, when they were not contradicting the scriptures. But finally, he announced absolute concepts as a proclamation of Christianity.

Adopting Athenian Concept as a Point of Contact
Paul began his Areopagus address with an Athenian concept to build a bridge between himself and his audience. It is a point of

contact which Paul used to reach the minds of the Athenians. In chapter seventeen, verse twenty-three Paul says, "for as I walked around and looked carefully at your objects of worship, I even found an alter with the inscription: TO AN UNKNOWN GOD. Now what you worship as something unknown I am going to proclaim to you." What Paul says in this verse has caused much controversy and misinterpretations among Christians. Some have deduced from this verse that Christ is in other religions as well. For instance, Raymond Panikkar insists that "in the footstep of St. Paul, we believe that we may speak not only of the unknown God of the Greeks, but also of the hidden Christ of Hinduism"(1964:137). He goes to the extent of believing that "the good and bona fide Hindu is saved by Christ and not by Hinduism, but it is through the sacraments of Hinduism, through the message of morality and good life, through the mysterion that comes down to him through Hinduism, that Christ saves that Hindu normally." But such presumptions are contrary to the rest of the Bible, for the person and character of Jesus Christ is totally different to that of the gods of Hinduism. It is unthinkable that Christ of the Bible is hiding himself in Hinduism or in any other religion. Even though the presence of Christ is universal, he abides with people who gather in his name (Matt.18:20, 28:19), and does not hide in other religions to save its adherents. According to 1 Corinthians 1:18-25, "the highest form of religious paganism still falls short of the knowledge of God...God is not found in images...They reflect ignorance of the greatness and omnipresence of God" (Panikkar 1964:54). In fact, non-Christian religions "are not witness to the deeds of the God who saves" (Goldingay and Wright 1991). Therefore, they "do not prepare their adherents for the revelation of Christ" (Cotterell 1993:51) for they have grown, as Romans 1:22-25 explicitly states, out of a "fundamental rejection of God's self-revelation" (Sproul 1982:55). Therefore, it cannot be maintained that Christ hides himself in other religions and reaches their adherence within their religious spheres. Likewise, Panikkar's thesis that Christ has other names in other religions is not biblically founded, but formulated by misquoting the Bible (Wright 1994:35).

Likewise, many falsely think that Paul is not introducing a new God to the Athenians. They see a continuation between other religions and Christianity. Hence they wrongly conclude that "converts, who turn to Christ from a non-Christian religious system, usually think of themselves not as having transferred their worship from one God to Another, but as having begun now to worship in truth the God they were previously trying to worship in ignorance, error, or distortion"(Stott 1994:285; Talbert 1984:74; Haenchen 1971:521). But this contradicts what Paul had said about converts in 1 Thessalonians 1:9. In fact the Thessalonians "turned to God from idols to serve the living and true God." Christian converts were people who like the Thessalonians, had renounced their old life completely (including the gods) and have come to participate in a new way of life in Jesus Christ, who cannot be compared to other religious deities. Their unconscious or ignorant worship was not now changed into a conscious and knowledgeable worship. Therefore, Paul's usage of an inscription concerning an unknown God is not an evidence to argue that there is a connection between Christianity and other religions except the Old Testament Judaism. If Paul's audience had been worshipping the one true God all along, it would be unthinkable that their ignorance was depicted as culpable, and Paul would have demanded that they repent (cf.17:27, 29-30).

By employing the term 'unknown God' Paul is not unveiling the God who is hidden to the Athenians. By having altars dedicated to unknown gods, the Athenians were not indicating that they do not know the true God. The inscription 'unknown God' is used by the Athenians just to make sure that they have not overlooked or left out and thus offended by any gods (Demarest 1992:138). Further, when a derelict altar was repaired and the original dedication could not be ascertained, they were simply dedicated to unknown gods (Deissmann 1926:287-291). The vagueness of such inscriptions "reflects ignorance of the divinity in whose honor it had first been erected"(Bruce 1997:336). Further, according to the accounts of Diogenes, when Athens was plagued by pestilence in the sixth century BC, after the city rulers had exhausted all their strategies to abate it, they had requested Epimenides, a prophet of Crete, to come and help. His remedy was to drive a herd of black and white sheep away from the Areopagus and, wherever they lay down, to sacrifice them to the god of that place. When the plague was stayed, memorial altars with no god's name inscribed on them were built throughout Attica (*Lives of the Philosophers* 1.110). Archaeological discoveries suggest that such altars were also built to appease the dead wherever ancient burial sites were disturbed by the building projects of latter generations (Wycherley 1968:619-621). Therefore it cannot be maintained that Paul was proclaiming the god whom the Athenians were worshipping. In fact, the well-known missionary author Don Richardson has misinterpreted and misled many by stating that the narrative of Epimenides' animistic polytheism as evidence that he was a prophet of the one true God and taught vicarious atonement (Richardson 1984:13).

Even though Paul employed a concept from Athenian religion, he did not utilize it in the sense it was used by the Athenians. This is an important point the missiologists need to consider when employing non-Christian concepts and phrases in their evangelistic message as contact points. Non-Christian concepts and phrases if necessary need to be modified, or redefined or even rephrased in order to avoid possible and potential compromises and misunderstandings. When Paul employed the term 'unknown God' he did not use it according to the beliefs of Athenians. He used it without compromising the fundamental tenets of Christianity. In Athens, there were several altars which were dedicated to unknown gods. Ancient writers point out that the inscriptions of the altars always had the plural forms such as 'gods' 'deities' etc., and there was never a single alter dedicated to a god which had the inscription in singular.[4] Hence it seems, as Jerome had proposed, that Paul had adapted the plural "gods" to the singular "god" in the light of his monotheistic sermon (Polhill 1992:371). Some think that Paul is referring to a particular altar, which bore a description in the singular. For instance, F.F.Bruce says, that Paul may have seen an altar dedicated exactly as he says. When a derelict altar was repaired and the original dedication could not be ascertained, the inscription "'To the (an) unknown god' would have been quite appropriate" (1997:336). Yet Jerome's suggestion seems more convincing, in the light of ancient writers. "There is no literary or inscriptional evidence for an altar dedication to an unknown deity in the singular" (Larkin 1995:255). Therefore Paul had modified the Athenian concept of unknown gods, when he used it as a contact point. Missiologists often use concepts of other religions to contextualize the Christian gospel, but they generally fail to modify the non-Christian terms and concepts to be in harmony with the

---

[4] *Beginnings.* 5:240-246; Pausanias, *Description of Greece*, 1.1.4 and 5.14.8; Philostratus, *Life of Apollonius of Tyana*, 6.3.5.

biblical message. Consequently the gospel is distorted and will not convey the Christian message to the people of other faiths.

It should not be forgotten that "what Paul picked out for comment was the Athenians open acknowledgment of their ignorance, and that the ignorance rather than the worship is thus underscored" (Stonehouse 1957:19). Paul used the term 'unknown God' to stress the ignorance of the Athenians concerning the true God. The true God was unknown to them, and their worship was in ignorance, hence Paul in his address, explained to them about the true God. "Paul stressed the ignorance with which they worship in order to raise the basic question, who is God?" (Williams 1985:297). For, "to worship an unknown god is to admit one's ignorance" (Polhill 1992:372). In the original text, "Paul did not express himself quite so personally, as if unreservedly identifying the "unknown god" of the inscription with the God whom he proclaimed. He used neuter, not masculine forms. The original text reads as "what you worship in ignorance, this I proclaim to you." Paul referred to "what" they worshipped, and not "who" they worshipped. They worshiped a "thing" not a god. They were totally in ignorance about the true God. To indicate such an ignorance Paul had used the phrase 'unknown God.' Hence the phrase unknown god was not employed by Paul in the sense the Athenians had used it. It is a point of contact to tell them that they do not know God at all and above all "a way of raising with them the basic question of all theology: who is God" (:305). Likewise, Christians need to find some point of contact in Buddhism in which the basic question of theology could be raised to Buddhists who deny or distort the concept of God.

As far as Buddhists are concerned, the doctrine of *anatta* is an appropriate contact point to reach them. In Buddhist thought, *anatta* means that there is nothing called self/soul or any unchanging abiding substance in human beings (Rahula 1959:52). Buddhism, while denying the self, ascertains that people have the power to attain *nibbana* by their own self-efforts. As Lynn De Silva has pointed out this is "one of the deepest dilemmas in Buddhism"(1974 :450). Hence he asks, "what is the self that denies the self and at the same time asserts that it alone can save the self?" (:450). In fact, "to deny the self and to affirm self-sufficiency is a contradiction"(:451). Therefore, it can be shown to Buddhists that the Bible takes what is implied in the doctrine of *anatta* more seriously than Buddhism does, for according to the Bible people are nothing by themselves, and can do nothing by themselves about their salvation. *Anatta*, therefore points to the truth that people cannot save themselves by their own efforts and they are in need of saving grace (De Silva 1974:451). Hence, by emphasizing the Buddhist doctrine of *anatta*, Christians could explain the necessity of divine help to Buddhists.

Acknowledged Athenian Concepts as a Process of Communication

After making an appropriate contact point to get the attention of the Athenians, Paul in his address, accepted certain Athenian philosophical concepts as a process of communication. It is an obvious fact, that if a dialogue or a discourse begins and continues only with disagreeing points, it will not have any positive reception at all. The Christian missionaries of the colonial era failed miserably in this respect, for they could not accept any good things from non-Christian religions. They totally discarded other religions and attributed everything in them to Satan. But Paul on the other hand, acknowledged certain Athenian philosophical concepts which were not in contradistinction to the Bible. For instance, in verse twenty-six Paul acknowledged common ground with the Stoics, affirming that God preserves and guides all of life. In verse twenty-seven he granted the correctness of Stoic belief that God was immanent in the world. And in verse twenty-eight he conceded a measure of truth in a Stoic poem that "we are his offspring." Paul thus "acknowledged glimpses of truth in the Stoic's understanding of God" (Demarest 1992:138). Likewise, Christians need to acknowledge glimpses of truth in Buddhism as well when communicating the gospel to them. Glimpses of truth in other religions are, however, due to God's general revelation to human kind through creation and human conscience (Cf. Ecc.3:11, Rom.1:19-22, 2:14-15). In fact, acknowledging Buddha's ethical teachings as divine truth derived via general revelation, Christians could find a common ground to continue their conversations with Buddhists. Since Buddhists generally see similarities between the ethical teachings of the Buddha and Jesus to some extent, dialogue with Buddhists on this premise is vital in communicating with them.

Christians need to be extremely cautious, when acknowledging glimmerings of truth, or insights from general revelation in other religions, for truth via general revelation found in other religions is often mixed with human errors and misconceptions. Therefore, Christians cannot just use non-Christian books as their sermon texts. Today many use non-Christian religious texts to preach about Jesus. By doing this they not only distort non-Christian texts, they distort the biblical concepts as well. In fact, they read Christian meanings into other religious texts.[5] It is true that Paul in his

---

5 For instance in India and Sri Lanka some identify a Hindu mythological figure called Prajapathi with Jesus Christ, and say what is said about Prajapathi in the Hindu texts are fulfilled in Jesus Christ (Cf.

address quotes from a non-Christian author, but his sermon text was the Old Testament and not the Greek book. It is to illustrate his point that Paul quoted from a non-Christian author in verse twenty-eight. He did not, identify Zeus with the God whom he proclaimed, even though the Greek poet wrote about his Greek god. Paul acknowledged the fact that the Greek poet had "some recognition of the true nature of God" via general revelation (Bruce 1997:339; Stonehouse 1957:30; Stob 1950:58-60). In fact, Paul's introductory remark, "in him we live and move and have our being," cleanses the Athenian quotation of both its reference to Zeus and its pantheistic metaphysic (Renehan 1979:347-353). Hence, what is left in the quotation is "some recognition of the true nature of God, especially what humankind's being made in his image says about the divine nature" (Larkin 1995:258). In fact:

> Paul is not suggesting that God is to be thought of in terms of the Zeus of Greek polytheism or Stoic pantheism. He is rather arguing that the poets his hearers recognized as authorities have to some extent corroborated his message. In his search for a measure of common ground with his hearers, he is, so to speak, disinfecting and re-baptizing the poets' words for his own purpose (Longenecker 1992:476).

J.Padinjarekara, *Christ in Ancient Vedas*, Canada: Welch Publishing, 1991; K.Abraham, *Prajapathi: The Cosmic Christ*, Delhi: ISPCK, 1997; J.Padinjarekara, *Gospel for Indians in Indian Cups*, Ontario: International Mukti Mission, 1993; S.Chellappa, *Is Christianity Necessary?* Madras: Agni Publication, 1995). This kind of missiology contradicts the Bible, which confines the divine revelation concerning Jesus Christ to both Old and New Testaments. Further, identifying Prajapathi with Jesus Christ contradicts the nature of Christ as well. For details see my "Expound Christ from Non-Christian Texts" in *Dharma Deepika* July-December 2000, pp. 5-20.

Announced Absolute Concepts as a Proclamation of Christianity

In his Areopagus address Paul not only acknowledged the glimpse of truth in Athenian philosophy, he also announced absolute concepts as a proclamation of Christianity. The Christian gospel is an absolute truth and it should be proclaimed to the people of other faiths without diluting it. Further, dialogue is not just a process of affirming the similarities between religions. It includes challenging the people with the truth as well. Hence in verse twenty-four, Paul stated that the true God is creator of heaven and earth, in order to refute the Epicurean doctrine of eternal matter. Likewise, in verse twenty-five he affirmed God's intimate concern for people to correct the Epicurean notion of distant and uncaring gods. In fact Paul explained the true nature of God to the philosophers who had distorted views on theology. His sermon contains some vital issues concerning God that the Christians need to confront with Buddhists.

God is the Creator

According to Paul, God is the Creator and Lord of everything. Thus he "challenged Stoic pantheism and Epicurean materialistic deism" (Larkin 1995:256). In verse twenty-four Paul pointed out this fact clearly when he stated that, "the God who made the world and everything in it is the Lord of heaven and earth and does not live in temples built by hands." Like the Buddhists, the concept of God as the absolute creator who is above everything is totally foreign to the philosophers of Athens. Such a God for them was "indeed an unknown god" (Polhill 1992:372). For the Stoics god is in everything, and Epicureans denied the involvement of gods in human affairs. Against Stoic thinking Paul pointed out that God is *the Lord of the heaven and earth*. Hence, he is above the world and not found within the material things nor could he be confined to humanly constructed buildings. Likewise, Paul pointed out to the Epicureans that God is not detached from the creation. He "does not live in temples built by hands" means he is omnipresence. The phrase that God "does not live in temples built by hands" is generally considered as a statement against idolatry (Williams 1985:305). Hence, "any attempt to limit or localize the Creator God, to imprison him within the confines of manmade buildings, structures or concepts, is ludicrous" (Stott 1994:285). Like Paul, we too need to correct the misconceptions Buddhists have concerning the world and its origin and the nature of God. They need to understand that the world was not a thing of chance, or came into being in any other way, but it is the creative work of God, who is Lord over everything he had created.

Buddhism has no God to whom it can refer as Creator, Lord, Savior etc, who can be described as eternal, omniscience, omnipotence etc. The Buddhist denies the validity of any reference from observation in the universe to its creation (Wijebandara 1993:108-109). When God is depicted as Creator who possessed of the characteristics of eternal, omniscience, omnipotence and infinite goodness, Buddhists say that they are atheists (Jayatilleke :104-105). In Buddhist literature the Brahma and other gods do not have the meaning and function they have in Hindu or Brahmanic religion. They do not have divine attributes and the enlightened-ones are superior to them. According to Buddhist cosmology, the gods are as much a part of the world of *samsara* as are the human beings or any other type of living beings. Buddhists, while denying the existence of the Creator God, generally accepts the Darwinian hypothesis of origin as a factual historical record. C. Wijebandara points out that "the cosmology of Buddhism does not provide room for a Creator God as it posits a universe that collapse and regenerates by nature in time. Distraction and contraction or disintegration and integration of the physical universe is understood to occur without the intervention of any supernatural agent" (1993:119-120). Hence it is necessary for Christians to disprove or at least point out the unacceptability or even the difficulties involved in the basis of Darwinian Theory while proclaiming to them about the creator God to them.

God is the Sustainer

Since God is the creator of everything, he sustains his creation too. In verse twenty-five Paul says that God "is not served by human hands, as if he needed anything, because he himself gives all men life and breath and everything else." Epicureans stressed God's self-sufficiency. Paul agreed with them saying that God is not dependent on the services of human beings (Neil 1973:191). Therefore, he "cannot be manipulated by human cult" as well (Polhill 1992:373). The word service in the original text (*therapeuo*) refers to "cultic ministry [and] consists in bringing of sacrificial fruits and any cultic action which might give the impression that the deity is referred to some human performance" (Kittle and Friedrich 1965:129). Buddhism, whether it is Theravada or Mahayana, has absorbed the local cults, rituals and ceremonies of the countries when it spread and grew throughout the centuries, which served the varied religious needs of the people (Ilangasinha 1992:183). In fact, contemporary Sri Lankan Buddhism is a "composite of canonical Buddhism, deity worship and magical animism" (Weerasingha 1989:45). Astrology, occultism and worship of territorial spirits and gods are common features of Sri Lankan Buddhism (Gombrich and Obeyesekere 1990:65-199). In rituals connected with these aspects of Buddhism, people try to manipulate various gods, demons and even the Buddha (Gombrich 1966:23). People supply the needs of the gods by offering flowers, food, fruits, vegetables and various other things to the idols. Such activities are unnecessary for God because he is not dependent on anything that people can offer to him.

> God continues to sustain the life that he has created and given to his human creatures. It is absurd, therefore, to suppose that he who sustains life should himself need to be sustained, that he who supplies our need should himself need our supply. Any attempt to tame or domesticate God, to reduce him to the level of a household pet dependent on us for food and shelter, is a ridiculous reversal of roles. We depend on God; he does not depend on us (Stott 1994:285).

Buddhists need to be confronted with the truth that God is not depended on people but "humanity is wholly dependent on God for everything, from life and breath itself to everything else" (Dunn 1996:235). Hence, they should depend on God instead of vainly depending on themselves in their spiritual pursuit.

God is the Sovereign Ruler

God who created everything, and continues to sustain it, is sovereign over the affairs of human beings. In verse 26 Paul says that "from one man he made every nation of men that they should inhabit the whole earth; and he determined the times set for them and the exact places where they should live." Since God is the creator of everything, he is the creator of human beings too. Paul confronted the Athenian philosophers with the concept of creation recorded in the book of Genesis. From one man God had made every nation of men. The Stoics believed that they 'sprung from the soil of their Attic homeland'. Hence they thought of themselves as indigenous and therefore different and superior to other nations. "This belief reflects the historic fact that the Athenians were the only Greeks on the European mainland who had no tradition of their ancestors' coming into Greece; they belonged to the earliest (Ionic) movement of Greek immigration" (Bruce 1997:337). But Paul pointed out to them that all nations came from one man and thus they were all equal. No single nation, or ethnic or religious group could claim superiority over other nations. "Although there are many nations, though they are scattered over the face of the earth, they are one in their ancestry and in their relationship to their creator" (Polhill 1992:374).

God has not only created all the nations from one man, he has also determined specific times for men and the exact places where they should live. Paul pointed out that God had determined the times set for them and the exact places where they should live. Some think that Paul is referring to the epoch of human history (the times) and the boundaries (exact places) of the nations. Even the phrase "the exact places where they should live" has been interpreted in different ways. Some think that it refers to the habitable areas of the planet and others take it as a reference to the boundaries between nations (Dibelius 1956:30-32; Gartner 1955:146-151). Accordingly they say the "times" in this verse refers to "the divinely appointed times for a given nation's flourishing" and the "exact places" are the "national boundaries" (Larkin 1995:256-7; Toussaint 1983:403; Stott 1994:286; Williams 1985:306). Such an idea is not foreign to the biblical writings (Cf.Deu.32:8, Ps.74:17), however, in this context, it seems that Paul is referring to individual people as a whole and their life within the sovereign plan of God, rather than God's dealings with nations.

Since the New Testament is concerned more with the fate of people as a whole than with individual nations, it is reasonable to conclude that Paul here refers to people and not nations (Marshall 1988:287). People's birth, death and dwelling places are not determined by human beings. They do not have any control over these matters. No one can choose the dates for their birth and death. Likewise they have no choice concerning their skin color, mother tongue and the place of birth and living. All these factors are divinely ordained aspects of human beings. Paul further pointed out that God did all this for a single purpose, namely that people might seek him and find him. Hence in verse twenty-seven Paul said that "God did this so that men would seek him and perhaps reach out for him and find him, though he is not far from each one of us."

God is within the reach of people; if they sincerely search for him, they will definitely find him. Since Buddhists deny the existence of the creator God, it is obvious that they are not searching for him. Hence the task before the Christian missionary is to create a desire within Buddhists to search for the true God. Some evangelical scholars are under the impression that due to sin nobody is able to search for God, unless God through his spirit draws people towards himself. But God has created human beings with a capacity to search for him. Through general revelation, via created world and human conscience God has left enough evidence about himself for people to search for him (Acts.14:15-17). What Paul says in verse twenty-seven confirms the fact that the general revelation was given "so that people would seek and perhaps reach out for him and find him" (Henry 1991:284). Among Paul's audience there were people who were depicted as "devout" as well (Acts.17:17). This description is important because "it shows that some were seeking God. In Acts, Luke applies this term to several groups (Acts.13:43, 13:50, 16:14, 17:4, 18:7, 18:13, 19:27), recognizing that just because people were not Christians or Jews did not mean they are uninterested in God" (Bock 1993:118). In fact people were "created to seek God" (:119). They have an inferred knowledge of God derived from nature (Rom.1:19-20), and an intuitional knowledge of God's moral law (Rom.2:14-15). Therefore they have a capacity to seek God. Paul further confirmed this fact saying, "for 'in him we live and move and have our being. As some of your own poets have said, 'We are his offspring.'" Since God has created the entire human race, they are all related to him in a father-son relationship; therefore Paul agreed with the Greek poets that all human beings are God's offspring.

Buddhists, of course, do not consider themselves as God's children. For Buddhists, life of a human being is the result of his or her previous life. A newborn baby, according to the Buddhist concept is a product of three factors: the female ovum, male sperm and *karmic* energy. *Karmic* energy is presumed to be sent by a dying individual at the moment of his or her death, which hits at a new mother's womb ready for conception (Nyanatiloka 1964:2). The nature of the *karmic* energy is conditioned by the good and evil volitional actions of that particular person's earthly life (Jayatilleke 2000:140). Hence the nature of the *karmic* energy which a newborn baby gets is subjected to its source in the previous life, and the life in this birth is conditioned by its *karmic* energy to a great extent. Therefore, one's life on this earth is viewed as the result of a previous life and he or she is the victim of his or her previous life. They do not know the divine involvement or purpose in human life. In fact, they do not know what the Athenian poets knew about their origins. Since God is the creator of the entire human race, he is the father of every one, including Buddhists who deny and do not recognize the existence of God. It is a greater challenge for Christians to confront Buddhists with the truth that they are indeed God's children and they too are the objects of God's fatherly love. "Although in redemption terms God is the father only of those who are in Christ, yet in creation terms God is the Father of all human kind, and all are his offspring, his creatures, receiving their life from him" (Stott 1994:286).

Conclusion

Paul concludes his address by challenging the Athenians to a radical personal change in view of God's judgment:

> Therefore since we are God's offspring, we should not think that the divine being is like gold or silver or stone – an image made by man's design and skill. In the past God overlooked such ignorance, but now he commands all people everywhere to repent. For he has set a day when he will judge the world with justice by the man he has appointed. He has given proof of this to all men by raising him from the dead (:29-31)

Since God has created human beings, "it is illogical to suppose that the divine nature that created living human beings is like an image made of an inanimate substance (Deut.4:28, Is.40:18-20, 44:9-20)" (Larkin 1995:259). Since images are the products of human design and skill, they cannot be analogous to God who created the human race. Further, being the products of human beings, the idols are inanimate and thus inferior to people. Therefore, they cannot be considered as gods. In fact idolatry "reverses the respective positions of God and us, so that, instead of our humbly acknowledging that God has created and rules us, we presume to imagine that we can create and rule God... [Idolatry] is a perverse, topsy-turvy expression of our human rebellion against God" (Stott 1994:287). Therefore, a radical change, i.e. renouncing idolatry completely and worshiping the creator God is extremely important.

As Paul pointed out, in the past God overlooked the folly of idolatry. Paul calls this as the "time of ignorance" which refers to the past generations from the first human beings until Christ, except Noah's generations, who were punished for their sins. During the time of ignorance, God overlooked human sin. This does not mean that he excused it or failed to notice it, but rather he did not punish it as it deserved (Rom.3:25, Act.14:16). In fact, "until the coming of the revelation of God's true nature in Christianity men lived in ignorance of him" (Marshall 1988:289-90). But now, Paul says that God commands all people everywhere to repent. As far as the Athenians here concerned "their ignorance had now ended. Now they knew the one true God through Paul's proclamation. He was no longer an unknown God" (Polhill 1992:376). Therefore they needed to repent and to make a radical turn from idolatry to the one true God (Acts.14:15, 26:20). "After sin has been judged in Jesus' death and resurrection, comes the 'day of salvation' in a gospel proclaimed in his name, calling for repentance and promising forgiveness" (Larkin 1995:259-260).

The call for repentance is urgent because the consequences for not repenting—a final judgment and eternal condemnation—are inescapable. "The offer of salvation in Christ carried with it the threat of judgment if that offer was refused" (Williams 1985:309). The judgment is definite, for God has set a day for it (Luk.17:24, 17:30, 21:34-36). It is universal, for he will judge the world (Acts.11:28, 17:6). It will be also a fair judgment for God will judge the people with justice. And the inescapable fact is that the savior of the world, Jesus Christ will be the judge (John.5:27, Acts.10:42). The proof Paul offers to establish his argument is Jesus' resurrection for by it Jesus was vindicated and declared to be both Lord and Judge. Likewise, "it establishes both the warning of judgment and the promise of salvation blessings (2:32-33, 5:30-32, 10:40-42)" (Larkin 1995:260). Ultimately all have to grapple with the inescapable truth that "all nations have been created from the first Adam; through the last Adam all nations will be judged" (Stott 1994:288). Challenging Buddhists with this truth is the most important issue in Christian missiology in the Buddhist contexts.

4

TELOS: THE THIRD TRUTH

RUSSELL MINICK

Christ and Buddha had some very similar experiences. From these experiences, they each taught some overlapping concepts about life. When talking with a Buddhist, addressing these similarities can facilitate communicating the uniqueness of Jesus. This paper will explore the use of the temptations and teachings of Jesus (the Messiah) and of Siddhartha (the Buddha) as a means of providing a relatively concise context for sharing the Christian message with Buddhists. Of particular importance are the issues of suffering, desire, impermanence and completeness as magnified by an apparent chiastic structure of the Sermon on the Mount as recorded in the Gospel of Matthew.

Temptation to Teachings: Siddhartha Gautama, the Buddha

Siddhartha Gautama was an astute observer and thinker. Though raised in an exceedingly privileged environment, the young prince came to see life differently than what his protective father had intended. While on an outing from his palace, Siddhartha encountered four passing sights. Sickness, aging, death and uncertainty provoked him to the conclusion that his hedonistic course in life was inadequate. He was compelled to pursue a better path than simply carving out an island of pleasure in a sinking swamp of suffering.

The disciplines and worldviews available to Siddhartha proved inadequate to the intrusive questions raised by the simple observations made in the market place. Something very fundamental was wrong with life, and only a fundamental understanding would offer a course of action substantive enough to deal with the problem and not just the symptoms.

Siddhartha's Temptation by the Evil One

When Siddhartha left the city, and later the religious companionship of fellow ascetics, he was tempted while alone. Mara, a Satan figure, was powerful due to merit he had earned, but which he used to seduce people into destructive desire and attachment so he could rule over them. A horde of Mara's minions, various forms of desire which included hunger, jealousy, pride, contempt and more, were rejected by Siddhartha. Mara used his own power from merit earned to try and move Siddhartha from his position of seeking enlightenment. In response to this attack Siddhartha touched the ground as a witness to his own merit gathered in countless lives. When he declared his merit, there was an earthquake and the intervention of the earth goddess "wringing from her hair a flood of water, accumulated in the past when Gotama (sic) had formalized good deeds by a simple ritual of water-pouring" (Harvey 1990:21).

Having vanquished the temptations of this world with the help of a goddess, Siddhartha was then able to meditate without interruption. The result was a clarity of thought, and enlightenment, thus the title "Buddha, the enlightened one". Again, it was the intervention of a spiritual being which guided Buddha to take his teaching and make it available to others. Though Buddha initially doubted there would be anyone who could understand, Brahma Sahampati, a compassionate god, told him there would be some who could follows his teachings.

Course Offered to Others

Though Buddha initially wanted to begin sharing enlightenment by finding his two yoga teachers, he was too late; they were already dead. He then chose to find his five companions who had exercised an ascetic life with him. When he found them he approached them with confidence. They initially considered him a failure because he had forsaken their way. He then told them, twice for emphasis, that he had transcended ignorance and all that came from it and that he could be their teacher. When their hesitancy was overcome, they washed his feet and submitted to be taught by him.

Teaching Four Noble Truths

Buddha then preached his first sermon. Like a doctor giving a cure for an ailment, the problem was diagnosed, the cause of the problem identified, and the removal of the cause recommended along with a course of treatment. What he ended up with are what are called the Four Noble Truths.

The first noble truth observes the fundamental problem of misery. Life is *dukkha*. *Dukkha* is sometimes translated suffering in English, at other times unsatisfactoriness. These ideas are clearly included, but usages in Buddhist writings indicate that *dukkha* is suffering from hopelessness in regard to satisfaction. This sense of being unsatisfied in life has a discernable cause: desire (*tanha*).

The second noble truth explains this cause of life's *dukkha*. People have cravings that cannot be adequately sated. We desire to grasp for and attach to things that seem to be good, but those things are elusive. That is because, according to Buddha, all things are impermanent (*anicca*): "This monks, is the holy truth of the cessation of *dukkha*: the utter cessation, without attachment, of that very craving, its renunciation, surrender, release, lack of pleasure in it." This is *nibanna*. No desire for that which one cannot have ultimately means a state in which neither mind nor body finds footing. Essentially, beyond existence is the hope to pursue. That is the third noble truth.

The fourth noble truth is how to get on with getting from the *dukkha* of a craving existence to the *nibanna* beyond existence. What is needed is to follow the Middle Path. Without extremes, desire subsides until full release occurs. This eightfold path is the way of living which results in the decreasing enslavement to ignorance (*avija*) and desire. Each of the eight is called 'right' or 'perfect' (*samma*). Being right (perfect, complete) is the means by which a follower of Buddha hopes to experience release from the misery of existence and desire. Similar words and ideas, with a very different conclusion, are found in the comparable story of Jesus' temptation and instructing of his disciples.

Temptation to Teachings: Jesus, the Christ

Focusing on the life of Jesus of Nazareth, there are some points of contact with Siddhartha Gautama's experiences prior to preaching his foundational sermon. There are also distinctions. Whereas Siddhartha was raised a prince in security, Jesus was born in a barn, had to flee his country as a child, and was raised under foreign occupation upon his return to his homeland. Siddhartha was confronted with the four passing sights as a young adult, and he was shocked. Jesus was born in the midst of suffering and hardship; he was well acquainted with sufferings and grief.

Temptation Sequence of Jesus

Like Siddhartha, there came a point when Jesus left town to encounter the ascetics. For Jesus it was his cousin, John the Baptizer, leading the call to repent (change actions due to a change in thinking). Jesus identified with those seeking purity before God and chose a course determined to fulfill all righteousness. God the Father affirmed him directly, but then drove him out into the wilderness to face temptation by the devil. During forty days of fasting the tempter approached Jesus three times.

The first temptation was a direct appeal to a specific desire Matthew records that Jesus had: hunger. The challenge was how to handle two competing realities: a real desire for food and a real belief in the access to the God of provision. Jesus' answer sets the tone quickly. Jesus does not deny that he has desire; he simply subordinates the desire of his flesh to the desire for faithfulness in accordance with the revealed scriptures. Life is not ultimately sustained by the impermanence of calories; life is sustained by the abiding Word of God.

Having resisted the lust of the flesh, the tempter takes Jesus to the most significant public place of worship. The temptation is for Jesus to be seen by others as the Son of God by means of a public miracle. Satan knows that one of man's greatest desires is to be seen as significant by others. This may be the dominant meaning of the term 'lust of the eyes'. Looking with lust on another is more an expression of the lust of the flesh attempting to be satisfied, even if just visually. The eyes we lust after, too often, are the eyes of others looking with admiration at us. When others do look upon us with awe, fear, reverence, admiration or any other elevating mindset, we feel a kind of pleasure. Jesus again rejects the temptation by referring to the word of God and his willingness to wait upon God instead of attempting to force God to serve him.

The ultimate temptation is the capstone of the other two. In order to compromise to his carnal desires and his social cravings, a reflective person has to devise a system to justify his own actions. This is the pride of life. What is offered by the tempter is a simple plan: acknowledge that Yahweh is not ultimate, that there is some authority other than the uncreated creator which is ultimate (all forms of this rebellion satisfy Satan's desire for worship) and the fallen world is yours to do with as you will. Jesus rejects anything but the will of the Lord as revealed in the Bible.

At this point, Jesus is attended to by angels. Though Siddhartha was tempted in similar fashion including lust, pride, and compromising rationalization, the responses were different. Siddhartha appealed to his own merit and was aided by supernatural beings in his conflict with Mara. Jesus appealed to the Word of God as the basis for truth, and no angelic beings or gods were included. Only after the engagement was settled did he get attended to according to the promises of angels being ministering spirits to those of God.

It is interesting that desire is the ultimate test given. Desire is the human problem of living rightly. All of us live life struggling with the various facets of desire. James, the half brother of Jesus, articulates this problem of desire quite forcefully:

> From what source do quarrels and conflicts among you come? Do they not come from this source, namely, from your inordinate passions which are struggling with one another in your members? You have a passionate desire and are not realizing its fulfillment;

you murder. And you covet and are filled with jealousy, and you are not able to obtain (James 4:1, 2).

Our strife with others, as well as within ourselves, is essentially because we cannot fulfill our desires wisely or with finality; true, lasting satisfaction. What are some possible worldview options in relation to this basic problem in life?

1. Resign to desire (and be embittered by the consequences) Nihilism

2. Embrace desire (despite its frequently negative consequences) Epicureanism (some Brahmanic; e.g. Karma Sutra)

3. Suppress desire (punish failures) Legalism (moral/religious fundamentalism)

4. Ignore desire (pretend to be above it) Stoicism

5. Fight for desire (blame others for non-fulfillment) Liberationism

6. Quench desire (pursue beyond being) Buddhism

7. Redeem desire (be made a new creation by the Creator) Christianity

Though this list is neither precise nor exhaustive, it is illustrative of the universal nature of the problem of desire and the type of primary strategies offered to deal with the problem. Both Siddhartha, the Buddha, and Jesus, the Christ, walked away from their own intense confrontation with the one who tempts our desires with a message: Light is available!

Gathering of Disciples

For Siddhartha Gautama his very title, Buddha, means enlightened one. What the Buddha offers is a way to experience clarity of thought beyond ignorance like he has. In approaching his former friends, the Buddha declared that he himself had experienced enlightenment, and that they could too. After a couple of appeals, they agreed to be his disciples. Buddha then preached his message, at the conclusion of which, the disciple Kondanna gained experiential insight into the *dharma* that was taught and was duly ordained the first member of the Buddhist *Sangha* (priesthood). Others soon experienced this as well, and the number of disciples grew rapidly.

Jesus came back to his people and by his very presence Matthew claims the fulfillment of the prophesy of Isaiah concerning a great light being made available to the people living in the shadow of death. At this point Jesus began preaching what was and is his message: "Repent, for the kingdom of heaven is at hand."

The message of Jesus is that our thoughts, and subsequently our choices and actions, are not right. People need to repent: change our thinking (and subsequently our choices and actions). The need is to understand that God is in charge of the very space around each of us right here and now. His rule is immediate in time and proximity despite our limited perceptivity. In order to teach this, Jesus calls out common people who, without hesitation, follow his command. Taking these disciples to engage the likes of the four passing sights, Jesus demonstrates the reality and significance of his message. Rethinking is in order; God really is near.

Jesus actively freed people from various hardships (illnesses, wrong thinking, demonic possession, etc.). His impact was astounding and quickly a large crowd followed Jesus. Though Jesus had been preaching that there is good news, and that the gospel is the rule of God (Mt. 4:23), he then stopped and laid out what is tantamount to his own manifesto. He gathered his disciples on a mountainside and gave his message.

Sermon on the Mount: Comparing Solutions to Life's Problems

What Jesus declares in the Sermon on the Mount is almost universally admired, but not universally interpreted. What follows is a possible understanding of the meanings in the Sermon on the Mount by focusing on the outline. It appears that there is an intentional structure presented in what we see recorded in Matthew that highlights truths in a way that allows emphasis. Of particular importance to this paper, is that Buddhist questions of right living in light of the problems of desire and suffering are addressed in significant ways.

The beatitudes are given as a vision of what is offered. Whereas Buddha to his disciples emphasized *dukkha* (misery), Jesus proclaims *sukkha* (blessedness). The beatitudes are given in sequence, 1-2-3-4-5-6-7-8, and then are exposited in reverse order, 8-7-6-5-4-3-2-1 (see chart below). In doing this, the first and the last blessings highlight the promise that "theirs is the Kingdom of the Heavens", the good news of Jesus according to what Matthew just previously declared was the point of Jesus' preaching (Mt. 4:23). What is more, the first and the last beatitudes form a chiastic structure such that the main point is the central verse (Mt. 5:48):

"Therefore be complete as your Father in heaven is complete."

A_1... is the Kingdom of Heaven

B_1

C_1

D_1

Be complete (Telos) before God

D_2

C_2

B_2

A_2... is the Kingdom of Heaven

What follows is a list of seven priorities of focus in implementing the experience of the blessing in living in the Kingdom of Heaven. These priorities begin and end with the priority of the permanent over the impermanent, and the central area of the seven refers to the way of life verses the way the leads to destruction.

There is no reason to believe that Jesus is addressing Buddhism directly. Rather, it is arguable that Buddha, with the exception of some of his Brahmanic cosmology, essentially perceives life "under

Sermon on the Mount Outline Chart

Who is Blessed?	How are they Blessed?	Blessed-ness Promised	Blessed-ness Explained	Chiastic Structure	Related need and response
Poor in Spirit	Theirs is Kingdom of Heaven	5:3	6:19-24	(A_2)	Discipline
Mourning	Comforted	5:4	6:16-18	(B_2)	Fasting
Meek	Inherit the earth	5:5	6:5-15	(C_2)	Praying
Starving for righteous-ness	Satisfied	5:6	6:2-4	(D_2)	Giving
Merciful	Receive Mercy	5:7	5:38-47	(D_1)	Stinginess?
Pure in heart	See God	5:8	5:27-37	(C_1)	Duplicity?
Peacemakers	Are Sons of God	5:9	5:21-26	(B_1)	Contempt?
Persecuted for right-eousness	Theirs is Kingdom of Heaven	5:10	5:11-20	(A_1)	Incomplete righteous-ness?

the sun" rightly. Jesus answers Solomon, Buddha, Tolstoy, Camus and any other thinker that realizes the futility of life as we experience it without genuine permanence. All these thinkers were right in saying that meaning in an impermanent world is ultimately futile despite our amazing abilities of distraction and self-delusion

> A_1 Persecuted for righteousness? Theirs is the Kingdom of Heaven
> [These are God's children who decide that maturity in God is worth suffering for.]
> B_1 Peacemakers (being mature in peace-making is worth suffering)
> C_1 Pure in heart (being mature in purity is worth suffering)
> D_1 Merciful (being mature in mercy is worth suffering)

Be mature/complete (Telos) before God (actually be transformed), not just perceived as righteous before men.

> D_2 give alms to affect needs (not to be perceived as righteous)
> C_2 pray to be purely dependent on God (not to be perceived as righteous)
> B_2 fast over the entanglements of conflict (not to be perceived as righteous)
> A_2 Poor in Spirit? Theirs is the Kingdom of Heaven
> [These are people who see the need to keep investing in their spiritual portfolio if they are to experience the blessings provided to them by their heavenly Father.]

There is hope, life can be blessed!

Blessed (Sukkha!)							
Poor in spirit	Mourn	Meek	Starve for right- eous- ness	Merci- ful	Pure in heart	Peace- makers	Perse- cuted for right- eous- ness
King- dom of Heaven	Comfort	Inherit the earth	Satis- fied	Mercy	See God	Sons of God	King- dom of Heaven
5:3 6:19- 24	5:4 6:16-18	5:5 6:5-15	5:6 6:2-4	5:7 5:38- 47	5:8 5:27- 37	5:9 5:21- 26	5:10 5:11- 20

For those who are sensitive to the ubiquitousness of human suffering, it is arresting to hear a repeated declaration of such broad and emphatic blessedness. This declaration of happiness is doubly perplexing when counterintuitive ideas like blessed poverty, grief and persecution are included. One wonders how such an introduction to a message would be possible if not for the powerful ways in which Jesus had just shown that his understanding and abilities are genuinely effectual for hopeful living. His audience certainly was willing to engage his paradoxes.

Having proclaimed blessedness, Jesus begins to explain his meaning. The last mentioned, is expounded first, "Blessed are they which are persecuted for righteousness' sake: for theirs is the kingdom of heaven" (Mathew 5:11-20). The emphasis is on righteousness, though being persecuted is significant as well. The problem of *dukkha* is not just suffering per se, but meaningless suffering. Jesus reminds his listeners that righteousness and suffering are not, and have never in human history been, mutually exclusive. The concept of karma is immediately challenged. Though this is a stumbling block to a Buddhist thinker, it addresses experiential problems. Everyone is aware of someone who is good in meaningful ways, and yet real hardship befalls them disproportionate to what would be expected in a just world. *Karma* is employed suggesting that when the good suffer it was because at some point, likely in a previous life, they really were evil and are just now receiving what is deserved. Natural disasters then, are sudden eruptions of *karmic* correction, leveling people's accounts for the time being, until continued existence and desire generate more *karmic* punishment. That is precisely the type of problem that leads to the Buddhist conclusion that there is no safe and satisfying existence.

The type of righteousness Jesus is talking about is unmixed and unhindered. Salt is salty unless it is impure, mixed with other things, and then it is worthless. Light is pure, but meaningless if hindered from being shared. The righteousness Jesus describes as worth being persecuted for is one where one's character is unmixed, pure, and unhindered, allow to shine naturally so that the Heavenly Father is glorified.

To address his Jewish audience and those attentive to its universal claim, Jesus makes it clear that he is not overturning previous revelation. He is fulfilling the intent of the history of God's revelation, which is a way for people to be and live rightly. It is not only possible— it is where blessedness is experienced. The message to a Buddhist is that Jesus claims a good existence is possible and not negated by the prospect of suffering. The distinction of Jesus' solution to meaningless suffering for those who is exist is not to lead to non-existence (or whatever is between existence and non-existence), but to lead to real life in spite of suffering. Suffering is not immediately remedied; purpose and meaning are.

Like the righteous man of Psalm One, the imagery is of maturity; completeness. What does this righteousness look like? Jesus goes on to give three illustrations of types of incompleteness contrasted with completeness. Each of these has three examples.

Blessed are the peacemakers: for they shall be called the children of God. Matthew 5:9

Expounded in Matthew 5:21-26

❖ A righteous person is a person who loves others by seeking their good by being a peacemaker the way God is with them.
  - Not murdering has a claim of righteousness, but is incomplete.
    - Not even having contempt for others is a more complete example of righteousness.
  - Going to honor God has a claim of righteousness, but is incomplete.
    - Loving people who you see as part of honoring the God you do not see is a more complete example of righteousness.
  - Not neglecting one's own rights has a claim of righteousness, but is incomplete.
    - Waiving rights for the purpose of reconciliation is a more complete example of righteousness.

Blessed are the pure in heart: for they shall see God. Matt. 5:8

Expounded in Matthew 5:27-37

❖ A righteous person is a person pure in their heart and actions, not duplicity in their heart and actions.
  - Treat her as a sister in public has a claim of righteousness, but is incomplete.
    - Treating her as a sister in one's heart is a more complete example of righteousness.

o Exercising Jewish matrimonial laws regarding divorce appropriately has a claim of righteousness, but is incomplete.
  ▪ Keeping a covenant of being made one flesh no matter what is a more complete example of righteousness.
o Persuading others by promising really hard has a claim of righteousness, but is incomplete.
  ▪ Being consistent with what one says and does is a more complete example of righteousness.

Blessed are the merciful: for they shall obtain mercy. Matt. 5:7

Expounded in Matthew 5:27-37
❖ A righteous person is a merciful person who endures wrong for the sake of love, like God has done for them
  o Hurting only as you are hurt has a claim of righteousness, but is incomplete.
    ▪ Absorbing wrongful hurt to overcome wrong is a more complete example of righteousness.
  o Tolerating hard situations has a claim of righteousness, but is incomplete.
    ▪ Utilizing hard situations for expressing love is a more complete example of righteousness.
  o Loving those who love you has a claim of righteousness, but is incomplete.
    ▪ Loving those who need love is a more complete example of righteousness.

Matthew 5:48 says, "So you should be *telos* (complete, fulfilled, mature, *samma,* perfect...) in the right way to be who you are (a created being), the way God the Father is in who He is (the Creator whose attributes are not just potential, but actual)."

But how can people experience such mature righteousness? What is described next are illustrations of disciplines which facilitate the inner transformation by God of a redeemed person's character. The warning is given that it is possible to do the right things for the wrong reason, and that the primary wrong reason is because of a wrongly chosen audience: people, not God.

Corresponding Disciplines and Goals of Maturity for a Child of the Heavenly Father

The disciplines of giving alms, praying and fasting were understood as basics for those who wanted to be righteous in the context of the hearers of the sermon. Jesus uses the existing forms as an opportunity for discussion. Buddhists, Christians, Muslims and others have variations of the same disciplines, or at least of comparable disciplines. Though the illustrations in Matthew 5 (set "1" below) parallel the disciplines in Matthew 6 (set "2" below), they are not exclusive matches of need and means.[1] Due to the brevity of this paper, only a caption of each discipline will be provided.

A_1 Persecuted for righteousness? Theirs is the Kingdom of Heaven
[These are God's children who decide that maturity in God is worth suffering for.]

---

[1] For example: There is a sense in which someone not at peace with others should employ the discipline of fasting, but there are other disciplines which help with peace-making. Likewise, fasting helps with other needs of maturity in righteousness as well.

B_1 Peacemakers (being mature in peace-making is worth suffering)
C_1 Pure in heart (being mature in purity is worth suffering)
D_1 Merciful (being mature in mercy is worth suffering)

Be mature/complete (*telos*) before God, not just perceived as righteous before men. (One's goal should be to actually be transformed and matured, not to just look like as though one were).

D_2 give alms to affect needs (not to be perceived as righteous)
C_2 pray to be purely dependent on God (not to be perceived as righteous)
B_2 fast over the entanglements of conflict (not to be perceived as righteous)
A_2 Poor in Spirit? Theirs is the Kingdom of Heaven
[These are people who see the need to keep investing in their spiritual portfolio if they are to experience the blessings provided to them by their heavenly Father.]

Blessed are they which do hunger and thirst after righteousness: for they shall be filled. Matthew 5:6
Is one starving (*tanha*) for things to be right (like have the widows and orphans cared for)?

> Do not give money for a reward from people for being so generous. Give to the needy to receive a "reward" from God (i.e. "Well done my good and faithful servant").

Blessed are the meek: for they shall inherit the earth. Matt. 5:5

Does one want to take charge of problems and challenges?

> Do not pray to be rewarded by people as a spiritual super warrior. Be meek enough to quietly call on God who knows what you (and others) need.

Blessed are they that mourn: for they shall be comforted. Matthew 5:4

Is one grieved over unresolved issues, like an unknown direction, or a person needing help?

> Do not seek to be rewarded by people for being so concerned. Seek to be rewarded by God for having your heart in the right place (where His is).

Blessed are the poor in spirit: for theirs is the kingdom of heaven. Matthew 5:3

Ultimate wealth, prosperity, is when one invests in lasting treasures, not elusive treasures.

> One's perception of value will determine one's master, choosing wisely is critical. If one chooses the impermanent as valuable, one's whole life will be *dukkha*.

The wealthy usually pursue wealth. Why? Many believe that no matter how much they have, they are living short of what they could or should have. They are "poor" in their portfolio, relative to what is possible, and may feel they need to keep investing. Poor in spirit, likewise, is a declaration that whatever we have in our spiritual portfolio is not enough. We need to keep investing in order to fulfill our purpose and experience the blessings we received freely in Christ. This should be the attitude of every Christian this side of paradise. As Paul put it:

> Not that I have already obtained this or am already perfect (*telos*), but I press on to make it my own, because Christ Jesus has made me his own. Brothers, I do not consider that I have made it my own. But one thing I do: forgetting what lies behind and straining forward to what lies ahead, I press on toward the goal for the prize of the upward call of God in Christ Jesus. Let those of us who are mature (*telos*) think this way, and if in anything you think otherwise, God will reveal that also to you. Only let us hold true to what we have attained (Philippians 3:12-16).

The preoccupation with the poverty of our portfolio is not in order to make a bid for entrance past pearly gates. The poverty of our portfolio is in our completion of having been conformed to the image of Christ, which is exactly what all who are justified are predestined to be:

> And we know that for those who love God all things work together for good, for those who are called according to his purpose. For those whom he foreknew he also predestined to be conformed to the image of his Son, in order that he might be the firstborn among many brothers. And those whom he predestined he also called, and those whom he called he also justified, and those whom he justified he also glorified. What then shall we say to these things? If God is for us, who can be against us? (Romans 8:28-31)

The message is that we can and should be able to experience an ever increasing satisfaction of the most meaningful desires, if we invest in the permanent, not the impermanent. Buddha would

almost surely agree, if he believed there was anything permanent
and good that was accessible.

> No god, no Brahma can be called
> The Maker of this Wheel of Life:
> Just empty phenomena roll on
> Dependent on conditions all
>> Path of Purification XIX (Khantipalo 1989:52).

However, he despaired of such, and declared that for any self to
find such satisfaction and wholeness, that self would have to be
truly perfect:

> The Buddha argued that anything subject to change,
> anything not autonomous and totally controllable by its
> own wishes, anything subject to the disharmony of
> suffering, could not be such a perfect true self. (Harvey
> 1990:51).

> Jesus Christ is the same yesterday and today and forever
> (Hebrews 13:8).

Jesus is the self-existent I-AM of the Old Testament. He is
exactly what Buddha said would have in order for there to be a
permanent self, the basis of permanence that does not lead to
dukkha. What Buddha would still stumble over, however, is
suffering, particularly when it is endured by the one proclaiming
freedom. What would need to be understood is the difference
between suffering for what is good versus suffering without
meaning.

Seven Priorities in the Pursuit of Completeness
How then does one pursue this righteousness that leads to a blessed
life where disciplines counter unrighteousness such that the

character of the permanent Christ is made more and more a part of our own experience? How does one become complete— *telos*? That is what is developed immediately after the beatitudes are given and explained. These admonitions appear to come in seven concepts, the divisions of which are suggested below:

Priority of seeking permanence	Priority of personal responsibility	Priority of Ask Seek Knock	Priority of path	Priority of character	Priority of relationship	Priority of building on permanence
Kingdom First and His righteousness	Do Not Start with Fixing Others	God will Provide	Pursue Life Do Not Drift to Destruction	Be Careful who you Follow	Be careful in what you trust	Build on what is permanent, not on impermanent
6:25-34	7:1-6	7:7-12	7:13,14	7:15-20	7:21-23	7:24-27

Permanence first (His Kingdom and righteousness) then impermanent things 6:25-34

Again the priority is in acknowledging that impermanence is inadequate. The beginning and ending of these practical exhortations relate to that concern. God's Kingdom, and righteousness that has its source and permanence in Him, is the basis upon which life is blessed. The lilies are glorious and the sparrows counted, but they die. Men too are like that. Our glory is fleeting, and then we are overwhelmed by impermanence. We must take shelter in God.[2]

---

[2] In order to save the 'self' we must find refuge in that which is permanent. This is almost full circle from Buddhism which argues there is no 'self' and certainly no safe permanence for 'self'. In God both the legitimacy of personhood and permanence are presented as a solution to

Having done so, we cannot agree with the position that the impermanent world in which we live is meaningless. We do need food and clothes. We do have impermanent needs and desires that are met with impermanent resources. That is not far from *dukkha*, in that it is an ongoing sense of needing more for satisfaction. There is suffering but not without meaning.

At times we confuse the meaning of life as being the acquisition (and in noble moods the distribution) of resources. But that is simply not the case. What matters is that our beings are transformed into the purposes intended by our creator and redeemer. What is true is that the transformation of our souls occurs in the process of exercising our will in the gathering of impermanent resources to meet impermanent needs. That life is real, but its meaning is of a permanent nature (for good or for bad!).

Pursuing completeness is what you need to do with God, not for other people 7:1-6

The excitement about the chance to live a blessed and righteous life can lead to some odd behaviors. As found in the Dhammapada, Buddha argued that we cannot be about fixing others:

> By oneself is evil done,
> By oneself defiled.
> By oneself it's left undone,
> By self alone one purified.
> Purity, impurity on oneself depend,
> No one can purify another (Khantipalo 1989:30).

---

the limited, but insightful observations that there is incompleteness in all people and that the lack of self (anatta) and the lack of permanence (anicca). If there were not a perfect, personal permanence, then there would be no adequate refuge for the non-self which in ignorance desired to be a self. Then Buddha would arguably be right to back away from desire and existence.

Jesus agrees in part. Self-salvation should be seen as a self-defeating proposition, especially to those who say there is non-self. Though Jesus says we as people are neither sufficient to exist by ourselves, nor to save ourselves, we are even less sufficient to save others. Yet, this is what religious people tend to do. Jesus lists two options of helping others, both with good intentions but less than good reasonableness.

One tendency is to pick at people's faults and problems, 'for their good.' Jesus makes a comical image of a guy with a plank extruding from his eye trying to get close enough to aid another with a speck. Jesus' admonition is quite practical: give attention to what you have responsibility and control over, which means yourself.

Others think that this restriction is limited to being negative, and though it may be wrong to focus on correcting the faults of other, they believe it is good and wise to provide unsolicited blessings for others. Again, the problem is that if we do not have mastery on what we ourselves need, then we certainly do not need to be presuming what others want or need. Thus, he says to stop pushing pearls on those who do not want them. The message is that we are our own main project before God, and that working towards completeness in our own character should be a primary job. One's character development may often be in service to others in that the trait we are pursuing is love: of God and others. The distinction is in presumption and posture.

God has what people need. We each need to ask, seek, knock to receive it from him 7:7-12

The way to work on our character includes disciplines, but those are not ultimate. In giving alms, everything we have comes from the

Lord. In prayer, he is our provision, our protector and our guide. In fasting, are we not crying out to him? What is needed is awareness that we are not alone. Our hope is in the permanent one providing what we need (including an awareness of what we actually need as opposed to what we think we need). We are to A.S.K: ask, seek, and knock. This is relational, and it is worship.

One very basic way of articulating the Good News is to say, "God has what we need (and he will give it if you ask!)."

> To Seth also a son was born, and he called his name Enosh. At that time people began to call upon the name of the LORD (Genesis 4:26).

> And it shall come to pass that everyone who calls on the name of the LORD shall be saved (Joel 2:32a).

> And without faith it is impossible to please him, for whoever would draw near to God must believe that he exists and that he rewards those who seek him (Hebrews 11:6).

The challenge then is to work on living in God's permanence by actively asking him for what you need (including wisdom), seeking to understand it, and knocking to take hold of that for which he has taken hold of you.

This is a significant departure from Buddhism, but it is so because of a difference on the existence of permanent self that is whole. If the latter is acknowledged, the former makes sense. What continues is a limited ability to affect others. Therefore, "do unto others" is included in this teaching on asking.

Path of Life! (fulfilled existence), not destruction (ruined existence) 7:13, 14

The central message of these seven points of focus is a call to a robust existence, not the extinguishing cessation of existence. There is a way to life, but it is defined and narrow, not open ended and subject to creative rationalization. Jesus did not come to save us from existence, but from futile and failing existence. He came that we might have life abundantly. Buddha says we are stuck in a swamp of *dukkha*, but he knows the way to a cliff where we can put an end to our misery. Jesus says we are in a swamp of dukkha, but he is the path to a mansion that is built on an unshakeable foundation, into which we are invited to be received as beloved children.

Be careful who you follow (character, not image) 7:15-20

If then one converts to Christ and wants to walk his path, who should he follow? The sangha (community of monks) is one of the refuges in Buddhism, is there an ecclesiastical equivalent in Christianity? The answer is yes and no. Jesus warns that images can be deceiving. Like wheat and tares, it is not easy to differentiate between the good and the bad. There is a way to tell what something is, however: observe its offspring, its fruit.

To determine the kind of fruit tree, inspect the fruit. If the fruit is an orange, then it is an orange tree. To determine what kind of animal (wolf or sheep) look at its offspring. (The same is said of elders). The admonition is to identify character, not image. It is not too difficult to imitate appearances; it is much more difficult to imitate essence.

Be careful what you are trusting in (relationship, not religious productivity) 7:21-23

This is a late warning that evangelical people tend to want up front. There may be a reason for the lateness of the warning. Yes, relationship, not apparent religious productivity is what differentiates those welcomed home and those left outside in darkness and hopelessness. Too often the focus on justification dominates our discussion such that the purpose of the relationship is neglected in the exuberance to distinguish it from a merit-based position.

When a child is born, it is a wonderful event. But there is more to a child than just having it born. In fact, the value of its birth is largely linked to the hope of its development beyond birth. The birth of a child is celebrated because that will lead to her first steps and words, her development in personality and abilities, and the beauty of maturing into the person God intends her to be. In the same way, we are born again by his righteousness so we can move from immaturity (babes in Christ) to complete, mature, actually righteous people (living out our positional, imputed righteousness) to the praise of his glory! The bulk of the sermon describes what growing up in God's household is like. The warning is that imitating a child of the household is not the way to be adopted as a family member. For that, a more complete exposition of asking, seeking and knocking needs to be explored (and of course is explored in detail later in the New Testament).

Permanence first (build on what is solid, not what is impermanent) 7:24-27

The end of the foundational sermon of Jesus is about foundations. Buddha could not have done better to articulate the futility of building a life an impermanent (*anicca*) base. Both views observe the certainty of hardships (though the reasons for the rain and wind are explained differently when explained at all). Both agree that it is hardly worth it to build on a poor foundation. In fact, the greater the desire and effort to build on the sand, the greater the tragedy of the certain collapse.

What Buddha did not have to offer was another option. If he had seen the firm foundation of the rock, would he have advised abandoning the hope of building? We do not know. What we do know is that Jesus and the life he teaches is that rock upon which are lives can be built. Hardships will come, but they will not be dukkha. Though we have hardships, we are not destroyed.

> So we do not lose heart. Though our outer nature is wasting away, our inner nature is being renewed day by day. For this slight momentary affliction is preparing for us an eternal weight of glory beyond all comparison, as we look not to the things that are seen but to the things that are unseen. For the things that are seen are transient, but the things that are unseen are eternal (2 Corinthians 4:16-18).

Conclusion

There are many concepts which are touched on too briefly in this short paper to provide a clear and unequivocal understanding. Questions have been raised for work in other discussions. What should be clear, however, is that the experiences and topics Jesus and Siddhartha encountered have similarities. These similarities are not synonymous, as if the same spiritual story were being repeated with different figures. On the contrary, the similarities of some events and some topics provide a relatively concise amount of information in which differences can be explored and understood.

Buddhism and Christianity have some very meaningful points of contact, but those points of contact are best used for appropriate differentiation, not of presumptuous syncretization. If Buddha is right about the four spiritual truths, then Jesus is an unacceptable teacher. He loved with real attachment and taught that others should seek attachment to what is permanent as well. Karmic-ly, Jesus seemed to live a good live, but he died a shameful and horrific death. If Buddha is right, then the rejection and crucifixion of Jesus demonstrate unrevealed evil in the being of Jesus, even if from another life.

Conversely, if Jesus is right, and there is a personal God who provides a permanent foundation for completed and satisfied selves, then Siddhartha is shown to be an a-buddha; a blind guide incapable of seeing passed the problem of the created world to the uncreated Creator. The two greatest commandments, according to Jesus, were to be lived, not extinguished. Loving God and man with unapologetic and passionate love is only a fulfillment of one of the two teachers' sermons. The Sermon on the Mount helps us to understand why and how children of God should desire to be more like Christ.

> Everyone who hears these words of mine and does them will be like a wise man who built his house on the rock. The rain fell, the floods came, the winds blew and beat on that house, but it did not fall, because it had been founded on the rock. Everyone who hears these words of mine and does not do them will be like a foolish man who built his house on the sand. The rain fell, the floods came, the winds blew and beat against that house, and it fell, and great was the fall of it (Matt.7:24-27).

PART II

SOCIOLOGICAL ISSUES

5

WORLD CHRISTIANITY IN BUDDHIST SOCIETIES

Stephen K. Bailey

What is at issue now is the surprising scale and depth
of the worldwide Christian resurgence that seems to
proceed without western organizational structures,
including academic recognition, and is occurring
amidst widespread political instability and the collapse
of public institutions, part of what it means to speak of
a post-western Christianity. Even church leaders have
been unable to comprehend fully, still less to respond
effectively to, the magnitude of the resurgence. In
some areas it's like being hit by a tidal wave and
unable to hold your footing. The fact is, no amount of
institutional organizing can cope with the momentum.
There necessarily will have to be ad hoc staging posts
and a good deal of unconventional religious re-housing
of converts until the pace slackens and the churches
can catch their breath (Sanneh 2003:3).

Reading these words from Lamin Sanneh's insightful book, *Whose
Religion is Christianity?* a missionary working among Theravada
Buddhists in South East Asia can do little more than sigh wistfully.
The tidal wave of new converts to Christianity since the end of
colonialism after WWII has caused little more than a ripple effect in
that area of the world. Many, including the contributors to this
volume are praying and thinking deeply in search of a plow that

will till the "hard soil" of Theravada Buddhist hearts. Admittedly there is more response to the gospel among the Thai, Khmer, Lao and Burmese Buddhists today than in the past but the pace at which these people are entering the Kingdom of God is at a crawl when compared to China, Indonesia, the Philippines and Sub-Saharan Africa.

In another article (Bailey 2003) I have taken up Charles Kraft's suggestion that what is needed today is not so much the contextualization of the informational content of the gospel but the careful contextualization of relationships (see Kraft 1999). Extending Kraft's idea into the Lao context I suggested that the slow response to the gospel there has more to do with the failure to shape communication along the lines of the social structural than it does with spiritual hardness. In fact, Buddhists of SE Asia are very spiritually sensitive people. Social allegiance to the group and the rules of social engagement within the group are issues that must be accounted for if the gospel is going to be communicated with impact in this context.

In this article I shift the analysis from how social structural issues should configure communication generally to how they are configuring the Lao Protestant Church.[1] While I use the Church in the Lao People's Democratic Republic (Laos) as my case study, I suspect that the findings here can be extended to other Theravada Buddhist contexts. Once I have described how Lao social structure is shaping the Lao Church I then bring these findings into conversation with Sanneh's ideas of "world Christianity" and "global Christianity." In his book mentioned above he briefly recounts the tremendous growth of the Church in the non-western

---

[1] For this point forward when I speak of the Lao Church I am speaking about Protestant churches in Laos unless otherwise noted.

world and then suggests that Christianity today can be characterized in by these two terms. He defines these two terms as follows:

'World Christianity' is the movement of Christianity as it takes form and shape in societies that previously were not Christian societies that had no bureaucratic tradition with which to domestic the gospel. In these societies Christianity was received and expressed through the cultures, customs, and traditions of the people affected...'Global Christianity,' on the other hand, is the faithful replication of Christian forms and patterns developed in [the West] (2003:22).

The thesis I argue is simply that Christianity will not grow significantly among the Theravada Buddhists in SE Asia until the Christian communities are more characterized by world Christianity than by global Christianity. But first I need to explain Sanneh's argument more thoroughly.

World Christianity

The incredible global expansion of the Christian Church during the past century and particularly since the end of colonialism is well documented (e.g. Aikman 2003; Barrett 2001; Sanneh 2003; Jenkins 2002). Today more Christians reside in Southern Hemisphere nations than in Europe and North America. In Africa, "the projections call for over 600 million Christians in twenty-five years...[by that time] Africa will have more Christians than any other continent, and that for the first time" (Sanneh 2003:41). China's engagement with Christianity while not as numerically staggering has nevertheless had a significant impact on the nation (see Aikman 2003 and Sanneh 2003:67). Ironically, Christianity in the missionary-sending West is anemic. Some "4,300 people were

leaving the church on a daily basis in Europe and North America"
between 1970-1985 (15).

Much of Sanneh's book is in the format of a free flowing
dialogue but he seems to suggest that there are at least two major
reasons for the emergence of world Christianity. First, world
Christianity has been fueled by the indigenization of Christianity by
local communities. Notice that in saying this he is emphasizing the
contribution of local communities to the contextualization of the
gospel rather than the efforts of missionaries in this regard.
Contextualization studies have too often been preoccupied with the
efforts of missionaries to communicate the gospel. In doing this
they overlook the fact that the appropriation and relevance of the
gospel is decided on by those who receive it and not the other way
around.

The key to the successful local appropriation of Christian faith
has been the translation of the Bible into local languages (see also
Sanneh 1998). Hearing the gospel in their own languages local
communities understood the gospel in terms of the cultural and
religious worlds that their languages activated. God was already
working among the local people before the arrival of missionaries
and the gospel expanded, fulfilled and critiqued this heritage
(2003:32). Sanneh points out that where there was a decision by
Bible translators to use the local word for God we discover the
successful growth of the Church in Africa. Whatever the
missionaries may have communicated about the gospel as important
the decisive factor was the meaning that local people found in it.

At the same time it is important to realize that contexts are not
passive but come preloaded with [their] own biases, ready to
contest whatever claims [they encounter]. Contexts, after all, are
"constructed strategies" (5). While Christianity landed into local

religious frameworks it did not lose its authenticity. Instead, local worldviews were also challenged and transformed (113-114). The resulting understandings and expressions of Christian faith in these new contexts have remained recognizably Christian (44).[2]

Another stage to this indigenization process was the emergence of African leadership in the Church. Where the institutional life of the Church was given over to local leadership the Church grew rapidly and the indigenization process deepened. Significantly, the emergence of women and young people in leadership has also marked world Christianity (18).

The second major factor in the growth of world Christianity has been its interaction with globalization. It is important to notice that globalization and world Christianity have emerged side by side. Christianity in the modern era attempted to safeguard religion by promoting the separation of Church and State. But the resulting emergence of a secularism armed with State power became combative and religion was increasingly characterized by private piety. Oddly enough, "Whatever the excesses of secularism as a political ideology, secularization as a cultural process does not

---

[2] This raises the question of what Sanneh considers to be authentic Christianity. "Conversion is a refocusing of the mental life and its cultural/social underpinning and of our feelings, affections, and instincts, in the light of what God has done in Jesus" (2003:44). At the same time conversion is not simply a private act. A person converts to God as a social act – identifying herself with a distinctive community of faith and with others called to the life of faith" (45). Christian conversion establishes a "theocentric notion of the equality of persons" which is the essential thread of the fabric of a free society based on the rule of law..." (73). "It is still with good reason then that world Christianity is suspected as a moral challenge to the political idolatry of the ideological state..." (74). In fact world Christianity offers a laboratory of pluralism and diversity" where faith and trust are foundational (75).

seem to be at odds with the religious resurgence today" (2003:9). As secularism has spread through globalization religion has found the space to flourish (10).

Sanneh acknowledges that this is still not the case in a few places such as North Korea (10). But even where the State has attempted to use its power to restrict world Christianity it has failed. Such is the case in China, Vietnam and Laos. "World Christianity is unarmed, and has been striking for its lack of political clout" (29). It has flourished most rapidly in societies, "marked by weak states and among impoverished populations, and where religious loyalties are stronger than political ones" (27).

By contrast global Christianity—fashioned philosophically in the Enlightenment—seeks to protect what it sees as the one essence of the gospel even as world Christianity "challenges us to pay attention to the dynamic power of the gospel and to the open-ended character of communities of faith" (35). World Christianity is a haphazard and unorchestrated movement to faith outside of and even as an antithesis to mainstream Christian bodies (28). "Small-scale societies insulated people from historical pressures and thus removed the need for adjustments in people's worldview. Christianity answered this historical challenge by a reorientation of the worldview so that the old moral framework was reconfigured without being overthrown" (43).

However connected the emergence of world Christianity is to globalization it should not be seen as simply an echo of globalization. In "some instances new Christian movements are a reaction to the ravages and threats of globalization, with concerted attention to the value of local cultures and economies, the challenges of social dislocation and marginalization, the interests and dignity of families, and the importance of community well-being" (75). In the days ahead world Christianity—in spite of its roots in private piety—will need to find ways to engage secular society in deeper ways (29).

In what follows below I relate Sanneh's arguments to the Protestant Christian Church in Laos. Specifically, I want to consider to what extent Christianity in Laos is indigenous and whether or not it can be associated with the emergence of world Christianity.

The Translation of Christianity into the Lao World

No one—including the Lao Christian Church—seems to know how many Christians there are in Laos. Although the number of Catholics is usually reported to be about 35,000, estimates of the Protestant community range from 50,000 Protestants to 150,000. The lack of statistical accuracy reflects a context in which administrative reporting is difficult given the remoteness of many Christian communities and the political liabilities of religious census taking in a country where the Lao People's Revolutionary Party (LPRP) has made it difficult to be a Christian. Clearly the number of Protestant Christians in Laos has grown significantly since 1990, the year that marks the slow emergence of Lao society into the global community.

Social Implications of the Lao Bible
Sanneh believes that the key to indigenous Christianity has been the translation of the Bible into local languages. The first thing to notice in this regard is that the Bible has only been translated completely into two of Laos' 130 plus languages. One of these

languages is of course Lao and the other is Hmong.[3] The decision to translate into these two languages was made for strategic reasons by missionaries. Lao is the most commonly spoken language in Laos and the Hmong made up the majority of the Protestant Church until shortly after the communists came to power in 1975. But the political and social significance of this decision has been enormous.

The Lao make up no more than 60% of the nation but at no point in the history of Protestant faith have they made up even a quarter of the membership of the Church. For this reason it is not difficult to see how the translation of the scriptures into Lao reflects and reinforces the political and social dominance of the Lao. For minority peoples education and religion (Buddhist and Christian) are accomplished largely in the language and social milieu of the dominant Lao culture.

Perhaps even more significantly the Hmong have been engaged in a long anti-communist resistance movement. Although few Christian Hmong in Laos today support the resistance movement almost all the Christian Hmong prior to 1975 were anti-communist but actively fought in partnership with the US military in the failed attempt to prevent the coming to power of the LPRP. These factors have established a situation in which most Christians in Laos do not read the Bible in their mother tongue. In spite of the preference for Lao in the Church community non-Christian Lao associate Christianity with minority groups and allegiance to the west.

A second important factor is related to the kind of language used to translate the Bible into Lao. Lao like other SE Asian languages has high and low languages. Traditionally the high language was used when speaking to the royal family and in government circles.

---

[3] The Bible has been completely translated into both Blue and White Hmong dialects.

Significantly, the first two translations of the Bible into Lao used the high Lao language.

The first done by Swiss Brethren missionaries before WWII was virtually incomprehensible given the high language and the low quality of the translation. The second translation done by an American missionary with a southern Lao church leader (early 1970s) was of better quality but retained the high language that even today is understood well only by a minority of Lao. It is even more incomprehensible among the minority groups. This by itself made it difficult for most Lao to read the Bible a fact that probably did not surprise most Lao because religious language at Buddhist temples is also mostly incomprehensible. Religious rituals in their experience are always associated with secret knowledge that only religious experts understand and properly use. This sentiment is still so deep that most Lao Christians feel uncomfortable if a non-Christian reads the scriptures aloud in a public setting. For that matter they prefer to ask only skilled readers to publicly read the Bible. Even today pastors use the high language to pray.

There are at least two ways in which the choice of the high language impacted the indigenous understanding of Christian faith. First, it perpetuated the Buddhist idea that religious scriptures are above and beyond the reach of the ordinary person. On the positive side it gave the scriptures an auspicious quality and placed Christianity high in the cosmological Buddhist hierarchy. Local pastors naturally became the vehicles through which the Word and will of God was communicated.[4]

---

[4] It is interesting to consider how the activity of Christians in reaching out to the lepers and those exorcised of spirit possession in southern Laos during the early years of Protestant missionary work contradicted the high social status of the Christian scriptures!

Second, the use of high Lao in the Bible acknowledged the relevance of hierarchy in religion generally and in Christian faith specifically. Locally this translated into Church politics so that in spite of the fact that the Church has been overwhelmingly made up of Khmu, Hmong and other minorities, Lao Christians have always dominated the leadership. Strangely enough non-Christian Lao have always associated Christian faith with minorities and colonialism while the Church's internal politics have reflected the structure of the larger Lao society almost perfectly.

Implications of Some Translation Decisions

The translators of the Bible into Lao made some other telling decisions that have shaped the local understanding of Christianity in important ways. I will look at just two of them. The first was the decision to translate the word God as *Pachao* (this was also done in Thailand). The other was the decision to make no reference at all to *khwan* when speaking of a person's soul or spirit. Both decisions were difficult ones to make and my point here is not to suggest that mistakes were made but simply to describe some of the implications of these decisions.

Pachao is much closer in meaning to the word "Lord" than it is to God. I know this because an elder in a village once referred to me as *Pachao* in hopes of winning my favor for a development project! A King and the Buddha are referred to as *Pachao*. It is often thought that the Lao have no concept of a high creator god but this is not the case. As in many traditional societies the Lao retain a pre-Buddhist era belief in a high creator god *Phii Thään* who is rather distant and uninvolved (Bailey 2002). The Biblical references, as well as Christian teaching and prayers to *Pachao* are ambiguous to non-Christian Lao ears. I once stopped a prayer meeting and asked two non-Christians who were in attendance what they understood we were referring to when speaking of *Pachao*. One of the young men confessed that he uncertain if we were speaking of Indra or Brahma. Given Sanneh's evidence from Africa that the Church has grown every where that the local name for God was used in translation one wonders what effect the use of *Phii Thään* for God would have made in Laos.[5]

The absence of any reference to *khwan* in the second translation of the Bible (1970s) is remarkable given the fact that nearly every anthropological study of Lao culture makes a point of stating how essential the concept is to the Lao understanding of the human person.[6] *Khwan* is the spiritual essence of life that every human being has when they are healthy and in a happy state of mind.[7] One of the earliest decisions made by missionaries was to associate *khwan* with evil spirit allegiances. This was a serious misunderstanding of *khwan* and *khwan* rituals. All *khwan* rituals are an attempt to bring blessing and well being to a person by recalling or affirming the presence a person's *khwan*.[8] Every major life event

---

[5] I am not suggesting at this point that a change be made. I suspect that the reason *Phii Thään* was not used in the Lao Bible was because the first part of this name – *phii* – is a Lao word that is generally used for ghost or evil spirit. However, its basic meaning is simply "spirit." Missionary and subsequently Lao Christian aversion to anything connected to this word is well established in Lao Christianity.

[6] See Bailey (2002:11) for a list of authors who point this out. More recently see the article by Patrice Ladwig (2003:46).

[7] Some animals and inanimate things associated with the sustenance of human life are also said to have *khwan*. For example the water buffalo that pulls the plow through the rice field is said to have *khwan*. Rice also has *khwan*.

[8] During the ritual white cotton string is tied around the wrist as a sign of blessing and the presence of *khwan*. This was most likely associated with

– whether in celebration or in crisis – is marked by a *khwan* ritual yet to this day the Christian community instructs its members not to participate in the rituals and never mentions *khwan* in its preaching.

When the most recent translation of the Bible was published a few years ago. The Lao translators working out of the refugee community in North America made a decision to include the word *khwan*. Psalm 103 was translated as follows:

> Praise the Lord O my *khwan*! Let everything within me praise His holy name! Praise the Lord O my *khwan*! Never forget the benevolent goodness of the Lord!

None of this should lead to the assumption that Lao Christians have stopped believing in *khwan*. In a survey that I conducted nearly all Lao Christians continue to believe that *khwan* is an essential aspect of each person. Nevertheless, the Church remains indifferent and often antagonistic to its place in Lao life. The word used by Christians for the spirit of a person or the Holy Spirit is the Buddhist term *vinnyaan*.

I would like to call attention to two implications of the above discussion. First, Christianity from the very beginning has associated itself (unintentionally for the most part) with the hierarchy reflected in Lao Buddhist society. While this may sound negative being positioned at a high place in the hierarchy is a favorable and auspicious thing from the Lao perspective. It has not however been conducive to the growth of the Church.

Second, the Church in Laos continues to struggle with finding an indigenized expression of the gospel that can be seen to gather into it, "whatever is true, whatever is noble, whatever is right, whatever

---

evil spirit fetishes that missionaries had either heard of or encountered in other contexts.

is pure, whatever is lovely, whatever is admirable..." (Phil 4:8, NIV) from Lao religious thought and practice. Rather than seeing the gospel as a fulfillment of the positive aspects of Lao religion Christianity has defined itself in opposition to and completely distinct from Lao religion. This of course is not a realistic stance. Christian faith is always appropriated in terms of what has gone before it. In fact Lao Christians often do express their faith in ways that are deeply connected to their traditional religious worldview. This has become more obvious since the exodus of formal missionary work in 1975 when the country was "liberated" by the LPRP. Since that time the Church has become increasingly power oriented in terms of its church polity and its emphasis on the power of Jesus to heal, deliver and provide. I will pick this issue up again after considering Lao social structure in terms of Sanneh's concepts of world and global Christianity.

Lao Households, Villages and the Müang

It is not possible to go into a full description of Lao social structure but for the purposes of this article I will draw attention to the three basic social spaces in which Lao life occurs. These are the household, the village and the *müang*.

Households are typically occupied by extended family that include three generations. Traditionally the maternal grandparents who once owned the home live in the house with their youngest daughter, her husband and their children. Often one of the older grandchildren is married and lives in the home with her husband as well since newlyweds will live with the bride's parents for a period of several years before starting a household of their own.

A Lao household is the property of the female line (matrilineal). Traditionally, men leave their homes at marriage to live in their wife's family home for a time (uxorilocal residence). But descent is traced through men as much as through women (bilateral) (Bailey 2002).

The village is the residence of households related through women, while the men have generally all moved into the village at marriage.[9] Men occupy formal roles of leadership and authority including government positions and as monks in the village temple. The village follows a complex ritual system that has four basic kinds of ritual areas: 1) Buddhist rituals that deal with merit making for the living and the ancestors, and funeral rites; 2) Guardian spirit rituals that are sometimes nature spirits and at other times important ancestor spirits; 3) malevolent spirit rituals; and 4) *khwan* household rituals. Villages are primarily oriented toward the household social space but they are regularly invaded by *müang* powers including powerful business people and government officials.

Any power relationship that is located outside the village may be considered to be part of the concept of *müang*. *Müang* is a Lao word that can refer to a series of villages that once shared a common water supply and political organization, a government district, an ancient kingdom or simply urban – non-village – life. *Müang* relationships are non-kin relationships and are utilitarian in nature. A villager hopes to avoid being harmed by these powers and aspires to being able to manage or even manipulate them for his/her benefit. *Müang* relationships are expedient and often contractual.

---

[9] Northeastern Lao tend to follow a more ancient Tai cultural system in which women move into their husband's homes / villages.

MORALITY AND POWER IN LAO SOCIET

Level of Existence	Undomesticated Dispassionate Non-Existence	Human Domestic Life			The Dead
Social Level	Temple	Household (kinship)	Village (government and temple)	Müang Power	The misfortunate
	Buddha	**Mothers** (fathers)	**Fathers** (mothers)	**Powerful Politicians Wealthy**	**The dead, forest, rivers**
Source of Spiritual Moral Power	*Dharmma* Wisdom	Selfless care as **mothers** birthing, raising children, Female ancestor spirits, rice goddess, earth goddess *Khwan*	Self-denial of men as **leaders** who care for the community and as **monks** who teach other and give opportunities to make merit *Khwan*	**Buddha Dharma Monks** *Vinnyaan*	Virtue (*Bunkhun*) of ancestors, especially grandmother
Source of Spiritual Amoral Power	None	Nature and guardian spirits	Nature and guardian spirits	Monks, *Pali* texts, Buddha images, Hindu deities, angels, nature spirits, ancestral spirits who are now guardian spirits	Fear that ancestors will be offended
Aggressive Immoral Power	None	Fear of offended, evil spirits	Fear of offended, evil spirits	Fear of offended, evil spirits	Anger of offended, evil spirits
Basis of Relationships	None	Promise between kin	Promise between kin, leaders' roles	Contractual	Fear

Above, in Table 1 these three social spaces of the household, village and *müang* are considered in terms of the Lao religious system. Households are clearly marked by the social power of women and are characterized by both moral and amoral power. In this case amoral power if appeased and ritually managed can bring blessing to the household.

If amoral powers are mismanaged and/or ignored they can bring harm to the household. Examples of amoral power available to the household are nature, ancestor and guardian spirits. Moral power is drawn from the *bunkhun* (gracious benevolence) associated with the self-sacrificing nature of mothers. *Bunkhun* speaks to a mother's willingness to put her own concerns aside for the sake of caring for her children and family. "At mother's side one is safe *pawt phay* and knows that one will be forgiven *aphay*. This goodness creates a moral debt that should be acknowledged; it is the source from which moral obligation arises" (Mulder 1979:119). One of the primary reasons that young men enter the Buddhist monastery for a period of time during their adulthood is to earn merit on behalf of their mothers (see for example Leffert's description of the ordination ritual in Xieng Khuang 1999:220).

The social space of the village serves as a kind of mediation between the household and social relations outside and larger than the village. It is characterized by both female and male social power. While villages tend to be a collection of households related through women, men are in formal roles of leadership and serve for various periods of time as monks in order to make merit on behalf of their parents—especially their mothers. It is the women of the village who feed and care for the monks. Moral power at the village level is located in mothers but also in monks. The monk's moral strength comes from his willingness to sacrifice the normal pleasures of life in order to provide opportunities for the laity to make merit. Their service to the community is also seen in their availability to teach the children, counsel laity regarding personal problems and perform various rituals of blessing and empowerment. But villagers also have available several sources of amoral power, the most important one being the local village guardian spirit.

Müang life is what lies outside the village in terms of social space and power. Men and women (but especially men) with political and economic power dominate *müang* relationships. While moral power can be seen in the role that the Buddhist community plays in legitimizing power (see Reynolds 1978) it is characterized by the use of amoral power. Relationships with people and spirits tend to be ritualized, contractual and manipulative. Hierarchy is at its peak and power centralized.

The matrilocal pattern of Lao society which forces men to leave home, coupled with the pattern of male dominance of formal leadership roles, work together to put men in contact with *müang* power outside the village much more frequently than women. That men can be seen to use amoral power more often is reflected in the fact that normally male ancestral spirits are housed outside the family house. It can also be seen in that the village guardian spirit is normally thought to be male.[10]

In summary, within the household and the *müang* levels of social life there is the tension between the use of moral and amoral power. The moral power of the household is primarily oriented towards the *bunkhun* benevolence of mothers but the amoral power of the spirits

---

[10] The guardian spirit is usually not only male but is thought to also have an appetite for human life unless appeased. This is reflected in the story of *Thao Dääng Awn* and the Giant *Yak.*

can be tapped into when needed. The level of hierarchy is considerably lower and relationships are based on kinship interdependence. As a result communication in the household is dialogical than in the *müang*. *Müang* moral power is available through the teaching (dharma or *thamma*) of male Buddhist monks but more frequently draws on the utilitarian use of political, economic and spiritual power.

At every level Laos is oriented toward power. The moral beauty of mothers and monks is held in high esteem but when they fail to provide what is needed to solve the problems of everyday life, the Lao readily move on to amoral sources. A distinguishing mark of Lao religion when compared to western religion is found in that religious teaching and ritual is relevant not because they are true but because they are powerful. In what follows I will try to show how this social structure impacts the configuration of Lao churches.

Lao Protestant Christianity Today

Things are changing in Laos. In 1990 the Protestant Church in Laos could be described as conservative, tightly controlled—both internally and externally—and reserved. It was gradually growing through the hard work of local evangelists who patiently taught the Word to a trickle of converts. Yet the growth remained largely among the ethnic minority groups and while more Lao were coming to Christ than at any time in the past the rate remained painfully slow.

Today the Protestant church is an increasingly unwieldy, increasingly Pentecostal movement of people into the Kingdom. In Vientiane you had better go early to one of the three Lao Evangelical Church (the LEC is the government recognized and largest Protestant Church) churches if you want a seat. Most of those attending are from the dominant Lao ethnic group. This movement to Christ is somewhat unorganized, even chaotic and could not be controlled should someone wish it. The Church is not only growing it is beginning to find its place in Lao society. Recently (January 2005) several key Lao government officials spoke with nearly 900 Christians in one event in Vientiane. In Laos this is a huge gathering of Christians and a sign of political and social recognition that has long been awaited.[11]

But the path ahead is clouded. The LEC has been attempting to funnel the swell of converts into old structures where authority is highly centralized in pastors. Teaching is largely based on translated materials[12] created in foreign contexts vastly different from Laos. There is very little if any theologizing since most pastors understand their role as passing on the established doctrines of the Church. Doing theology for new contextual concerns is not even considered. LEC pastors have seen their authority elevated by harnessing Pentecostal-style ministries emphasizing the power of the Holy Spirit to heal, bless, solve problems and transform lives. "There is no illness or problems in Jesus Christ!" proclaim the pastors. The impact in a country where spiritual power is sought out everywhere has been significant. People eagerly present themselves ready to give their lives to Jesus and look to His power.

---

[11] After the event mentioned above the response given at the event by the head of the LEC was aired on the government radio and public address system the next morning. Also significant are the numerous articles in the People's newspaper (controlled by the LPRP) highlighting the activity of the LEC.

[12] These materials are mostly translated into Lao from Thai materials which were translated from English creating a double distance.

But the movement to Christ is broader than the LEC can contain or control. It has overflowed into small groups that are led by disenfranchised LEC leaders and sometimes by groups sponsored by foreign organizations. Student ministries are successfully engaging the younger generation. There is also another group of professional Christians who do not attend any organized churches but gather irregularly with other Christians for worship and mutual encouragement.

This spill over is an on going frustration to LEC leaders. From the leadership's point of view all Christians—local and foreign—have a spiritual responsibility to work through the LEC. They have even been able to prompt the government to issue decrees making it illegal to plant churches that do not come under the authority of the LEC. They point out that questionable theological emphasizes are being taught and chaos is resulting from these renegade Christian groups. Yet, the flow continues to move over and past the LEC with increasing speed.

My purpose in describing the situation of the Church in Laos is not to criticize the LEC or Pentecostal ministry. Pentecostalism has brought revival and energy to many of God's people in Laos and it is a highly relevant theology in the Lao context given its power orientation. The LEC has successfully taken a scattered group of frighten Christians in the 1980s and established a growing Church institution that has been granted acceptance by the government of Laos. God has and continues to use the LEC. Having said that, I also want to suggest that Sanneh's observations regarding the growth of world Christianity considered against the situation in Laos can provide insight into why the new growth of the Church in Laos may or may not turn into a full fledge movement.

Church As Household or *Müang?*

The growth of the Church in Laos cannot be said to simply echo globalization. Nevertheless, globalization can be seen to have cleared a path for the expansion of the Church in important ways. It has given the Lao people access to information, capital and communication with the outside world that was formerly unavailable. In many ways globalization is the technological version of political democracy. It has empowered local communities even as it has connected them to global realities. It is both a threat to local meaning and identity and the means by which local populations can defend them. Most relevantly for this article the impact of globalization in Laos has been to connect the Christians with the resources, methods and ideas of the international Church. I would suggest that these relationships with the global Church and international missionary organizations have allowed many Christians to escape the *müang* power of the LEC (and global Christianity) and birth Christian communities that are more characterized by household life (and world Christianity).

It is my observation that there is a tension in Laos today between a model of Church that reflects household relationships and a model that reflects *müang* relationships. To some extent both kinds of relationships can be found in every Protestant Church or group in Laos. But it is still possible to draw some generalizations.

First, Church life within the LEC reflect *müang* relationships more often than they do household relationships. This is particularly true in the urban areas but it can also be seen in the countryside. The LEC is a highly structured organization that reserves authority for (male) clergy. It demands absolute obedience of the laity to the extent that sermons regularly list failure to obey the pastor and attend a LEC church as a serious sin. The relationship between government and LEC leadership grows stronger by the year. Communication is unidirectional and the Christian life is clearly evaluated in terms of one's external participation in the Church and separation from Lao Buddhist society. To the extent that this assertion is true the LEC reflects global Christianity to a larger degree than it does world Christianity.

The small group/house church movement that has emerged on the margins and even outside of the LEC carries many characteristics of household relations and by extension world Christianity as described above. These groups are low in structure and involve laity in ministry much faster and more easily than does the LEC. The leadership of women and young people also marks these communities. These groups are evolving even haphazard communities. No pre-programmed blueprint guides them and their theology is thoroughly grounded in the interaction between scripture and experience. The Christian life among these people is evaluated by one's testimony of faith and the active power of God in one's life. Informal, spontaneous expressions of faith through the network of kin relationships are the single most decisive means by which the Kingdom is growing among these communities. This feature, more than any other marks its connection with world Christianity.

I have drawn the lines in the description above more ideally than the reality on the ground to help discern some general patterns. Neither the LEC nor the house church movement can be categorizes so neatly. The emergence of world Christianity is flooding the doors of the LEC in spite of its traditional forms and structure. Many of its rural churches reflect more of household religion than they do *müang* power. The shear size of the Church today makes it difficult to control and structure. Ironically, given what Sanneh has

	LAO CHURCH MOVEMENTS and SANNEH'S TYPES	
Sanneh's Types	**World Christianity**	**Global Christianity**
Lao Christian Church Movements	House Churches / Small Groups Low Structure Laity Empowered Women in Leadership Youth in Leadership Informal Spontaneous Evangelism Grace = Child of God Kingdom Ethic emphasized but Pentecostal Power present	Lao Evangelical Church Highly Structured Laity Obedient Male Pastoral Teaching Government Sponsorship Program Orientation Performance = Obedience to LEC Pentecostal Power emphasized but Kingdom Ethic present
	TRADITIONAL LAO SOCIAL ORIENTATIONS	
Social Level	Households Ancestral spirits Village Maternal kinship relations	***Müang* Powers** Buddhism Powers larger than village Non-maternal kin networks
Social Dimension	High Group Community well-being Presence of each person's *khwan*	High Grid Individual pursuit of power within a *müang* power system
Gender Orientation	Female (Male)	Male (Female)

Power Source	Moral	Amoral	Amoral	Moral
Ritual Focus	Restoration for well-being	Blessing for well-being	Blessing for success	Merit for ancestors
Spirit Type	*Khwan*		*Vinnyaan*	
Key Ritual Specialist	*Mawphawn*		Monk	
***Khwan* Ritual Symbol**	Rice, meat offerings, cotton string	*Pali* chants *Tonbaasii,* cotton string, marigolds	*Pali* chants, Buddha images, cotton string, marigolds	
Life Focus	Life		Life/Afterlife/Death	

described, any effort to control and bring order may work against the momentum of people into the Kingdom. In the same vein the house churches are sometimes found to have leaders who lead with almost dictatorial power and influence.

Conclusion

The encounter between Christians and Theravada Buddhists in SE Asia has been frustrated by a lack of indigenous expressions of Christian faith and the failure to shed hierarchy and empower the laity. The Church has been uneasy with putting down roots in the soil of dharma, ancestors, and nature spirits. We have preferred to truck in our own soil and failed to see the secularism, materialism and colonial triumphalism that lay within it. Converts to the Christian faith have had to choose Jesus and a foreign identity that has alienated them from their friends and relatives leaving them dependent upon foreign missionary structures. It is time for the Christian faith to take root in the soil of SE Asia and find the sustenance it needs grow into a great tree "so that the birds of the air come and perch in its branches" (Matt 13:32b). These birds will be the sign that the Church belongs to the land. We need not fear the impact of the soil on the tree. This tree of life is strong and its leaves, having fallen into the soil, will transform and nurture the ground.

Indigenization of the meaning and expression of Christian theology requires a release from the control of western theological paradigms. This has happened to some degree by default as the LPRP has refused to allow foreign involvement in Lao churches. It lives on however in the constant translation of western Christian materials into the Lao language. The current generation of Lao Christian leadership trained by foreign missionaries in theological fundamentalism in the pre-1975 era also keeps the colonialism of theology in Laos alive. Even the new generation of Church leaders are affected through their training in foreign Bible Schools whose curriculum remains saturated with western Christian concerns and assumptions. At the same time there is a need for the Church to increasingly move in the direction of decentralized lay driven household assemblies of believers. The decentralization of the Church in Laos requires a relinquishing of power by local clergy and foreign missionaries. It is needed most urgently in the LEC but also in some non-LEC groups whose leaders (Lao and/or expatriate) carry denominational agendas. Both LEC and foreign denominational Christian communities continue to carry many of the traits of *müang* power and global Christianity. These churches will expand to the limits of the ability of their leaders unless the laity is empowered.

At the heart of the tension in the Church in Laos is the issue of power that presents itself on the one hand as Pentecostal power and on the other as the centralization of social power in the hands of church leaders. In Laos the power Jesus can too easily slip into an amoral use of power; the use of power to enforce my will. Any demonstration of power in Laos draws a crowd but interest in power does not necessarily translate into allegiance to Jesus and a life lived according to the ethic of the Kingdom. This ethic demands that Jesus' disciples put the interests of others before their own (Luke 22). Authentic Christianity requires the presence of both spiritual power and Kingdom ethic but it is the ethic lived out in Christian lives that set Christian power apart from other kinds of power. In the Church power is to be used on behalf of others and then given over to others. This has relevance for local church leaders and for foreign expatriate missionaries.

In some emerging Christian communities in Laos a volunteer force of empowered laity are already making their mark calling on the power of Jesus while recognizing that this power is available to every believer who calls on His name. Their converts are turning around to impact others in their kinship network and a movement is emerging. In this way and in the ways already described above an increasing number of Christian communities are bearing the character of world Christianity.

The need in SE Asian Theravada Buddhist societies is not for more missionaries to implement strategic planning. Neither do we need stronger national church organizations with funded national plans. Above all else missionaries and national church leaders alike need the discernment to relinquish control, empower the laity by teaching them the authority they have Jesus' name and the requirements of the Kingdom ethic. In this way the flames of the emerging world Christians will be fanned into a movement that will carry the potential of transforming Laos. Doubters of this recommendation need only look to China to see what the Spirit can do when uninhibited by the shackles of both foreign and local attempts to bridle Him.

6

EXPLORING SOCIAL BARRIERS TO CONVERSION AMONG THE THAI

Alan R. Johnson

In this paper I am making what I consider to be preliminary observations that I hope will serve to stimulate further research on a subject that has been alluded to in the past two SEANET missiological forums. In Paul DeNeui's paper "Contextualizing with Thai Folk Buddhists" he argued that the strongest barriers Thai folk Buddhists faced in coming to Christ were social and not religious (DeNeui 2003:130, 134-135). In last year's forum I argued that it is our ways of "doing church" that create more problems for people coming from Buddhist backgrounds than their own doctrinal understandings (Johnson 2004:1). I want to pick up this theme of barriers to conversion that are not religious, doctrinal, or philosophical, but rather are social in the sense that they have to do with the dynamics that grow out of our interrelationships with other people.

The importance of this issue was driven home to me again through two experiences that happened in this past year. In one case I was chatting with a Thai friend who has been attending church for several years now, and who was planning on marrying a Christian girl. In the course of our conversation I asked when and how he had become a believer. He was quick to reply that he was not a follower of Christ yet. I was quite curious and questioned him about what he thought was keeping him from professing Christ, since he had such a positive attitude about Christianity in general and attended church regularly. A second incident happened while I was sitting in front of a local school.[1] A teacher walking out saw me and stopped to ask if I needed anything. When she found out that I worked with a Thai Christian organization she asked me if I knew certain people. It turned out that the two or three people she mentioned were very well known people in the broader Christian movement in Thailand. She identified herself as the *luuksit* (disciple) of one of them. So I asked her if she was a Christian and how she became one and she immediately replied, "No, I am a Buddhist. My family is Buddhist."

These two incidents reminded me of the fact that even where people have a chance to hear the Gospel over a protracted period of time and are in relationship with solid believers and groups of Christians, there are still things that act as barriers to their coming to faith. The problems are more than conceptual (in terms of not understanding key doctrines) or structural (in terms of not having long term exposure to solid believers); I believe that they illustrate

---

[1] We had this conversation while taking a long driving trip together so I was unable to make any notes on what he said. Recently I asked him to recount what we talked about in terms of things that were barriers to him becoming a Christian. He told me that he is now a believer and, quite interestingly, said that he has forgotten much of his initial reactions that he had when he first went to church. I think that this is a very common process where time and distance from a once held set of beliefs and values makes remembering precisely what our feelings were in the face of a new belief system rather difficult. This normal "forgetting" process means that unless there are conscious attempts at reflection on our former beliefs in light of our new ones that we will be less sensitive to shape our message to those outside the faith and instead relate things in terms of our Christianized categories, terminology, and social contexts.

the fact that there are social barriers that make it difficult for people to become followers of Jesus.

Delineating Types of Barriers

At this point I want to make a few clarifying remarks about the whole enterprise of critically examining how people respond to the Gospel of Christ and then attempt to explain what I mean by social barriers. If we use a theological lens, it is clear that conversion is a work of the Holy Spirit. It is the Spirit who convicts of sin and who draws people to the Father. On that basis there are some who feel that this implies that we should simply "preach the Gospel" and let the Holy Spirit do the work. The problem with this view is that it ignores the issues of encoding, decoding and social context that make communication meaningful. There are no culturally neutral renderings of the Gospel for either those who are sharing it or those who are listening because it can only be encoded and decoded through perceptual filters that are based on our socio-cultural context. The practical outgrowth of this is that what the Gospel messenger may intend as her meaning is not what the receiver may understand.

It is this reality that means there is great benefit to increasing our understanding of both the conceptual and social worlds of our potential listeners so that we can render the Gospel message and all that goes with it in terms of being a community of believers on this earth in a way that is as easily understandable as possible. While it is the Holy Spirit who is ultimately drawing people to Christ, we have a role in either making that process easier or harder by the way that we communicate the Gospel, and here I am thinking of the Gospel in its broadest sense including not only verbal propositions but the entire structure and practice of the Christian community. Most Christians understand this reality when there is an obvious language difference. For instance, I do not know of anyone who would seriously defend the preaching of the Gospel in Russian to a Swahili speaker and expecting that the Holy Spirit could use that message to bring a person to Christ. However, the power of socio-cultural context is often neglected when we are speaking the same language. The assumption being that since we are encoding things in the same language as our listeners (Thai language for a Thai listener) that everything will be quite clear.

Another way to express what I am saying here is that we can be confusing both conceptually in terms of the ideas of the Gospel message and socially in terms of what we are asking people to do or join. Although there are probably other ways of looking at this, one way of thinking about "barriers" would be to think of them in terms of where they are located. Thinking of those who are sharing the Gospel, there are barriers in the way that we conceive church, and do ministry and leadership. Thinking of those who are receiving the Gospel message, there are barriers that are conceptual in nature (inside the person) and those that are social (where the locus is both internal and external to the person in the networks of relationships they live in).

What exactly am I thinking of when I use the term social barriers? In talking about things "social," I want to be clear that ideas about the nature of the social, social structure, and society are very problematic and notoriously hard to pin down in a concise definition. Anderson says that social in the broadest sense has to do with behavior or attitudes influenced by past or present behavior of others and that is oriented towards other people. He distinguishes the social as having to do with interaction, while the cultural has to do with normative and cognitive patterns for action rather than interaction (1964:643). There are those who would take issue with this mentalist view of culture and see it as much more connected with behavior and interaction as well (Knighton 2003:90; Carrithers 1992 for his mutualist view of culture).

Let me say first that we experience the flow of life as a totality and not in compartmentalized segments. So while I am separating conceptual problems and social problems analytically for the purposes of discussion, they are wound intimately together. In terms of lived experience it is much more a package deal. Let me make an example of the kinds of distinctions I am drawing here. If a Buddhist is puzzled about what we mean by God, or sin, or the significance of the cross at least in part due to their understandings of these subjects in the light of Buddhist teaching about their being no single creator God, merit and demerit, and karma; then we are dealing with a conceptual problem. By way of contrast, if a person does not want to become a Christian because he sees it as joining a foreign religion, or because his family would be against it, you are dealing with social barriers. A person could believe everything about the Gospel but not want to make a response publicly known because of the way other people in their social networks would respond. Again, social barriers could be classified as being fairly abstract (Christianity is a foreign religion, I violate my Thai identity to become one) to very concrete where a person hesitates to respond to the Gospel because specific relationships will become problematic (I cannot become a Christian because I have to become a monk temporarily in order to make merit for my mother).

The table below represents one way of representing these various types of barriers.

Type of Barrier	Conceptual or Doctrinal	Social	Church Life
Location	Primarily within a person	Primarily in interaction between persons	In the assumptions and practices of church life
Examples	Confusion about the nature of God, sin, salvation etc. Use of amulets	Thai identity–to be Thai is to be Buddhist Merit making ceremonies with the family.	Strong emphasis on trained, full-time leadership Building-centric church life versus being out where people live in the community

An Examination of Some Social Barriers

In this section I will now briefly overview some areas that I have come upon in personal experience that are social barriers for people and conclude with some material from a few interviews with young Thai believers and seekers. The concluding section will pick up on some of the implications that these barriers have for Christian witness.

Thai Identity

When you share your Christian faith with a Thai Buddhist, you will invariably run up against a wall which can be best summarized in the sense people have that to be Thai is to be a Buddhist. Although it will be expressed in a number of different ways (for example the ideas that Christianity is a foreign religion, that to become a Christian is to leave the paths of the elders, that one's parents would be horrified if a person became a Christian), at the core is the self-understanding that "Thainess" is in some way connected with being Buddhist. This sense of identity combines with the common saying that "all religions are equally good, they teach us to be a good people" to build a wall so that people do not see becoming a Christian as a life option at all. It is something for foreigners; it is "their" religion, while "our" religion is Buddhism.

This sense of identity that is reinforced and reproduced over and over again in social relations can be seen as the reason why it is so easy for Thai people who become Christians while in a foreign country to be reabsorbed into Buddhism upon their return. When they are outside of Thailand, it is permissible to a degree to adapt to local custom, to do as the Romans do in Rome so to speak and check out what the locals do for religion there. It is a case of where Thai identity can be marginalized in the effort to fit in with the new setting, and this includes religious practice as well. However, once they return to Thailand, even though they may have been very sincere in their desire to follow Christ, the overwhelming assertion of Thai identity, the call to fit in and be part of the group, means that many people abandon at least the outward practice of their new faith to conform to the appearance of Buddhist practice.

For those of us who have been raised in western cultures that are very individualistic, it is extremely difficult to understand how it feels to step outside of the mainstream in a much more collective cultural setting.[2] When a person does convert there is often a period of intense pressure from family and friends to bring them back into the fold of Buddhism. While for the most part this pressure is not violent (although there are some exceptions) it is still extremely difficult for people to bear up against it as they feel like they are standing alone against the entire social system.

I think that this has much to do with the interesting observation that I have made, at least in the churches in the Christian group I am associated with, that hardly anyone who attends a given church actually lives in the immediate neighborhood of the church. They all come from somewhere else farther away and attend the services. When I have asked Thai Christians about this they have indicated that if you live close by everyone knows that you are going to church. But if you live far away and someone asks where you are going on Sunday you can easily dodge the question by answering with a generic line such as going on business, or going out for fun. The anonymity afforded by urban areas helps people to deal with the pressures of going against acceptable Thai identity and associated practice.

---

[2] It is important to remember that the individualism that is noted about the Thai and that led to Embree's famous and controversial description of Thai society as "loosely structured" is not the same as individualism in the West. On measures of individualism and collectivism like those used by Hofstede (Hofstede, 1982) the Thai score on the collective side of the continuum. Cohen argues that hierarchy and individualism for opposing cultural codes that are ever present in Thai society and are continually reconfigured and reshaped without ever actually disappearing. Thai individualism is based on individual independence and an opportunism for advancing personal interests, it is both anarchic and present oriented (Hofstede, 1982:42, 46).

Listening to some Young Thai Voices

My thinking about the subject of barriers has led me to start an ongoing project of collecting data from informants who are either new Christians or people who have attended church but not made a profession of faith. I am interested in probing what in their minds were the major obstacles to their becoming a believer. As part of the preparation for this paper I asked a Thai friend who is planting a church to ask some people about the obstacles they experienced as they were coming to faith. In December of 2005 Pastor Brayun Maiwong spoke with four people on this subject. Three of the people were new Christians, while a fourth had attended church for about two years without yet becoming a Christian. The question was "What were/are the barriers that you were afraid of and that would be a problem if you became a believer"?

It was no surprise to me that their answers covered the spectrum of my threefold barriers typology. On the conceptual/doctrinal side, one person said that the Gospel was hard to understand, another that it is was humorous and not very believable. They both used the terminology of the Gospel not having right reasoning or rationality *mai mii hetpol* which they felt was part of Buddhism. On the barriers within the church, the one person who attends church but has not yet become a believer completely lays the blame for this on Christians. He said the he was impressed with Jesus but not with Christians. They were no different with others, they say they will help you but they do not, they are not like Jesus, they have too many activities and actually neglect their families, and they say one thing but do another.

The three who have become believers all said that their biggest problem had been social in nature. One person did not want to change their life as things were already going good and they did not want to create problems. The second said that her mother was violently opposed to Christians and said she could be anything but a Christian. This person is afraid of hurting her mother's feelings and since the mother is in ill health and she does not want to upset her and has hidden the fact that she is now a Christian. Finally, one person said that he was afraid of losing his friends.

In all three of these cases it goes back to the issue of Thai identity as being Buddhist. It is an irrelevant point as to how serious they are in practicing Buddhism, but what is important is that they maintain at least the minimal identification with the essence of Thainess, of which identifying oneself as a Buddhist is a core part. Becoming a Christian creates problems by putting a person at odds with the broader Thai Buddhist community; it jeopardizes friendship not because people are zealous in the practice of Buddhism but because it threatens one's identity. A person can no longer join in activities that are part of defining as person as Thai.

Addressing Social Barriers in Christian Witness

In my opinion it is the sense that to be Thai is to be a Buddhist and its corollary that Christianity is a foreign religion that comprises the greatest barrier to people becoming Christians here. Following Jesus is not even seen as an option, because in order to do so one must stop being Thai. In light of this fact it is interesting to me that so little is done in Christian churches to argue for an essence of "Thainess" that is not bound up in religion. Over my nearly nineteen years of association with Thailand I have been involved in literally hundreds of situations where Thai people have been sharing the Gospel with their fellows Thais. This has ranged from one on one encounters, to public church services, to open air meetings where the Gospel is being preached. In my memory there has never been a single time that I have heard a Thai Christian make any formal argument at all that they did not shed their "Thainess" when they became a believer.

It is almost as if Thai Christians assume that because they are Thai that their listeners are going to assume that you can still be Thai and follow Jesus. However, personal experience and the interview evidence provided here would indicate that this is still an issue that looms large for the Thai person being exposed to the Gospel. What might explain this disconnect between a Thai Christians experience as a non-Christian and subsequent neglect of dealing with this issue as they share their faith with others?

While in fact there may be some Thai Christians who do not "feel" very Thai I think it is wrong to assume that this applies across the board in the absence of some empirical data. This in fact would be a most interesting study, to talk with Thai Christians about how Thai they feel post-conversion and document how they come to understand themselves as a Thai and a Christian. I think that there is too much vibrancy in the Thai church to posit that Thai Christians in general feel like they have lost their "Thainess."

Another possibility, which does have empirical backing is the work of Nantachai Mejudhon, is that Thais have bought into western ways of formulating and sharing the Gospel. Since in the West we do not typically deal with identity issues for our listeners Thais have picked this up and simply tell the story in the same way they received it. While I think this definitely has something to do with the situation, Niels Mulder makes an observation that may be more germane to this apparent disconnect. In his book *Thai Images: The Culture of the Public World* he explores the social construction of the public world through examining dominant ideology as embodied in the social science curriculum of the public schools and into the college level, in popular newspapers, fiction, and material from the Thai National Identity Office. He notes that there "is a tendency to shy away from critical analysis of things Thai, a weakness for which more than the experience of a narrow-minded formal curriculum appears to be responsible" (1997:25). Mulder points out the gap between the matter of fact reporting of the problems of public life in the news and Thai ideals and suggests that "as long as the king, national and religious ceremonies, and beautiful traditions keep existing, there is enough to identify with" (201). It is when taboos are breached that image anxiety occurs, where the key institutions are questioned, or certain Thai customs come under scrutiny by foreigners (201).

It is quite possible that having in one sense breached a taboo—leaving the ancestral paths to become a Christian, people feel in themselves and in the social world around them this "image anxiety" and find it extremely difficult to probe publicly into the generally unexamined bases that form the construction of Thai identity. But this reticence to examine things Thai creates a vicious circle where both Christians and those they are sharing with keep the very things off the table of debate and discussion that hold the potential for creating an articulated Thai identity where religious affiliation is not solely connected with Buddhism.

There are three things that come to mind immediately that I think it would be very healthy to add into our thinking about discipling Christians. The first is to begin to explore with Thai believers just what it means to be Thai and Christian and to work at articulating an apologetic that can be incorporated into personal and public presentations of the Gospel. It is safe to say that if it is never verbally expressed, our listeners are in the back of their mind wondering and worrying about how to negotiate relationships in a social world that is hostile to the idea of them becoming a Christian. This is part of being sensitive to local context as we share the Gospel.

A second point is that I think leaders need to work with people early in their Christian experience about what it means to *ruam muu* cooperate with others in Thai society. I have noticed in working with a Thai Christian church movement that their concepts of cooperation are very different than those of us who come from the West. We tend to view cooperation as being a separate issue from belonging, thus it is possible to for instance be a part of a denomination and not cooperate in everything they do, yet still be a member in good standing. I have noticed though that here *ruam muu* means that you must be involved in all the things that are going on or else you are accused of pursuing personal over group interests. A key part of what makes a person *naachuathuu* (trustworthy) in Thai society is that they *ruam muu* with the group or community that they are a part of.

When people become Christians they often cut themselves off from social life, in which many things are related to Buddhist ceremonies or practices. By not being *ruam muu* with the community they increase the perception that they are now "other" and have moved away from being Thai. There is a place for working out in specific situations how Christians will position themselves in order to have maximum participation in social life without compromising their faith.

Finally I think that it would be good to encourage some Thai theologians and pastors to discuss the issue of Thai Christian identity with the goal of doing some writing on the subject in order to help both believers and non-believers to see that it is possible to follow Jesus and be fully Thai.

Dealing with Implications of the Gospel for Social Life Issues

My suggestions here follow in the same vein as those dealing with identity issues. For many listeners, there are specific social situations that they are thinking about when assessing whether or not to follow Jesus. Part of training people to share their faith should be how to handle questions such as what to do about temple attendance, merit-making activities, and the pressure to enter the monkhood for young men. We need to help people move beyond sharing only cognitive aspects of the Gospel to looking concretely at the implications that it has for a person in their network of relationships and daily life.

Another action point is that churches and leaders should examine how they can develop ceremony and celebration that conveys rich meaning to people, and is fun *sanuk*. I had this brought home to me while doing a participant observation on the parade put on during Thai New Year (Songkhran) in the slum community in which I have been doing research in. What I initially thought was a brief walk through the community turned out to be a two and a half hour street closing event, where a special image from the local temple was paraded around a major city block complete with a brass band, drums, water throwing, and lots of drinking. Well over a hundred people made the journey on foot while many more followed along in trucks and motorcycles. What struck me was the way that the old people so reverently crowded in around the image being carried on poles in order to briefly lend a shoulder to carry it or to reach out a hand and touch the poles, or even lay their hand on the back of someone touching the poles.

When I got home and was reflecting on this event I realized really for the first time how bland Christian worship is in comparison to an event like this which is just one of many the community does through the course of the year. The typical church service is exceedingly tame next to that, definitely not *sanuk* in the way Thais count fun. Not only that, but I was recently teaching a Sunday School class at a church and was asking the people in the class about how they share their faith with other people. One person said that they tell people that Christians don't have any ceremonies like Buddhists do. This reflects not only their own experience in church, but also the fact that rather than looking for connecting points and thinking culturally like a Thai they are emphasizing the radically "other" nature of Christianity from Buddhism which just exacerbates the problem of identity discussed above.

Beginning with baptism and the Lord's supper Christians should be finding ways to practice these ordinances that convey meaning and at the same time bring the group together so that there is a feeling of *samakhii* harmony and accord as well as fun *sanuk*. Next we should look at developing other ceremonies that are uniquely Christian (churches do very well with Christmas in this regard) and also find possible areas within Thai custom and tradition that can be drawn upon.

Finally all of this needs to be done in a much more collective sense than we usually approach things. Thais appear to have bought into our individualistic approach to sharing the Gospel, focusing on winning individuals and forgetting that people are embedded in networks of relationships. Developing venues where the Gospel is presented naturally in a group where communication is not directed at the non-believer is more effective than inviting a person to join a "community" that she cannot see and has never experienced. People need to experience what the Gospel means in real life, seeing what reconciliation to God and then to each other looks like on the ground, experiencing God's grace and power in the company of others. If this new community has a rich symbolic life as well then we are not inviting them to leave a vibrant social world to enter some kind of vacuum, instead we are inviting them to a new community, one that is manifestly Thai, which has beautiful ceremonies that are also fun.

As we work with seekers there needs to be a concerted effort to build trust with their personal network that consists of family and friends so that we are not seen as "pulling them away" from the community. The methods described by Ubolwan Mejhudon in her integrated model for evangelizing Buddhists and illustrated from their own local church show that this approach is effective in helping people come to faith and creating acceptance among family who are not yet believers (Mejudhon 2003).

Conclusion

In thinking about barriers to responding among the Gospel, I see the clarification and discussion of such issues as being very helpful and creating a sense of hope and expectation for the future of the Gospel among Thai people. First, when we start to set out more precisely what the obstacles are, we can pray for the guidance of the Holy Spirit to help us in rendering the Gospel in a way that is understandable and relevant. Second, it makes us realize that people have not responded to the Gospel for specific reasons, rather than defaulting to the murky notion that they are simply resistant. It also makes us realize that the task is one that can be done, these are not insurmountable walls, and in fact elements of social organization and culture can actually facilitate the spread of the Gospel rather than hinder it if we will be open to understand and use them. Finally, I am confident that within the Thai Church itself lies the resources to take up the task of articulating what it means to be fully Thai and fully Christian and that there will be a day in the future when choosing new life in Jesus will be an acceptable option for millions of Thai people.

7

THE STRUGGLE OF ASIAN ANCESTOR VENERATION

Alex G. Smith

Recently in Mongolia the long-standing power of ancestral veneration in Asia was clearly highlighted. Almost eight hundred years after his warring exploits that cut a swath through the nations of his day, Genghis Khan is still revered as the legendary hero of the Mongolians. After successfully uniting warring tribes, the great Khan took over half the known world of his time. In two short decades, he built an empire that was larger than Rome's—from Korea to the Black Sea. In August 1227, Genghis fell from his horse and died. He was buried in a secret location. All traces of it were erased as thousands of horses raced over the area around his final resting place. Those attending his funeral were massacred to keep the site secure—not uncommon practice in ancient Asia.

Finding Genghis Khan's gravesite baffled archeologists for centuries until 2001 when a team headed by a University of Chicago professor believed they had located the Khan's burial area. Associated Press revealed how deeply ancestral veneration can permeate a nation. The archeological work was brought to a halt after Mongolia's former Prime Minister, Dashiin Byambasuren, wrote to the current President, Natsagiin Bagabandi, accusing the archeological team of desecrating and defiling the remains of the dead. He wrote: "I regret that our ancestors' golden tomb has been disturbed and the purity of our burial places tainted for a few dollars." Earlier in 1993 Japanese archeologists ended the search for Khan's tomb because of the unpopularity of the project among the general populace in Ulan Bator, the capital. "According to Mongolian tradition, violating ancestral tombs destroys the soul that serves as protector." A local student summed it up poignantly, "Genghis was the greatest khan of them all, and I pray that his soul will protect Mongolia" (Oregonian, August 14, 2002). Ancestral practices and influence are powerfully perpetuating.

This paper will follow three approaches for investigating ancestor practices: first, comprehending and understanding concepts underlying ancestor rites, second analyzing and evaluating data concerning them, and third applying and experimenting with practical approaches towards solving problems encountered.

A Phenomenon of Universal Value

One widespread belief that affects many Asian peoples is ancestral cults with various forms of overt or covert worship. This is more engrained and commonly practiced than most westerners realize. Offering to ancestors was a central tradition that predated formal systemized religions. Herbert Spencer suggested, "Ancestor worship is the origin of religion," processed through reverence to ancestors or their ghosts. This worldwide phenomenon is deeply rooted in many Asian peoples. It was a prevalent practice down through the historic ages in many sophisticated societies, including the former empires of Greece and Rome. Ancestor worship is performed at special sites, in temples, at shrines, and on home altars. Rites, sacrifices, prayers and offerings are usually involved in a myriad of expressions of ancestral veneration. Professor

Hwang declared, "There are perhaps more people who practice ancestor cult than people who live the Christian faith" (1977:340).

Most ancestral practices arose around the concepts of death and the afterlife. Bronislaw Malinowski calls death "the supreme and final crisis of life." Death is the last turning point every human must face. The general belief in the immortality of the soul, and the subsequent belief in social interaction between the living and the dead, especially in monistic worldviews, helps to develop practices of ancestral cults. While death brings normal social relations to an end, vivid memories of the deceased continue. Death rites are universal. Ancestral worship and rituals are common in Asia.

The Concept of Ancestral Veneration

Veneration covers two aspects: respect and worship. Christians only accept the first as biblically legitimate. Ancestor worship is worship directed to deceased parents or forefathers based on the belief of the immaterial and immortal part of humanity, along with the belief that these ancestors continue to have the same kindly interest in the affairs of the living as when they were alive.

Many believe that their ancestors uphold family tradition, provide family survival, and protect the family. Therefore it is right for the living members of the family to remember the ancestors and make offerings to them. Since, when alive on the earth the ancestors ruled the family, functioned as head over it, protected it and rewarded or punished the family members as needed, these ancestors are therefore seen as continuing to carry out these functions after death. The Chinese believe that the spirits of the ancestors fly above and around the house of the living relatives. The ancestors may provide protection, blessings and prosperity or if neglected, bring misfortune.

The initiation of ancestral deification has a long history. Anthropologist E. B. Tylor (1889) describes how the dead ancestors are deified as ghosts or saints and are consequently worshipped. In ancient Rome's religion, this developed as manes worship. In other societies and tribes arose a belief that the members were all descendants from a common non-human ancestor. This may be a god, spirit, animal, or person of myth. This prime ancestor then became the clan's totem. One expression of this kind of thinking was found in Japan where, under State Shintoism, the Emperor was ardently believed to be the incarnation of the Sun goddess.

John V. Taylor noted that ancestors are considered part of the social group and are not cut off at death (1963:103-105). In the minds of relatives, these "living dead" still exert a powerful influence, recognized as very real and intimate. The belief that the souls of dead ancestors may become ghosts is also strongly held. These ghosts exercise power over current situations and are involved in many forms and functions among the currently living relatives. The ancestors take up residence in some abode of souls. This is like a parallel kingdom to earth. That similarity is viewed as a counterpart reflection of it. As an expression of this the Chinese, Vietnamese and others burn paper offerings of money, cars, houses and other items to the ancestors. These are meant to help comfort them in the abode of dead souls and also to keep them kindly disposed towards the living. In some cultures the ancestors may be regarded as guardian spirits over the family, clan, or tribe.

The cohesive continuity in worldview reinforces the ancestral cult. Since this perception is learned early from the cradle, its perspectives, perceptions and values continue persistently on till the grave. The permeation of education, thinking and daily life produces a comprehensive and continuing connection with the ancestors. This is so much so that the dead are seen as having an ongoing, intimate relationship with the generations of the living. In Sri Lanka the "rice-name" ceremony is performed usually about seven months after the birth of a child. An auspicious date is calculated and all the relatives gather. The grandfather places a handful of rice in the child's mouth and gives his grandchild its name. This reinforces the perpetuation of ancestral continuity (Peiris 1956:226; Weerasingha 1989:93).

The pervasive control of cultural tradition also fosters ancestral cults. One example is the Damal tribe in the Indonesian jungles of central Irian Jaya. Damals view the spiritual world as more real than the physical realm. Their ancestor worship is consequently most vital to them, and they offer many items to their ancestors including stone axes, dogs and pigs. For Vietnamese Mahayana Buddhists ancestor worship and shamanism are more essential to daily living than tenets that direct them towards countering their *karma* to overcome suffering, ignorance and illusion.

The Importance of Ancestor Worship in Asian Thinking

The experience of ancestors is highly valued and respected. Ancestors founded many things in the family lineage, both methodological and moral. They have experienced common problems in the past and so can empathize with living relatives now facing similar difficulties. The knowledge and achievements of the ancestors provide a rich pool of resources from which to draw. Their priority of headship provided experienced leadership in decision-making in bygone days.

Ancestors' presence in the dreams of the living also points to reminders of their importance. These are to be noted, not ignored. Keeping ancestors alive in the memory by frequent reminders through visions fosters a feeling of continuity and connection with the deceased. It is not uncommon for Asians to interpret dreaming about ancestors as warnings from them of some impending danger. Dreams are taken seriously.

The ancestors' perpetuity in living memory is powerful. Often only ancestors known from memory are venerated—usually back to grandparents. In some cases statistical ancestral lines are recognized to seven or more former generations. Names are usually recorded on some kind of ancestral tablet or lineage record. Ancestral founders of clans or tribes initiated much, leaving legacies of learning. Cult and totem practices are maintained in almost endless perpetuity.

Ancestors are recognized as part of the current social group and identified as "the living dead." Deceased forebears live in a spiritual world but they are believed to have an ongoing interest in the material world. Normally there are locations or sites where the ancestors are accessible and can be contacted or consulted. This may be a high mountain, a body of water, or some centralized ancestral shrine. Gravesites are also chosen carefully, usually through some form of geomancy such as *feng shui*. This includes peoples such as the Chinese and Vietnamese (Reimer 1975:158; Hickey 1964:38f).

Ancestral powers are believed to be available to the living who may invoke them. Ancestors have already trod life's path, experienced its problems, faced and surmounted its difficulties, and made important decisions. Therefore they possess a wealth of knowledge, achievement and power that the living family believes it may draw upon. These are at the disposal of the family provided they are accessed correctly—through offerings, sacrifices, libations, prayers, incantations, or other appropriate forms of ancestral worship.

The Motivations Behind Ancestor Worship

Filial piety or respect and affection for deceased ancestors have a high value among peoples such as Chinese, Japanese, Korean and Vietnamese. The motivation for this veneration has strong ethical and social implications. It includes gratefulness to the ancestors for their care, training and provision for the family. Usually filial piety is expressed in three primary ways:

1) Proper burial and funeral rites for the deceased,
2) Offerings before the ancestral tablets and
3) Correct care of the ancestral graves.

First, culturally acceptable decorum and appropriate ceremony with the rightful administration by the eldest son and/or priests and shamans are required. This is both a public social event and a private family affair. Due respect and correct procedure dignify the final rites of passage for the deceased, sometimes accompanied by professional mourners as well as feasts and other activities.

Second is the worship at family altars, known in Japan as *butsudan*, set up in each family home. This entails some form of ancestral tablets inscribed with the names of forebears going back a number of generations. These are placed on the altar. Generally these tablets are wooden, stone or occasionally paper. Often a photograph of the ancestor is placed at the shrine. Living family members make daily offerings of food, drink, fruit, flowers and other items, before the ancestral tablets or the altar. Incense is burned. Candles are lit. Often a perpetual light is kept burning. These offerings allow the ancestors "to eat" and so preclude the deceased from becoming hungry, unhappy, miserable and unfortunate ghosts (Hung 1983:32). Where deceased kinsmen are deemed to possess enough interest and power over human affairs they may be regarded as deities and often are worshipped (Taylor 1973:392). Family members direct prayer requests for their current problems to the ancestors and also plead for their assistance in any difficulties that the family may be facing. This kind of worship is maintained daily or weekly. After the sacrificial rituals are completed and the ancestors have partaken, the living members then eat the food from before the altar. In this manner they also partake in a communal sense with the ancestors (Lowe 2001:4f).

A third way of showing filial piety is the ritual ceremony of visiting the ancestral graves at least annually at special times of the year to honor the dead. The graves are cleaned and spruced up at this time. This is known as "sweeping the graves." Special offerings are made and veneration of the ancestors is performed. In China, this festival on April fifth, is known as *ching ming*. In similar fashion the Japanese celebrate *bon* festivals in summer, as well as popular *boson*—frequent visiting of family graves (Shibata 1985:247).

Another dominant motivation behind ancestral worship is fear of ancestral ghosts. Death is a serious event in Asia because of the dread of ghosts and spirits. If not treated properly the disembodied entities may cause all sorts of havoc, trouble and even curses for the living thus the departed ancestors are viewed with terror. Consequently the living meticulously provide for the recently departed by offering money, houses, possessions and means of transportation to help them in the abode of the dead. Usually these are only models made of paper or perishable materials, which are burned as offerings along with joss sticks. Fulfilling these duties is like insurance for the family, even if due respect and true love for the departed are absent. Thus selfish desires may be at the true root of some ancestral practices. The proper rites of passage, appropriate funeral, and adequate sendoff are deemed essential for the efficient transportation of the dead to their spiritual resting place. This is also necessary to protect the living relatives and their families. Daniel Hung lucidly described the fear behind ancestral cults: "Failure to worship ancestors is not only considered to be a great sin and an act of rebellion against one's ancestors, but is also believed to result in disasters and misfortune for the living" (1983:33).

A third motivation reinforcing the ancestral system is conformity to social customs. Confucian teaching established and institutionalized prescribed forms, expectations and ceremonial rituals. To neglect the ancestors produced strong social stigma. Among many peoples, especially in North and East Asia, not following the prescribed patterns for honoring ancestors is considered a major disgrace, a most despicable sin. This posed a dilemma for Christian converts, criticized as deviants for disrespecting their own ancestors. Abstaining from society's ancestral rites brought persecution. In Vietnam, Christianity is ridiculed as "the religion that is ungrateful to the ancestors" (Reimer 1975:156).

A fourth motivation for ancestral practices is maintaining the bonding of the family. The ancestral celebrations and rites give the relatives an opportunity for family gatherings and provide a sense of togetherness. This reinforces the strength and unity of the extended family. Often help for field labor, aid in financial crises, and assistance and advice in major decisions comes first from immediate family members and relatives. This is true both in rural and urban communities. Gatherings for ancestral veneration not only show the value of communal respect but also remind families of these close bonds, their common unity and the obligation for interrelated dependence on each other and the ancestors.

So far the focus has been on comprehending and understanding the concepts underlying ancestor rites. Now we turn to some analysis and evaluation of contexts and data.

The Comparison of Two Differing Worldviews

It is crucial to comprehend the divergent perceptions of two outlooks—that from a biblical analysis and that from a culture developed around ancestors. The general biblical view describing the flow and process of life simply is summarized in diagram 1 below. This shows a duality separating the spiritual from the physical realms. God as Creator is outside the process but works within it. He is not part of the creation itself. Not neglecting the human physical factors in the process, one can grasp a biblical answer to the question "Where do babies come from?" In scripture it seems clear that the unborn come from the blessing of a sovereign Creator God, the source of all life. According to considerable illustrations and verses in the Bible, the Lord is the One who opens or closes the womb (Genesis 29:31, I Samuel 1:6). So babies are recognized as a gift from God. They come into the world of the living by the blessing of God through His command for humankind to procreate and multiply (Genesis 1:27-28).

Normally each person has an allotted lifespan of "three score years and ten" (Psalm 90:10). At the end of each life it is then appointed "once to die" (Hebrews 9:27). This is a radical break with life, with a fixed state of no returning (Job 10:21; Luke16:13).

The terms *sheol* (Hebrew) or *hades* (Greek) are similar in their focus as the abode of the dead. Like most religions, there is also a sense of final accountability. The future state of the dead seems to be either paradise (Abraham's bosom) or *hades/sheol* (a place of discomfort and pain). Afterwards, at the appointed time of the end comes the climactic judgment, followed by assignments in heaven or hell. Commentators have differing views of what these terms mean, ranging from literal to allegorical, physical to spiritual, or figurative to actual.

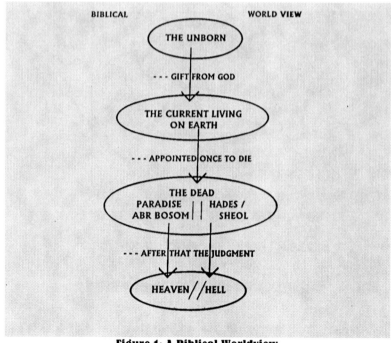

Figure 1: A Biblical Worldview

This somewhat simple explanation of the process and flow of life from a biblical perspective is in considerable contrast to that of the cult of the ancestors, diagramed in figure 2 below.

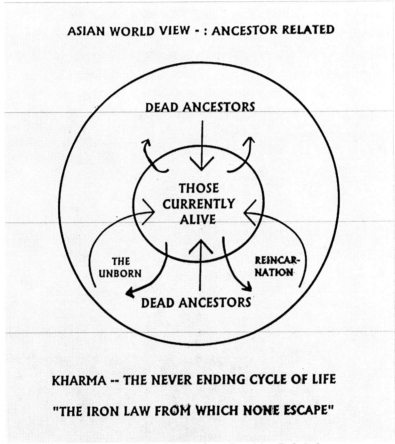

ASIAN WORLD VIEW - : ANCESTOR RELATED

KHARMA -- THE NEVER ENDING CYCLE OF LIFE

"THE IRON LAW FROM WHICH NONE ESCAPE"

Figure 2: Asian Worldview: Ancestor Related

Generally the Asian worldview is monistic rather than dualistic in its orientation, where all is part of the whole. In this view dead ancestors are believed to be part of the sphere of life that includes those currently alive as well as the departed ("living dead"), and even the "not-yet-born." Berentsen analyses the relationship between the performers of rites and their ancestors under three interrelated aspects of cosmic-monism: 1) The community of obligation, 2) The community of interdependence, and 3) The community of cosmic continuity (1985:264-269). So the outer circle above contains the broader pool of relationships recognized as true viable life where interaction and communication take place, not just the inner circle of those actually alive on the earth. Even where Buddhist concepts reject the entity of human soul, this view of the world recognizes that the ancestors are living entities who can affect the affairs on earth for good or evil. In their spiritual state the ancestors still are intimately related to the material world and integrated with it. These "living dead" still have an influence on the current live family. When humans die they go to the abode of the ancestors, awaiting reincarnation, depending on their accumulated *karma*. As shown in figure 2, the newborn come from the pool of the ancestors by means of reincarnation or rebirth. This recycling motif indicates more of a cyclical life process than the linear one common to the orientation of the West.

The Means and Causes for Consulting Ancestors

Where ancestral cults are prevalent, established patterns of approach to the deceased must be followed. These include a kind of priesthood or mediators. Frequently the head of the household as family mediator performs the rituals in the home. In other situations the eldest son in the extended family acts in this prescribed function. Where Buddhism became dominant through its cultural accommodation of integrating ancestral and animistic practices, Buddhist priests also took on similar roles in performing some of those ritualistic tasks.

The main reasons ancestors are consulted include:

1. *Biological concerns for human fertility.* This relates to the physical extension of the tribe or family line. Infertility or barrenness becomes a cause to consult the ancestors. One example is the Kaguru tribe of East Africa, who illustrate this belief clearly. First, the Kaguru marriage rites affirm that the ties of marriage "will continue beyond the life span of the couple involved." Second, if a woman has difficulty conceiving or retaining a pregnancy, a diviner is consulted in order to identify the cause of the difficulty. Usually the problem is diagnosed as "disruptive forces associated with the ghosts of the ancestors who do not want the unborn to leave the land of the ghosts of ancestors and go to the land of the living" (Grunlan 1981:50-51).

2. *Fertility and fruitfulness of the land.* Since the land is inherited from the ancestors, they still have an interest in helping preserve it for the current family and causing the harvests to produce prodigiously.

3. *Personal relationship between the living and the dead.* There is high affection for the ancestors and/or a considerable fear of them—usually a combination of both. This ambivalence of the ancestors being predictable and unpredictable, exhibits something quite human about them. Like a mirror, the ancestral cult reflects the kind of dynamics found in the living family. A mediator with special knowledge, aptitude and experience considers how to approach the ancestors in ways that are like human to human, in order to placate them, plead with them or trick them on behalf of the living.

4. *Sickness and disease.* The deep reason or hidden cause divined behind illness is usually identified as neglect of the

ancestors. Because he was angry or dissatisfied, the ancestor failed to protect the living. The family examines themselves to see why the ancestor disapproved of their behavior. A similar process and cause is traced in cases of drought, famine or natural calamity. Where these or an epidemic is widespread throughout the tribe or people, it is often interpreted as a matter of national significance. The cause is usually determined that all in the group neglected their religious duty to the ancestors, so renewed ceremony and ritual is called for so as to correct the general neglect of ancestors.

An Evaluation of Biblical Principles

First, the problem of idolatry in ancestor worship is raised in the first Commandment. "You shall have no other gods before Me" (Exodus 20:3). The question is: "Do ancestral cults worship their forebears as gods and thereby violate this primary command?" (Kraft 1991:309). On the other hand one must also ask: "Is all sincere reverence of ancestors, with their practices and rites, necessarily elevating their position to that of gods, thereby competing with Jehovah?" How does one distinguish between the two? In what ways can one discern when the fine line has been crossed from valid respectful veneration to veritable idolatrous worship? These are most difficult missiological questions.

The belief, common in China, Japan, Korea and Vietnam, is that after death the ancestor's spirit actually returns to enter the ancestral tablet. Sometimes a hole or a slit is made in the tablet for this purpose. After a short time the deceased soul is located in three places simultaneously: in the abode of the dead in "heaven," at the coffin or gravesite, and in the ancestral tablet in the home (Liaw 1985:186). The living relatives worship the ancestors with incense, candles, flowers, spirit money, prayers and offerings before the ancestral tablet and altar. This can contravene the second commandment "You shall not make yourself an idol, or any likeness... You shall not worship them or serve them" (Exodus 20:4-5). This is a notable concern, especially where incense is burned, for in North Asia joss sticks and incense automatically indicates worship to a deity (Tan 1985:221-223; Hung 1983:36).

Reginald Reimer points out that the Vietnamese cult of the ancestors is founded on their complex "beliefs concerning the soul" (1975:155-156). This is likely true of other Asian peoples also. Interestingly the Hebrew word for soul, *nephesh,* does not distinguish clearly between soul and body. In cultures where ancestors are venerated, it could be argued that though the physical body has died, the spiritual soul lives on and is thereby potentially accessible for communication with the living. Most ancient nations and waves of civilizations believed in life continuing after death. Consequently humans developed elaborate systems to provide for their ancestors and to assure harmony for the afterlife. The nation of Israel did not establish any formal practice of ancestral worship, though they highly respected their ancestral forebears as frequently commanded in scripture. Israel was strictly to worship only one God, Jehovah.

A second problem concerns adequate respect following the fifth Commandment. "Honor your father and your mother, so that you may live long in the land the Lord your God is giving you" (Exodus 20:12). Here Asians might rightly ask local Christians and especially those in the West: "Do Christians neglect respecting their ancestors? Is the first commandment more important than the fifth? Or is the fifth less inspired?" western theology relegates little attention to ancestors, though a large volume of scripture talks about them (Hiebert 1985:210). The repeated ancestral maxim, "The God of Abraham, Isaac and Jacob," is a vital statement of ancestral veneration and continuity. What of the West's lack of showing true filial piety to the forebears used of God to prepare the heritage we have today? Christians should excel in respecting parents, in caring for their elderly relatives, as well as in nurturing their own families.

Furthermore, the only one of the Ten Commandments that was given with a promise of blessing was the fifth, calling for us to respect our parents, despite their weakness, inadequacies and sinfulness. In fact being classed in the first five, which seem to relate God-ward, the fifth commandment also reflects the honor due unto God.

The Missiological Challenges of Ancestral Practices

When the Gospel entered North and East Asia, cult practices for the ancestors were among "the most critical problems, which Christianity had to face" (Ro 1985:4). Like "a giant rock blocking the flow of water in a river," Hung wrote, "Ancestor worship is the greatest obstacle to the Christian mission among the Chinese" (1983:32).

The complex, eclectic stewpot of Chinese religion contains a broad list of deities including "Heaven" (*Shang Ti*). "The great mass of Chinese worship Buddha, the bodhisattvas, the Taoist immortals, Confucius and their own ancestors, with equal vigour" (Samagalski 1984:69). A similar though modified consensus could describe Korea, Japan, and Vietnam, as well as most other parts of South East Asia.

Significantly in Japan, Buddhist sects such as Nichiren, and "new religions" like Tenryko, have incorporated ancestor worship (Shibata 1985:253). Similarly in Vietnam the Hoa Hao, Cao Dai and Coconut religions have a heavy focus on ancestor veneration (Reimer 1975:165). Actually most religions of Asia are neither "pure" nor "pristine." They are mostly conglomerates of Buddhism, Hinduism or Islam, their dominant components, with various forms of animistic mixtures, including the cults of the ancestors.

Ancestral practices among other Asian peoples are not always as obvious as those of the Chinese or Japanese. For example, except for those of Chinese extraction, the Thai do not appear to have codified ancestral cults. But when significant adversity strikes a family, their first reaction is to make sacrifice and obeisance to their angry ancestors. Similarly, though nominally Christian, the Filipinos pay homage, make sacrifices and offer prayers to their dead ancestors "so they would respond favorably to the needs of living family members" (Henry 1986:8). In Cambodia the festival of *Pchum Ben* is held for fifteen days in the autumn. During the celebrations all families are expected to travel around to seven Buddhist temples (*wats*) to gather together and make balls of sticky rice, which they throw around the *wats* to feed the famished spirits of ancestors. For rural Cambodians, ancestral ghosts are among "the spirits they most fear, and with whom they are concerned on a day-to-day basis" (Bowers 2003:48). In Laos and nearby lands, when a death occurs in a *Taidam* family, animal sacrifices are made to provide offerings to the spirit of the deceased ancestor. The corpse is placed on a stand in the house. Then in communal fashion the living attendees at the funeral partake of the sacrificed food. One could multiply scores of examples from other people groups of Asia, but this is sufficient.

These illustrations identify the heart of the problem concerning ancestral practices. The worldviews affected by ancestral influences are so deeply engrained in the psyche of many Asian peoples that a simple dismissal of the issues is not only inadequate but also ineffective. In the war torn devastation of South East Asia during the 1970s, ancestral sites and altars in homes were destroyed and the people forced to flee across borders. Yet within a few weeks, ancestral altars reappeared in the refugee camps of east Thailand (Reimer 1975:163). The powerful, persistent influence of the ancestors permeates the hearts of many Asians and penetrates their deepest culture. Meeting these deep felt-needs requires considerable research and understanding.

Ancestral Cults Incorporated into Buddhism

In Buddhism, rites for the deceased have a long tradition from earliest times. Once King Bimbisara invited the Buddha and some priests to a meal at his palace and offered robes to the Bhikkus. The king dedicated "his merit to his deceased kinsmen." The Buddha announced that the offerings "will go to benefit the deceased" and assured the king, "A great merit you have done in performing your duties as their relatives, in worshipping the deceased through this fruitful kind of worship and in strengthening the Bhikkus in doing so." In Brahmanism ancestral offerings were limited "only to three former generations," but Buddhism sets no limit for transferring merit to all previous generations. The Brahmin practices of using lumps of rice and pouring water oblations for the deceased were incorporated into Buddhist rites for the deceased in Thailand and elsewhere. Buddhism set three qualifying conditions for effective transfer of merit to ancestors: 1) While giving charity, donors must make a mental note to dedicate their merit to the deceased. 2) Only deceased ancestors who have taken their place in the planes of hungry ghosts can appreciate and share this merit. 3) The acts of merit are effective when dispensed towards those who are worthy, namely first, Buddhist priests and second, others in need (Nyanasamvara 1993:125-133; Berentsen 1985:267).

Professor Wei's excellent historical analysis of Chinese ancestor worship traced its roots back to primitive animism and totemism. In the Hsia (Xia) dynasty 2,000 years before the entry of Buddhism, worship of ancestors was only a little less important than the worship of Heaven. The heart of ancient rites was the belief that "all things originated from Heaven; people originated from their ancestors" (1985:119-125). Over time, changes transformed ancestor worship. Though China's contact with Buddhism started from 200 B.C., the most significant changes came with its official introduction during the Han dynasty (65-73 A.D.), around the time of the destruction of the Temple in Jerusalem. Wei reports the Chinese classics had no recorded use of incense. "The practices of burning incense, candles and paper money were added to the ancestor worship ceremonies after the introduction of Buddhism to China." Originally the meaning of ancestor worship was "to revere Heaven, to enlighten moral virtues, to edify filial piety, and to show gratitude to the ancestors." Buddhism also encouraged "the worship of the deceased" so as to help them enter the western Paradise (1985:128-130).

While fundamentally rejecting all spiritual entities as inconsequential, Buddhism is most accommodating and highly syncretistic, strongly influencing Asian cultures at the grass roots. From a historical perspective, Arnold Toynbee stated: "Buddhism has transformed every culture as it has entered, and Buddhism has been transformed by its entry into that culture" (Maguire 2001:207). Consequently the majority of Folk Buddhists views their ancestral cults as part of their Buddhism, whether in China, Korea, Japan, Taiwan, Vietnam and elsewhere.

After understanding the concepts related to ancestral veneration, and evaluating their contexts, we finally suggest practical approaches for applications and experimentation, towards solving problems encountered in ancestral rites.

The Need for Functional Substitutes

Historical controversies in the Church over this sensitive issue have been well documented (Ro 1985:149-160). Generally church and missionary responses to ancestral veneration have been either to condemn all or to condone all. The first results in isolating Christians from society as outsider aliens to the culture. The second is so accommodating that syncretism takes over in the Church. The first can be too ethnocentric, unfeeling and unaware of the deep felt needs of Asians. The second is compromising, confusing and lacking understanding of both scripture and culture. The goal is to find solutions that are both thoroughly biblical without compromise, and truly cultural while satisfying deeply felt needs of Asians.

Current scholars encourage a middle way that demands determined development of adequate functional substitutes, specifically appropriate for each people's ancestral practices. Functional substitutes overcome blocking barriers by building bridges. It is safer to take old forms and transform them with new meanings, than to bring in new forms, which tend to transfer and retain old meanings. Discarding key elements may also leave frustrating voids. Discernment is surely needed for three actions: 1) Retaining things which one can follow, 2) Rejecting things one cannot practice, and 3) Recognizing things that can be transformed and adapted through functional substitutes. Serious experiments and evaluation are required on the third, so that efficient solutions are implemented. Past examples on these were made in Liao (1972:130f), Hwang (1977:353f), Hung (1983:36f), and Ro (1985 part IV). Crucial solutions find answers, which do not leave empty voids in the hearts of believers, and still keep the Church in close cultural proximity to society. It is futile to continue denying the depths of the emotional grip that ancestral practices hold on Asians. Below are some ideas for functional substitutes that may provide models for experimenting, testing and evaluating. Since each cultural situation is different, we offer only possibilities. Creativity is required.

1. *Funerals and disposal of the body.* All proceedings related to the coffin, and the services for funeral, burial or cremation must be dignified, solemn and sober. They are also to uplift the attendees with comfort, peace, hope and joy. The best of local forms should be used rather than outside imports. Make them cultural not western, Christian not cultic. Setting up a memorial altar with items such as a large photo of the deceased, a family Bible and tastefully arranged flowers is helpful. Display large banners with fitting Scriptural texts or words of appreciation for the deceased. Wear proper cultural dress and symbols of grief. Though not offering joss sticks, Christians should first pay respects to the dead and give condolences to the family before helping with meals, drinks or refreshments. Where culturally appropriate, church bands or choirs should perform eulogies honoring the deceased delivered, and a history of his/her accomplishments, provision, care, giftedness and

value to the family given by various attendees. Other cultural trimmings and practices that are not proscribed can be added. All should fit as thoroughly as possible with the culture of the local society, within biblical bounds. Non-judgmental attitudes are important, as some will probably perform practices unacceptable to believers. Here is a chance to show acceptance and love to them. Be patient, not unkind. Tasteful tombs, grave markers or headstones honoring the ancestor should be set up afterward.

2. *Memorials to the deceased.* These are held at different times and places. Initial memorials and death anniversaries call for much creativity in expressing honor and thanksgiving for the ancestor's nurture and good for the family. Make provision for memorial meals and for sharing feelings and appreciation for the deceased. These are times for families to show their solidarity and mutual love and concern. Play cultural games, music or drama, as deemed proper. Togetherness and unity are the watchwords. Give donations to charities in the name of the deceased towards needy projects of community and Church. Plant trees or shrubs in honor of ancestors, adding memorial plaques. It is important to maintain fellowship with those who are not believers at family or clan gatherings and anniversaries. Remembering ancestors at annual, lunar or New Year festivals stretches one's imagination for ways to show respect. Where relatives still insist on ancient rites for unbelieving ancestors, Christian families can hold a final ceremony. On that occasion they tell the ancestors before all relatives that this is a respectful, final, special celebration of veneration to the ancestors. As God's children Christians are giving the deceased the highest honor now by entrusting them to Creator God, and committing them to His power and eternal care. The family should express much sincere gratefulness to the ancestors for their nurture in the

past as they bring closure to ancestor worship. Also tell the ancestors what kinds of respect Christians will continue to give them, excluding the old fearful spirit ways. Then close and put the ancestors to rest.

3. *Care and cleaning of ancestral graves.* Family or clan gathering for festivals, such as *ching ming* or *bon*, can be unifying events, full of fun for the members. Identity and unity are keys. It is also a solemn time to remember the ancestors and to honor them with words of gratitude, written tributes for their value, and blessings of flowers or balloons. After meticulously cleaning up the gravesite and restoring its luster, hold hands around the grave while members offer prayers of thanksgiving to God and maintain a minute of special silence. Christians can excel others by doing this at least one extra time a year to honor their ancestors.

4. *Family altars in the home.* Suggestions made earlier for funerals are proper here. Add special meaningful items such as a list of ancestors recorded in the family Bible. David Liao even designed a model of a "corrected" Hakka ancestral tablet (1972:124). Hold family devotions near the altar and praise God for placement in that family and in His Church. Thank the Lord and for His provision of protection, health, food, shelter and clothing. Consider displaying photos of the ancestors for several generations on the wall nearby. Produce a family history of the ancestors with significant details and place it on the memorial table. Read sections of it to the members for devotions. In times of crisis or need for decisions gather near the family altar to call upon God for His direction and blessing. Praise Him for His grace, mercy and will. Tell God all the troubles, confess sins and commit the future to Him.

Conclusion

This paper has attempted three things: 1) to apprehend the complex concepts driving ancestor veneration, 2) to analyse the societal context behind the cult, and 3) to apply practical suggestions in the use of functional substitutes. We conclude with eight actions that will hopefully point the way to better understanding, evaluation and experimentation.

1. *Recognize the complexity of ancestral rites and practices.* Understand them. Simplistic responses or polarized antagonism do more harm than good. Reinforcing the importance of this issue Charles Van Engen succinctly writes, "A careful, culturally-appropriate, biblically-faithful, and missiologically intentional theology of ancestor veneration still cries for development" (1998:66).

2. *Exemplify strong models of genuine Christian filial piety.* Believers are to excel in expressing true respect for their ancestors, especially while they are yet alive. Paul Hiebert's "unfinished business in mission" includes "ancestors and traditional life-cycle rites." These are "once again living issues that church leaders must confront. The debate surrounding these issues has been heated" (1993:258). Elsewhere Hiebert notes that people of different cultures "ask different questions. For example Africans and Asians ask, 'What shall we do about our ancestors?' Western theology gives little attention to ancestors, although much is said about them in the Bible" (1985:210). Creating examples and practices that honor parents and forbears may be a vital key to church growth in Asia.

3. *Empathize with heartfelt understanding and compassion.* Behind the disturbing elements in ancestral cults are deep feelings of desperate psychological need and spiritual pain. Differing views

call Christians to sensitivity, patience, love and prayer, not contention, criticism and judging. Accepting people as they are and empathizing with their need and motives is paramount. Listen to their heart.

4. *Focus on whole family evangelism.* Asian family consciousness and extended relationships produce strengths for social unity and kinship continuity. "One by one" evangelism disturbs this, producing fractures in families and protective reactions. Practice the biblical approach of reaching and baptizing whole families. Change strategy by planting churches around households. Produce literature, videos and radio dramas that tell of family conversions. Evangelize with families in mind, rather than individuals.

5. *Conduct sound research.* Serious socio-anthropological, theological and missiological investigations provide data on the current beliefs about ancestor worship. Indigenous leaders can conduct in-depth studies and surveys at the grassroots. Cross-cultural comparative studies would enhance understanding regional variations of ancestor practices among people groups, providing a pool of possible models for new approaches and cross-fertilization of ideas. Interview unchurched folk especially.

6. *Build on contact points.* The capacity of ancestor worshipers through such concepts as belief in the soul, life after death, prayer, worship, relation with the invisible beyond, and spiritual communal sharing provide bridges to be explored and applied in the worship of God. Many positive points of honoring fathers relate to the heavenly Father.

7. *Develop appropriate functional substitutes.* Undertake experiments using the above bridges. With national believers' input create and test new approaches that give assurance and visibility to

Christian respect for ancestors. Evaluate and recycle lessons learned.

8. *Instruct new converts—educate church members*. Teach believers (new and old) and missionaries about new approaches. Train them to be models in honoring. Instruct them how to relate to their relatives, and use functional substitutes. Learn to differentiate between worship of the Creator God and dutiful respect due to ancestors. Understand both monistic and biblical worldviews. Especially teach how to handle fear by trusting God's power and depending on believers' position in Christ.

8

CHRISTIANITY AND BUDDHIST MARRIAGE IN SRI LANKA

G.P.V. Somaratna

Marriage is the socially recognized and approved union between two individuals, who commit themselves to one another with the expectation of a stable and lasting intimate relationship. Marriage is commonly defined as a partnership between two members of opposite sex known as husband and wife. The wedding ceremony formally unites the marriage partners. A marital relationship usually involves some kind of contract, specified by tradition, which defines the partners' rights and obligations to each other. In addition to being a personal relationship between two people, marriage is one of society's most important and basic institutions. Marriage is the state in which men and women can live together in a sexual relationship with the approval of their social group. Every culture of the world recognizes some form of the institution of marriage. In most cultures a man or a woman is not considered complete without a spouse when they reach the age of maturity.

In Christianity and many theistic religions, marriage is considered a sacred act. In the Bible marriage is traced back to the union of Adam and Eve. As a blessing of God, the Biblical concept of marriage is not only for the purpose of perpetuating humankind, but also to enhance and complete the partners' personal growth.

Christian marriage has always been characterized by the practice of monogamy and official resistance to divorce. Traditionally, marriage was justified primarily for producing children, with partnership in the background, and avoiding fornication. The Roman Catholic Church classes marriage as a sacrament. Denunciation of marriage has usually been regarded as an error, except by extreme ascetics (Hinnells 1995:301). Catholics entering wedlock have been expected to understand it as a permanent commitment, lasting for a lifetime.

The Christian Church in Sri Lanka

Sri Lanka has been identified as a Sinhalese Buddhist country for over two millennia. However, the presence of Christians in the Anuradhapura Period is indicated by archaeological and literary evidence. We are, unable to ascertain the nature of their contribution to the culture of Sri Lanka. The assertion made by Senarath Paranavitana in the *Story of Sigiri* connecting the sixth century Sigiriya fortress with Christianity has not been popular amongst historians despite the fact that the Persian origin of the garden layout of the city of Sigiriya has been accepted by archaeologists. The arrival of Franciscan missionaries from Portugal in 1543 in the Kingdom of Kotte, at the invitation of Bhuvanekabahu VII (A.D. 1521-1551) marks more clearly the beginning of Christian influence on the life of Sinhalese Buddhists. Apart from those who embraced the Roman Catholic faith during this period, the Sinhalese Buddhist population generally also came under Christian influence (De Silva 1959). Thereafter, under the Dutch administration of the maritime provinces of the island the process of Christian cultural contact with Sinhalese Buddhist

Society continued (De Silva 1959). The expansion of missionary activities in the nineteenth and twentieth centuries under Protestant missionary organizations resulted in further cultural influences to Sinhalese Buddhist society.

In this article we shall examine one important area in which Christianity made a lasting impact on Buddhist culture in Sri Lanka. The institution of marriage has undergone vast changes as a result of Christian impact during the last four centuries. We shall attempt to identify some of these areas in which Buddhists acquired Christian practices and made them part of their heritage.

Sinhalese Buddhism

Buddhism in Sri Lanka is referred to as Theravada, the School of the Elders. It was officially introduced to Sri Lanka in the third century B.C. Ever since that time Buddhism has played a pivotal role in forming the culture of the Sinhalese, who were regarded as the sole occupants of the island until about the thirteenth century, and have remained the dominant ethnic community of the island until today. The identification of the Sinhalese with their hereditary religion has been strengthened by the conscious efforts of the Buddhist activists of the nineteenth century. It is therefore not surprising to hear from political platforms that "Sinhalese are Buddhists," where an attempt is made to preserve national and communal identity with the hereditary religion. The Sinhalese Buddhist leaders since the second half of the nineteenth century in their struggle for national identity had to grapple with the presence of a Christian community amongst them. The Christians who formed nearly ten percent of the Sinhalese population in the nineteenth century became a stumbling block to their idea—a "nation of Sinhalese Buddhism." The "Protestant Buddhism" which raised its head in the second half of the nineteenth century has acquired Christian social and cultural aspects to modernize Buddhism in order to compete with the aggressive Christian missionary activities.

Buddhist Monks

Canonically, Buddhism is not at all involved in the changes of status that sociologically mark the individual's passage through the life cycle. Although contemporary Buddhism pays great attention to these points of transition, it has less involvement in them than is characteristic of other religions. Except for certain death ceremonies, Buddhism is only peripherally concerned with the life cycle. Birth, puberty and marriage are not marked in Sri Lanka and other Buddhist societies by rites of passage deserving religious involvement. They most certainly are life cycle ceremonies, but outside the purview of the otherworldly religion of Theravada Buddhism (Spiro 1971:232).

The *sangha*, according to its rules of discipline, was not able to get entangled in the ritualistic services of laymen (Bechert and Gombrich 1991:135). It essentially forms the Buddhist priesthood, which unlike Christianity, has no distinct secular clergy. The *sangha* need only provide the opportunity for the laity to seek their salvation, even by offering the chance to accumulate merit through pious gifts to the *sangha*. Buddhist priests conduct funerals and memorial services for the dead, which involve the transfer of merit for the benefit of the deceased. Naturally then, the monastic *sangha* plays a prominent role in the funeral proceedings.

There is an indifference to lay customs in Sri Lankan Buddhism. Buddhists monks as well as Buddhist sacred objects have not had any part in the rites of passage in traditional Sri Lanka until its encounter with Christianity in the sixteenth century. The third precept of Buddhism enjoins the abstention from illicit sexual behavior. This precept undertaken by lay Buddhists states "I undertake the course of refraining from wrongdoing in respect of sensuality (*kama*)." In the Buddhist view there is nothing uniquely wicked about sexual offences or failings. Failure in this respect is neither more nor less serious than failure to live up to the other four precepts. The fourth precept, to refrain from all forms of wrong speech, is the most difficult one to live up to (Walshe 1986:3). Because of its ambiguity, the precept against sexual misconduct (*kamesu micchacara*) has been variously interpreted in different Buddhist societies (Obeyesekere 1991:298, Gomrich 1991:298).

Buddhist precepts are not commandments. They are regarded as rules of guidance. It is the undertaking by the person to do their best to observe a certain type of restraint. It is undertaken because the person thinks it is good. But if the person finds it unattractive he or she is free to abandon it, believing that it would have bad *karma* in the future *samsara*.

The Pali word *kama* means sensual desire. It is not exclusively confined to sex. The plural word used in this connection would be equivalent to "lust of the flesh" in the biblical vocabulary. Therefore the precepts refer to the desire for pleasure from the other four senses as well. It is *tanha* (craving) which leads to *dukkha* (sorrow). It is the root of man's desire and craving. It is the intension of the five precepts to control these desires and craving so that one would experience less and less *dukkha*. Therefore both rigid puritanism and total permissiveness have been regarded as extremes in the Buddhist teachings. Specificity regarding lay ethics is absent in Buddhism. Some scholars have stated that this facilitated the spread of Buddhism among the peasant societies with diverse and contradictory moral codes (Obeyesekere 1971).

Buddhism and Marriage

Buddhism is not concerned with the ceremony of marriage, but non-Theravada school of Buddhism, and monks of the Mahayana Buddhist orders, may be called in to recite scripture at a birth, marriage or funeral (Humphreys 1984:125). In Buddhism, priests are regarded as renouncers of lay life. Hence, they are not expected to play any role in important areas of lay life such as birth, marriage and sickness. In Buddhist doctrine, though the rules of conduct for the *sangha* are minutely regulated, there is no systematic code of lay ethics. Therefore rituals specified for these important areas of lay life have been left for popular religion to fill. The only Buddhist text dealing with lay life is the *Sigalovada Sutta*, the householder's code of discipline, as described by the Buddha to the layman Sigala. This *sutta* offers valuable advice on how householders should conduct themselves in relationships with parents, spouses, children, pupils, teachers, employers, employees, friends, and spiritual mentors.

These guidelines are not adequate to provide institutions like marriage with ceremonies that could be regarded as religiously prescribed. Such affairs of lay life do not appear to have been dealt with in canonical writings as matters of importance. The Sinhalese marriage ceremony is entirely secular. In itself it contains no Buddhist elements. When this vacuum, as compared with Christian practice was realized, Buddhists made an attempt to appropriate institutions from Christianity.

Sinhalese Buddhist Marriage before Missionaries
According to the contemporary reports it is clear that the Sinhalese Buddhists had a very lax sexual life prior to the introduction of Christianity. In the Kandyan territories (which did not directly come under Christian influence until 1815), this situation continued well into the latter part of the nineteenth century. T. Berwick, reporting on the judicial aspects of marriage in 1870, was appalled by the Kandyan practice of marrying and dissolving marriages (1870:50). It is stated that marriage began with one glance and ended with a kick! The traditional family was a social institution. It was not regulated by law. A man could meet a woman, enquire about her consent and start a sexual relationship (Ellawala 1962). Sociologists state that sexual relations are one thing and marriage quite another. However, since there was an absence of legal demarcation, marriages became fluid affairs during this period (Harvey 2004:206). Buddhism from its inception has not defined the right kind of marriage to lay people. Therefore the prevalence of monogamy, polygamy and polyandry have been reported in many Buddhist societies (Obeyesekera and Gombrich 1990:28). All these practices have been accepted by Buddhists of Sri Lanka.

Polygamy
For economic considerations polygamy has not been popular among the lowest strata of the Sinhalese society. The laxity of sexual moral codes made it unnecessary to maintain a number of wives. For the same reason, sociologists have found no trace of the institution of professional prostitution in the Kandyan kingdom (Peiris 1956:207). Polygamy, however, is found in the historical

records as an accepted fact in the upper strata of the society. For example, the Sinhalese Chronicle *Rajavaliya* records that Vira Parakramabahu (1476-1489) had two sisters as his chief wives in addition to the concubines that the kings of Sri Lanka used to have (Suravira 1976:212). The usual form of fraternal polygamy is for sisters of one family to be married to one man. This practice is common among the *binna* method of marriage, where the man goes to live in the wife's house, among the Kandyan Sinhalese (Peiris 1956:207-232).

Polyandry

The Sinhalese custom of fraternal polyandry where a wife would be shared in common by several brothers has long fascinated those interested in Sinhalese Buddhist society and culture. The practice referred to as '*eka-gei-kema*' still survives in some remote areas in spite of its condemnation by contemporary marriage laws.

The practice is also known to have existed among other Asian communities such as the people of Tibet and Sikkim, the Jats of the Punjab, the Tidying of Kerala and the Todas of the Nilgiri hills until fairly recent times. Some scholars have suggested that its existence among the Sinhalese was due to a common origin. It is likely that it is an independent development on parallel lines.

M. B. Ariyapala referring to the medieval social practices of Sri Lanka states: "polyandry and polygamy may have been rare occurrences. We get a few references to co-wives and miseries known to them. Reference is made to a man marrying a second time if the first wife proved to be barren" (Ariyapala). However, the Sinhala writings of the medieval period speak of the loose nature of

Sinhalese marriage.[1] The eminent archaeologist, S. Paranavitana, states that the genealogy of king Parakramabahu II (1236-1270) has confused in the contemporary accounts because of the prevalence of fraternal polyandry (Ray 1959:615).

Although the practice of polyandry may have been of early origin the earliest clear record we have of polyandry among the Sinhalese is the Magul Maha Vihara inscription of the fourteenth century where we find the queen calling herself the chief consort of the two brother kings named Perakumba (Liyangamege 1968:84). This information is confirmed by the *Dalada Pujavaliya* of the same period (Thera 1954:35). The practice was also found in the time of the arrival of the Portuguese in the Island as Vijayabahu VI (1513-1521) and his brother Rajasingha had married one wife, and from her they had four sons and one daughter (Suravira 1976).

The European writers of the colonial period, who have been fascinated by this practice, have left us vivid descriptions of the custom as it existed then. The elaborateness of the ceremony of marriage, if there was one, varied according to the social class and place in the caste system of the families of the couple.

Fernao de Queyroz whose work *The Temporal and Spiritual Conquest of Ceylon* (1645), which has been regarded as the history par excellence of the Portuguese period of the island, records (Abeyasinghe 1966:7):

> They also have taken from the Malavaras the most
> barbarous custom that exist among those nations; for it
> is a common practice for four or five brothers or more
> to marry one single woman, and on the contrary one

---

[1] Most Sinhalese scholars of the modern era were ashamed by the absence of a proper marriage among the Sinhalese in the past. Therefore when the issue of marriage came in their studies they glossed it over by making some sweeping statements

single man may marry many sisters, and the youngest ever holds the first place in authority and power in the house and even in love. But in order to separate, each one's wish is sufficient, who taking what was brought to the household may go back and marry at pleasure; and if they had children the males are entrusted to the father and the female to the mother; and if all are males or females then they divide, each one taking what falls to him by lot. And Bento da Silva relates that when he was *ovidor* of Ceylon, there appeared before him a woman married to seven brothers to complain of the ill treatment she received from so many, and begged in good earnest to be relieved of some of them. And as they were still subject to their laws and customs, the *ovidor* asked her whether two would be enough for her, and she replied she would take four; and choosing those she liked, the case was settled. Such are the fruits of paganism (Kumaa 2001:24, 91).

The Portuguese historian Juao Ribeiro says in his *Fatalidado Historica da Ilha de Ceilao* (1685) that once the marriage ceremony is concluded, the first night of consummation is allotted to the husband, the second to his brother, the third to the next brother, and so on as far as the seventh night, when if there be more brothers, the remainder are not entitled to the privilege of the eldest six. He further states:

A girl makes a contract to marry a man of her caste for they cannot marry outside it, and if the relatives are agreeable they give a banquet and unite the betrothed couple. The next day the brother of her husband takes the place, and if there are seven brothers she is the wife of all of them, distributing the nights by turns, without the first having greater right than any of the others. These first days being past, the husband has no greater claim on his wife than his brothers have; if he finds her alone, he takes her to himself, but if one of his brothers be with her, he cannot disturb them. Thus one wife is sufficient for a whole family and all their property is in common among them. They bring their earnings into one common stock, and the children call all the brothers indifferently their fathers (Pieris 1910:140).

The Dutch missionary Philip Baldaeus in his Description of Ceylon (1672) regarding the Sinhalese in Galle says:

Incest is so common a vice among them, that when husbands have occasion to leave their wives for a long time, they recommend the conjugal duty to be performed by their own brothers. I remember a certain woman in Galle, who had confidence enough to complain of the want of duty in her husband's brother upon that account (1996:841).

On another occasion he states that "They marry as many wives as they think fit"(1996:822). Robert Percival, who stayed in the island from 1796 to 1799 reports:

In some respect the accounts given of the matrimonial connections of the Ceylonese are incorrect. It has in particular been said that each husband has only one wife, although a women is permitted to cohabit promiscuously with several husbands. This however is not always the case; many of the men indeed have but one wife while others have as many as they can maintain. There is no positive regulation on the subject, and it is probable that the case with which promiscuous intercourse is carried on, and the case with which marriages are dissolved, is, together with their poverty, the true cause why polygamy is not more general among them (1803:129).

James Cordiner, who served as the chaplain of the British garrison in Colombo and the principal of all the schools in the island from 1799 to 1804 reports:

> The custom of several brothers marrying amongst them but one wife undoubtedly prevails amongst the poorer sort of people who are not Christians, and although not sanctioned by their religion, seems approved by the immemorial usage in the country (1807:96).

John Davy (1815-24) reports:

> Though concubinage and polygamy are contrary to their religion, both are indulged in by the Sinhalese, particularly the latter: and, it is remarkable, that in the Kandyan country, as in Tibet, a plurality of husbands is much more common than of wives. One woman has frequently two husbands; and I have heard of one having as many as seven. This singular species of polygamy is not confined to any caste or rank; it is more or less general among the high and low, the rich and poor. The joint husbands are always brothers (Parker 1982:10).
>
> The apology of the poor is, that they cannot each have a particular wife; and of the wealthy and men of rank, that such a union is politic, as it unites families, concentrates property and influence, and conduces to the interest of the children, who, having two fathers, will be better taken care of, and still have a father though they may loose one. These reasons were once assigned to me by a very acute old Kandyan chief, who, with his brother, had one wife only in common. The children call the elder brother, 'great papa' and the younger 'little papa" There appeared to be perfect harmony in the family (1987:215).

The last substantial account of the practice is perhaps that of Sir James Emerson Tennent in his monumental work *Ceylon* (1859), where he says that polyandry prevails throughout the interior of Ceylon, chiefly amongst the wealthier classes of whom one woman has frequently three or four husbands, and sometimes as many as seven. He notes that as a general rule, the husbands are members of the same family, and most frequently brothers. The custom was however not to remain legal for long for the British outlawed it the same year, though it is known to have survived for a considerable period thereafter.

Ponnambalam Arunachalam observed in *Twentieth Century Impressions of Ceylon* that:

> Polyandry, though illegal, continues to exist among the Kandyan peasantry, especially in the case of brothers. The law against polyandry is evaded by not registering the union at all or by registering it as with one brother only (Wright 1907).

The maximum number of husbands has been seven. If there were more than seven they had no claim over the woman. It is generally believed that a woman with five husbands was a fortunate person (Peiris 1956:205). The woman who is the wife of many husbands was similar to a royal queen (Ribeiro 1685:118).

The men who shared one wife in common did not say that they were married to one wife. Their statement was 'that they protect her in one house' (Peiris 1956:205). Similarly the woman would not say that they are her husbands. Instead she would say, "I cook food for all of them" (:205). The children would refer to the men as father using the epithets indicating their chronological order.

Looseness of Marriage

From the reports available, through local and foreign informants, it is clear to us that marriage was not a serious and well-marked institution amongst the Sinhala Buddhists. We may quote the statement of Queyroz, "among them there is no stable marriages (sic) nor union, except that which arises from personal inclination"(1645:90-91). In addition to the practices of polygamy and polyandry there was a disregard for the marriage bond both among men and women.

Robert Knox writes:

> But their marriages are but of little force or validity. For if they disagree and mislike one the other; they part without disgrace...Both women and men do commonly wed four or five times before they can settle themselves to their contention (1681:248).

Robert Percival, further states:

> It is also customary for those who intend to marry, previously to cohabit and make trial of each other's temper; and if they find they cannot agree, they break off without the interference of the priest, or any further ceremony; and no disgrace attaches on the occasion to either party. But the woman is quite as much esteemed by her next lover as if he had found her in a state of virginity (Percival 1803:129).

There is no tendency in Buddhism to regard sexual irregularities and deviations as wicked. Adultery was regarded as something that was to be avoided. It was widely considered that premarital sex was a good thing for young men but bad thing for girls. In traditional Sinhalese Buddhist society marriage was not a sacrament and often divorce was by mutual consent (Gombrich and Obeyesekere 1990:256). Researchers report that adultery was not a very serious offense in the society before the impact of Christianity (Gombrich and Obeyeskere 1990:4,150).

Robert Percival states:

> The marriage ceremony, which, among nations with stricter ideas of chastity, is looked upon with a degree of mystery and veneration, is a matter of very small importance among the Ceylonese, and seems to be at all attended to only with a view to entitle the parties to share in each others goods, and to give their relations an opportunity of observing that they have married into their own caste. The marriages are often contracted by the parents while the parties are as yet in a state of childhood, merely with a view to match them according to their rank and are often dissolved by consent almost as soon as consummated (1803:129).

Change was Necessary

Roman Catholic missionary activities since the sixteenth century terminated the historic equation of Sinhalese Buddhist identity. During British times Protestantism was the dominant religion. Protestants became the economically dominant class but the middle of the nineteenth century saw a revival of Buddhism. Buddhists made every effort to emulate the Protestant Christian model in order to give Sinhalese Buddhists a respectable status. Among those methods were imitation of organizational forms and tactics of the Protestant Christians. The rising middle class, which had their education in Christian Schools and were closely liked with the British administration made their attempt to reinterpret Buddhism in harmony with modern concepts. Therefore "Protestant

Buddhism" is a direct result in Sri Lanka of Christian experience over several centuries.

Christian Marriage

The institution of sacramentalized lifelong monogamous marriage was a Christian concept, first introduced to Sri Lanka by the Roman Catholic missionaries in the Portuguese period. Marriage in Christianity is an exclusive relationship. The total unity of persons—physically, emotionally, intellectually and spiritually—is comprehended by the concept of "one flesh" and is encapsulated in the concept of holy matrimony. This eliminates polygamy and polyandry as options. The indissolubility of marriage has been the biblical principle guiding this lifelong union.

The Introduction of Christian Marriage

The registration of marriage, which this concept necessarily entailed, was done in Sri Lanka in the *Tombo* registration books under the supervision of the Roman Catholic clergy beginning in the sixteenth century. Therefore, marriage has been referred to as *casada* in Sinhalese, this word being a derivation from the Portuguese word *casado* meaning marriage. Marriage, thus, became a sacrament to those who embraced Christianity, unlike Buddhists to whom marriage, at which nonreligious dignitary was present, were not a sacrament (Disanayake 1999:121).

The Dutch administrators continued the practice of the registration of marriages are connected it with the legitimacy of children for purpose of inheritance. The registration of marriages together with births and deaths was done by the school masters under the guidance of the *Predikants* (ministers) of the Dutch Reformed Church. The system of registration of marriages, births and deaths continued to be the privilege of the state church until 1860 when civil registration was introduced.

The introduction of monogamous lifelong marriage was not readily accepted. It was broken at the slightest opportunity by Sinhalese Buddhists used to a system of lax marriage. The change of colonial power from the Portuguese to the Dutch during the period between 1642 to 1658, and later from the Dutch to the British in 1796 and the disruption caused by the period of transition from the East India Company to the British Crown, also provided an opportunity for the people to lapse into traditional practices. The presence of an independent kingdom of Kandy until 1815 also encouraged the law to be broken as the Kandyan laws did not have any rules to regulate marriages.

Sri Lankan Buddhist Reaction to Christian Marriage

Ordinance number six of 1847 introduced the formal registration of marriages, births and deaths. Severe penalties were imposed any who dared to treat lightly the social responsibilities of the marriage contract whether he or she be Tamil, Sinhalese, or western. Marriage was regarded as a very important social matter. Prior to this period Sinhalese Buddhist as well as Tamil Hindu marriages were not regulated as monogamous lifelong affairs. This ordinance became a hindrance to the current practice of polygamy and polyandry and established the system of registration of marriages (Senaratna 1999:97).

The Buddhist priests were the first to object to the formalized monogamous marriage. This may be because they did not have a role it. Bentara Attadassi Thera, writing in the early 1850s in reply to the Wesleyan missionary Daniel Gogerley's criticism of Buddhism entitled *Kristiyani Prajnapti* (1849), refers to the introduction of monogamous marriage from the point of view of the traditional Sinhala Buddhists. Attadassi further elaborated that monogamous marriage created individual families, cutting them off from other family members who could be a source of support. The law enforcing monogamous marriage was often violated in many devious ways as indicated by reports of missionaries and the police reports.

Marriage, being an extremely important social institution, was affected by the socio-economic and cultural developments in the country. The pressures which arose from the alteration of the socio-cultural milieu with the rise of a new middle class and missionary education, greatly influenced the institution of marriage.

The *Buddhist Catechism* published by Colonel Olcott in 1881 was very popular among Sinhalese Buddhists educated in Christian missionary schools. As a result the book underwent several reprints in the nineteenth century. It incorporated many Christian concepts of marriage in to the Buddhist system of values. These views were popularized among the Buddhists through the schools run by the Buddhist Theosophical Society. For example question 205 of this catechism is, "What does Buddhism teach about marriage?" The answer is:

> Absolute chastity, being a condition of full spiritual development, is most highly recommended; but a marriage to one wife and fidelity to her, is recognized as a kind of chastity. Polygamy was censured by the Buddha as involving ignorance and promoting lust.

These are not teachings of the Buddha or the instruction embodied in the Buddhist canon (Wickremesinghe 2002:31).[2] They

---

[2] According to the *Lalita Vistaraya*, Prince Siddhattha had three wives, Yasodhara, the daughter of Dandapani, Mrgadja and Utpalavarna.

are the innovations of Olcott, which he derived from his own Christian upbringing. In fact the view of the Buddhist scholars is that there is no Buddhist text referring to the preference of monogamous marriage. Buddha did not teach the validity of monogamous marriage over other forms of marriages prevalent in North India in his time (Gombrich and Obeyesekere 1990:253, 273).

The *Poruwa* Ceremony

The meaning of the Sinhala word *poruwa* is a plank. *Magul poru* is the plank where the married couple is expected to stand in order to perform the wedding rituals. But Sinhala writings before the eighteenth century make no mention of *Magul Poruwa* even when they refer to royal weddings (Senaratna 1999:50). Robert Knox (1681) does not mention the *Poruwa* even in the case of the royalty and nobility neither is the *Poruwa* is mentioned by Percival in his account of Ceylon published in 1803. Cordiner also makes no mention of it in 1807. But Alexander Johnston who was the Chief Justice in the Maritime provinces of Ceylon wrote sometime between 1811-1819:

> The manner of marrying, according to the Cingalese custom, is, when a bridegroom comes, together with his relations, to the house of the brides' parents, for the purpose of marrying, there shall be spread a white cloth upon a plank called *Magoolporoewe*, and upon that white cloth there shall be scattered a small quantity of fresh rice, whereupon bridegroom and the bride shall be put or carried upon the said plank by the uncle of the bride, who shall be on her mother's side—if there is none, by any other nearest

---

According to Chinese tradition, the three wives of Siddhattha were Yasodhara, Gotami, Mrgadja. According to Tibetan tradition they were Yasodhara, Gopa and Utpalavarna.

relation—and afterwards there shall be delivered by the bridegroom to the bride a gold chain, a cloth, and a woman's jacket, besides which there shall be changed two rings between them; at the same time, the bridegroom gives a white catchy cloth to the mother of the bride, according to his capacity; after which ceremony, and while the bridegroom on the right and the bride on the left are standing upon the said plank, by the uncle of the bride, or by any of her nearest relations, as above stated, shall be tied the two thumbs, one of the bride and one of the bridegroom, by a thread, and under the knot of the said thumb there shall be holden a plate, and some milk or water poured upon the said knot, and then shall the bride be delivered to the bridegroom. In some places, the two little fingers of the bride and bridegroom are tied, and the said ceremony performed; and, in some places, a chain shall be put by the bridegroom on the bride's neck, a cloth be dressed, and then rings be changed. In some places the marriage is performed without these last mentioned ceremonies (Upham:323-324).

In this record there is no reference to a religious dignitary, auspicious times, consulting of horoscopes, *jayamangala gatha,* or various decorations done to the poruwa. It was mainly a family gathering confined to the families of the two parties.

D'Oyly also refers to a simple *poruwa* ceremony which was performed by the upper class Kandyan Sinhalese. It had no religious significance. There was no religious dignitary officiating it. There was no religious text chanted or song of blessing sung. It is also clear that the common man was not aware of such a ceremony.

> The happy moment being arrived, the Bridegroom throws a gold chain over the Bride's neck and then presents her with a complete set of apparel and

ornaments—and the Bride being arrayed therewith steps up along with the Bridegroom on the *Mogool Poroo* or wedding plank which is covered with a white cloth. The Bride's maternal Uncle or some other near relation then takes a gold chain and therewith ties the little finger of the bride's right hand with that of the Bridegrooms left, and the couple then turn round upon the plank three times from right to left—the chain is then taken off, and the Bridegroom moves to a seat prepared for him—Magool Pata or wedding plate is then brought in from which the Director of ceremonies take rice and cakes and making balls of them give the same to the Bride and Bridegroom who make a reciprocal exchange thereof in token of conjugality (D'Oyly 1938:124-125).

The Development of Poruwa

It was later in the 1870s that the *poruwa* ceremony was introduced to commoners. In this period Buddhist leaders made a conscious attempt to imitate several Christian institutions in order to bring honor to the Buddhist marriage ceremony. The Sinhalese Buddhist leaders, lay and clergy, in the first half of the nineteenth century believed that the Christian sacrament of Holy Matrimony was one of the attractions that drew Buddhists to Christian churches. The Buddhist leaders viewed this with great alarm. On the other hand the new bourgeoisie found the sexual mores implicit in the British legal system fit well with their expectations. This new middle class was a product of the missionary educational system and the introduction of the capitalist economy by the British. In order to bring the Sinhala marriage ceremony closer to Christian ideals and make it more respectable it had to be sacramentalized (Obeyesekere and Gombrich 1990:256).

The Buddhist newspaper, *Lakmini Pahana*, proposed the *poruwa* ceremony which was current among the Sinhalese Buddhist society, especially prevalent among the Kandyan nobility as a Buddhist counterpart to the Christian sacrament of marriage. In 1869 the *Lokarathasadhaka Samagama* (the Society for the Welfare of the World), which was the Buddhist educational society headed by Dodanduwe Piyaratna Tissa, met at Sailabimbaramaya at Dodanduwa and resolved to advise Buddhist laymen on the validity of the practice of the *poruwa* ceremony as a Buddhist invocation, in order to solemnize Buddhist weddings (Sri Lanka National Archives 1968).

Dodanduwe Piyaratna Tissa had a special reason to spearhead such a move as he lost his only brother, David Weerasooriya, on his conversion to Christianity (Darling 1991:5). David Weeasooriya was the father of Arnolis Weerasooriya Colonel of the Salvation Army. David Weerasooriya's conversion in 1862 at the height of religious controversies made Piyaratana Tissa indignant. In fact the person selected as the headmaster for the first Buddhist school organized by Dodanduwe was a Sinhalese Buddhist convert from Christianity who had had his education in a missionary school (Malalgoda 1976:234).

By 1907 the *poruwa* ceremony had acquired more fertility rites as indicated by D.J. Subasingha:

> A special dais, termed the *magul poruwa*, is prepared in the centre of the hall. On the floor is spread a mat, over which is drawn an octagonal diagram divided into eight equal parts. Over this is placed a wooden board, which is covered with a carpet, and this in its turn is covered with a cloth.
>
> Over the temporary platform described, gold and silver coins, pearls and fried paddy, and five different kinds of flowers are scattered. A canopy is suspended over the

dais, at the four corners of which four pots, half filled with water and holding outspread coconut flowers placed. On each flower is an earthen lamp burning with coconut oil. At the auspicious moment announced by the astrologer, the bride and groom are conducted to the *magul poruwa*, and as they mount, a coconut is split in halves with a wood chopper. Benedictory verses are now repeated, after which the bridegroom is handed a cloth, to an end of which is tied a gold coin that goes to the dhoby is a present. Spreading out the cloth, the bridegroom wraps it around the bride's waist; she in turn presents him with a suit of clothes. This called the *Piliendavima*. The maternal uncle of the bride now mounts the dais, ties together the right thumbs of the bride and bridegroom with silver threads, whilst learned relatives of both families chant *Astaka* verses containing Buddha's attributes and blessing. The uncle them pours water from an ewer over the joint thumbs, and thus gives away the bride. As the wedded couple dismount a coconut is again split into halves (Wright 1907:191-192).

In this description one can see the new addition to the simple *poruwa* ceremony. A religiosity has been added with the chanting of praises of the Buddha. However, the *poruwa* itself was still placed on the ground. There was no elaboration of the *poruwa* into the shape of a throne.

The Contemporary Poruwa

Today Buddhist weddings are influenced by Hindu culture which gives prominence to *Nekath*, auspicious times. The *Nekath* is derived from the horoscopes of the bride and the groom which are created based on their dates and times of birth. Of the many traditional events that take place during a Buddhist wedding, the *poruwa* ceremony is the most important. Therefore it is strictly guided by *Nekath*. The *poruwa* is a beautifully decorated wooden platform on which the traditional Buddhist marriage ceremony takes place. Therefore this event is called the *poruwa siritha*. The origin of the modern *poruwa* ceremony goes back the nineteenth century when Protestant Buddhists made every endeavor to counter Christian cultural influence. Ever since its introduction, many innovations have been introduced to the *poruwa siritha*. By and large, the men and women of present day society consider it their heritage and are motivated to protect and preserve something of their past for posterity. Today's *poruwa* ceremony has been influenced by both upcountry (Kandyan) and low country (maritime) customs of Sri Lanka.

The *poruwa* is a decorated marriage platform that is used for the bride and the groom to stand on until the traditional wedding ceremony is completed. According to Sinhala rites and customs, the platform is prepared by covering it with a clean white cloth and placing rice, five kinds of medicinal herbs, a coconut and a few coins to bring prosperity to the couple. Four pots known as *pun kalas*, upon which four lamps are lit, are placed on the four corners of the *poruwa*. The lamps are lit before the ceremony to invoke the blessings of the gods in charge of the four zones (Wijetunga 1984:1668).[3] The Master of Ceremonies, sometimes known as *Gurunnanse* or *kapuwa,* presides over the ceremony.

Kandyan or Low Country drummers would herald the ceremony as the bridesmaids watch. At an auspicious time, known as *nekat*, the bride is escorted to the hall by her father to stand before the *poruwa* till the groom joins her. At an auspicious time the couple ascends the *poruwa*. Traditionally, the groom is escorted to the

---

[3] These are the traditional four guardian deities of the Sinhalese. They are Upulavan, Saman Boksal, Vibhisana and Kataragama.

right side of the *poruwa* and the bride to the left. With the reciting of the *Ashtakas* or eulogies, blessings are invoked upon the couple. After that, seven betel leaves are dropped on the dais to symbolize unity, cooperation and friendship. The little finger of the right hand of the bride and left hand of the groom are tied together with a blessed thread and water is sprinkled on the hand to denote oneness. Four virgins wearing traditional half saris sing the *jayamangala gatha* or auspicious songs, invoking health, wealth, prosperity and happiness upon the couple. This is followed by the exchange of rings and the couple is led to the *poruwa*, each of them putting the right foot forward. The beating of drums known as *magula bera* by the Low Country drummers or Kandyan drummers is an auspicious way to herald every important occasion of the wedding ceremony. These drummers accompany the couple to the dais and each important step in the ceremony is marked by the beating of drums (Herath 2004).

The newly coined words such as *Poruwa siritha* (poruwa custom) have confirmed the significance of the *poruwa* in the modern Buddhist wedding. The rites associated with it have become elaborate. *Gok* (coconut) leaves and banana bark which were associated with festive occasions in the past are being introduced to the wedding *poruwa*. Some of the wedding *poruwas* today resemble royal thrones.

Today the bride is accompanied by her father to the assembly of friends and relatives in front of the decorated *poruwa*. When the father leads to bride to the hall, the assembly rises, imitating the pattern of the church service. This practice shows how far the Buddhist mind was attracted by the Christian sacrament of Holy matrimony and its rituals.

The Meaning of the **Poruwa**–*Then and Now*

Traditionally the wedding *poruwa* was a simple plank which was covered with a white cloth for the occasion. According to Johnston rice was sprinkled over it at the time of the ceremony. The *poruwa* being simply a plank was used for various purposes. *Porewedanda* meant a plank placed to cross the stream. The plank which was used in the paddy fields to smooth the muddy ground after ploughing is also known as *poruwa* (Leach 1982). Some anthropologists have regarded *poruwa* as a fertility symbol because of its association with rice cultivation (Gombrich and Obeyesekere 1990:262). The fact that seeds of rice are spread on the *poruwa* before the couple ascend it may be taken as further proof to this hypothesis. According to Davy's account, the couple stand on a plank of jak wood. The *jak* (*Artocarpus integrifolia*) being a tree which oozes milk is also treated as a fertility symbol in the Sinhalese society.

Adaptations and Innovations in Buddhist Marriage Ceremonies

Today the rituals connected with the *poruwa* ceremony are based on auspicious times calculated to the minute. This, of course has been made possible only with the introduction of clocks in the twentieth century. In the era before the use of clocks the auspicious times were not kept to the minute (D'Oyly 1938:124).

Kapurala, and *Gurunnanse* who have become the officiating priests owe their origin to the post-independence era. They now dress and act like the Royal Purohita Brahmins described in the Buddhist literature. In Subasinha's account (1907) the chanting of *astaka* was done by the relatives. The *jayamangala gatha* was not known even at that time.

The practice of singing *jayamangala gatha* by virgins is of much later origin. These innovations were motivated by the desire to emulate various aspects of the ritual of a Christian wedding, which proved to be attractive and a status symbol to many Buddhists.

Although the term *poruwa* is used for the modern structure used in connection with Sinhalese Buddhist weddings, its original meaning is forgotten. Hardly anyone would be willing to adapt that it has origins in fertility rites. According to Obeyesekere these are royal symbols that have been attractive as a result of association with the Kandyan aristocracy (Gombrich and Obeyesekere 1990:263). The couple receive something similar to consecration of royalty. The accompaniment of drumming and music also add pomp to the occasion. The modern wedding would have hired dancers, traditional or modern, in their wedding ceremonies to add color to the occasion.

The Bride Wears White

The Christian custom is still seen in the use of a white veil by brides in many parts of the island. The color white symbolizes the union of Christ to the Church. The bride also wears a white sari. However, in the Sinhala tradition the color white is not auspicious. It has been used on polluting occasions such as funerals, puberty, births, and weddings. The *magul poruwa* is covered with a white cloth. Alexander Johnston's report indicates that the bridegroom gives a white catchy cloth, indicating the polluting aspect of the marriage act, to the mother of the bride, according to his capacity. Traditionally widows and widowers wear white. According to Sinhalese Buddhist tradition the color white is clearly connected with sorrow. Yet following the Christian custom, Sinhalese Buddhist brides wear white in the *poruwa* ceremony disregarding the example of the colorful outfits worn by Hindu brides.

Blessings Chanted

There are two types of chants mentioned in connection with Buddhist weddings today. The *ashtaka* are sung in order to ward off evil powers emanating from gods, demons, evil spirits and humans (Senaratna 1999:51). While the couple is on the *poruwa,* maids dressed in white chant the *jayamangala gatha.* Although there is no accepted order they do this usually at the end of the *poruwa* ceremony. The *Jayamangala Gatha* (meaning victorious auspicious songs) consists of nineteen four-line stanzas in the Pali text. It celebrates the Buddha's triumph over evil and passion. These songs were traditionally sung after the gathering of the paddy harvest. It is intended to expel malevolent spirits (Gombrich and Obeyesekere 1990:264-265).

According to Obeyesekere, "To have these Buddhist verses sung by pre-pubertal (i.e. infertile) girls dressed in sterile white is a symbolic proceeding that from the standpoint of the traditional culture annuls the sexual and procreative aspect of marriage" (:265). It is interesting to note that while in the traditional Christian wedding white is confined to the dress of the bride, in the context of the Buddhists even the other participants who sing *jayamangala gatha* are also in white.

Participation of the Clergy

According to traditional beliefs, Buddhist monks, being celibate men, are symbols of sterility. Their yellow robe is associated with impermanence and death. The mere sight of a Buddhist monk is generally regarded as inauspicious therefore the Buddhist monks have been kept apart from the marriage ceremonies. However in the recent past in Sri Lanka, as in Myanmar, Buddhist monks have been invited to chant *pirit*, an all purpose tradition to ward off any ill fortune, after the wedding ceremony is over. It is also reported that on rare occasions monks have been invited to chant *pirit* at the wedding ceremony itself. Worship of the Buddha by the couple before or after the *poruwa* ceremony is also another innovation to receive religious blessing to the couple.

The Post-Christian Era

In the post-independence era much of the Christian contribution to Sinhalese Buddhist social life has been taken for granted as Buddhist heritage. Most of the Christian practices acquired by the Buddhists in the colonial era have been baptized into the Buddhist system by giving them high-sounding Sinhala names. The monogamous sacramentalized institution of Christian marriage is one of them. Present-day Buddhists condemn the western culture as being sexually promiscuous and pride themselves on having higher moral standards from time immemorial. Monogamy, which is the only form of marriage advocated by the Christian church throughout history is now being thrown at Christians as a Buddhist heritage.

Modern Christian Adaptations

Some modern Christians who are not aware of the origins and the intentions of these social institutions have tried to imitate or incorporate them in the garb of indigenization and contextualization of Christianity in the Sri Lanka soil.

White or Yellow?

Among other Christian practices connected with the wedding ceremony adopted by Sinhalese Buddhists is the wearing of a white sari and face veil by the bride. The white sari was the usual wedding dress even in the case of Kandyan weddings where the veil was not often used. As a result of the research done by Gananatha Obeyesekere, Buddhist leaders during the last decade have made a deliberate attempt to shun white as the color of the *poruwa* bride even though the veil is still retained. On the other hand the Christians wear white because it symbolizes Christ's union with his bride, the church. However, there is a growing trend among the Christians who are unaware of their tradition and symbolic value of white in the sacrament of marriage to opt to go with the trends of the day. It is interesting to note that some brides now unwittingly use shades of yellow which is the color of impermanence and death according to the Buddhist tradition.

Magul Poruwa *in Churches*

During the 1960s in the Catholic Church some leaders who were interested in the process of accommodation with the local culture vehemently agitated for enculturation and indigenization. They questioned the validity of not permitting the *poruwa*, *jayamangala gatha*, *pun kalas*, *hewisi* music, the national flag and other traditions that constitute the hallowed Sinhala customs at Buddhist weddings, for church weddings as well. In 1967 on the occasion of his daughter's marriage, Santiago Fernando was very keen in observing the Sinhala customs and traditions with all of the intricacies of the *poruwa* ceremony etc. in the church. However, he failed to obtain permission from several churches. Ultimately, a French priest gave him full permission in his church in Bolawalana, to have the church wedding with all cultural regalia of Sinhala traditions. Santiago had to fight with his back to the wall to withstand the tremendous challenges in and outside the Church for his radical innovation. Some Catholics, who strongly opposed Santiago, labeled him as a Marxist rebel and Satan. Ever since that time *poruwa* structures have been seen occasionally in Roman Catholic and Protestant Churches at wedding ceremonies. Many of them who make these requests are unaware of its association with fertility rites.

Jayamangala Gatha

Jayamangala Gatha is a collection of Pali stanzas which eulogizes the Buddha and is sung in the hope of obtaining various victories and blessings in the Buddhist way. Today one can find Christian hymns of blessing sung according to tune of *jayamangala gatha* at the Christian marriage ceremonies by the choir. They are sung at the most sacred part of the sacrament of marriage while the vows are repeated and the rings are exchanged.

Parental Blessing

Buddhist critics have pointed out that the Christian wedding ceremony has no place for the parents of the couple. Their complaint is that the mother of the bride has no place in the Christian ceremony. It is only the father of bride who has an official role in the ceremony. The groom's parents also do not play any part in it. According to the critics the couple does not pay homage to their parents and receive their blessing on this special occasion. The fact that the roles assigned to the parents of the bride and the groom is a very recent innovation to the series of *poruwa* customs is not known to the modern onlooker. Taking this to be a valid omission in the Christian marriage ceremony some Christian churches have included hymns in Sinhala thanking the parents for nurturing and bringing up the couple.

Drums

Churches are often decorated with young coconut leaves. Flowers are kept in two large pots filled with water known as *pun kalas,* and a clay lamp lit with coconut oil is found. Those who can afford hire drummers for an auspicious *hevisi* session. Some do it inside the church before the couple enters. However, some of these practices have fallen out of use as a result of the difficulties of obtaining labor and raw material.

Conclusion

When Christianity was prestigious and powerful in the colonial Christian era, Buddhists tried to imitate and acquire Christian practices and values. Today being the post-Christian era, the trend has reversed. Christians, being unaware of their own heritage in Sri Lanka, have fallen into the lap of Buddhist resurgence and have acquired many of the Buddhist practices without knowing their origins. There is a tendency to follow the contemporary popular practices without knowing the non-Christian symbols attached to them. Many critics of this tendency have stated that this is a part of the syncretism that the church is undergoing. Others have indicated that it is necessary to make the Christian marriage relevant and pertinent to today's social demands as long as they do not contradict the basic Christian values.

The *poruwa* ceremony has become a very colorful and attractive event that would provide lasting memories to the couples who take part in it. Even foreigners have been attracted to the pomp and pageantry of the *poruwa* ceremonies and the rituals attached to it. The *poruwa* ceremony, being a folk innovation, can keep on adapting to suit the trends of the time and yet give a mysterious and religious touch to the event. Since the *poruwa* can be hired at a comparatively low cost and since the ceremony can be performed without its astrological and fertility symbols, some Christians would be attracted to it in this post-Christian era. It is unavoidable that some young couples would prefer to go with the trend of the day.

The intention of the institution of *poruwa siritha* as a counterpart to the Christian wedding ceremony has not only achieved its original purpose; the dreams and aspirations of its original innovators have far surpassed their intended purpose. Now they have been able even to challenge the Christians. Christians have mistakenly capitulated to the view that only Buddhists have contributed to the cultural heritage of Sri Lanka, thus undermining their own heritage as "foreign" despite its five hundred year history. The Christians are not aware of the fact that they have enriched the cultural heritage of this island. The Sri Lankan Christians have been pushed into a predicament that they feel guilty about their historical past. They wrongly think that the fathers of their faith acted destructively by demolishing the Sinhala culture. They do not know their own contribution to the enrichment of the culture of Sri Lanka. Monogamous marriage and the dignity that they introduced to the chaotic family life of the Sinhalese is one such major contribution.

PART III

STRATEGIC ISSUES

9

Beyond Karma: a Model for Presenting Freedom in Christ in the Buddhist Context

Paul Wagner

The primary purpose of this paper is to present a model for sharing the Gospel that communicates to Asian Buddhist thought patterns and language. This model begins with the Buddhist worldview within the context of an Asian value system. From there it proceeds to the more uncharted sphere of similar or divergent concepts of teaching and experience where terms may be used with some overlap in meaning to bridge the gap between cultures and worldviews. This model is based on my forty years of personal experience interacting with Asian Buddhists of different backgrounds as well as with communicators of the gospel. In part, I have come to similar conclusions that other observers of Asian people groups such as Kirsch (1975), Mulder (1970), Spiro (1970), Sponberg and Hardacre (1988), and Tambiah (1975) have made.

Finding a Common Point of Reference
Asian Buddhists view themselves within concentric circles of influence beginning from the core with family and gradually moving out to peer groups, society in general, and the supernatural world (Mulder 1978:90). This supernatural world includes the Buddhist concept of karma which is an outcome both of merits and demerits from past and present lives. According to the Buddhist

teaching the law of karma is the ultimate regulating principle governing the outcome of human existence (Spiro 1970:114). In it every good action brings merit and every bad deed demerit or sin as well as retribution or punishment. It is proverbial that in the course of one's life demerits or sins normally accumulate faster than merits (43).

Religious law, as given in the Old Testament, teaches that it is not able to bring salvation but rather brings people into an understanding that sin is bondage and that there is a need for a Savior. In a similar way, for a Buddhist, the law of karma encases the practitioners in a legal system where punishment consists of having to live in various hells. This is in some way in agreement with the biblical teaching that death and judgment is the result of sin (Romans 7:10). In a way, the Buddhist view of the individual in relation to the natural and supernatural world is similar to the view of the Bible. Religious law, as found in the Old Testament or Buddhist precepts and rituals, is therefore a common point of reference for both Buddhists and Christians.

Starting from this common moral perception we attempt to show a larger worldview. In doing this we build on the worldview that already exists. We do not replace it but enlarge it because people are generally reluctant to embrace radical change, but are open to absorb and apply new insights.

Using Familiar Illustrations

Much of Asian Buddhist thinking is expressed in circles or cycles referred to as *samsaric* existence (Spiro 1970:73). My observation in the Buddhist world is that many Buddhist rituals and the reading of graphic religious displays tend to begin on the right and move in a clockwise circular movement to the left. I prefer to use circular illustrations in this model to visualize the message we want to communicate. In cultures that stress linear thinking, the flow and description of thought moves from left to right in its core parts. It is up to the communicator to decide which method of communication is best for the context of the receptors.

This model of sharing the Gospel is not intended to be an oversimplified presentation that leads people to a quick conversion experience. It is intended as a guide for conversation between the communicator of the gospel and an Asian Buddhist recipient in order to help bridge the gap between bondage to karma and freedom found in a personal relationship with God. Just as a diagram appeals to the person who thinks visually, so an example or story may appeal to an individual who tends to understand better by hearing a spoken illustration than by viewing a picture with an abstract application. Both approaches can effectively lead the listener to experience the ultimate reality which is God. Examples of each will be given in the following explanations.

Emulating the Apostle Paul

Just as Jesus and Paul identified with the people of their time, so the messenger of the Gospel must enter the world of Buddhists and identify with them and their current environment without becoming a part of any wrongdoing. The apostle Paul said:

> Though I am free and belong to no man, I make myself a slave to everyone, to win as many as possible. To the Jews I became like a Jew, to win the Jews. To those under the law I became like one under the law (though I myself am not under the law), so as to win those under the law. To those not having the law I became like one not having the law (though I am not free from God's law but am under Christ's law), so

as to win those not having the law. To the weak I became weak to win the weak. I have become all things to all men so that by all possible means I might save some. I do all this for the sake of the Gospel, that I may share in its blessings (I Corinthians 9:19-23 NIV).

When applying these principles to Buddhist cultures we start from their worldview, learn to understand and speak their language, and use their forms of communication. Thus the communicator can say: "To Buddhists under the law of karma, I became like one of them to win them. To those under that law I became like one under the same law, reaping what I sow. To those who are weak and cannot keep all the precepts I also am weak and acknowledge my limitations and inability to keep the precepts. I identify with the fear of the law of retribution, having myself feared to be condemned to a future existence in hell." It can be observed among most Buddhist groups that they are conscious of many hells and suffering in various forms as a result of their bad karma (Spiro 1970:41). This understanding of the future existence in punishment of hells is more prevalent in Asian Buddhist cultures than in western cultures today. By identifying with Buddhists in this way they can see our compassion and understand our honest testimony which then can lead them to experience deliverance from the consequences of karma. This is the salvation which the Gospel offers to people of every culture. By presenting oneself as a personal example and by sharing in lasting relationships, the Christian messenger becomes the key for God to open the Buddhist heart.

The protector of a Buddhist monastery related to the author that, according to his understanding of Buddhist scriptures, because of his own karma he would have to suffer many thousands of years in hell. Even his knowledge of the promised compassionate Savior did not comfort him since that compassionate one would come to this world only and could not save him from hell. Fortunately, he got to know about the present deliverance available through the compassionate one in this life before he left this world.

Procedure for Presentation

The way in which the Gospel was originally communicated to the people in Asia Minor during the first century can teach us how to do the same in our time. The apostle Paul took special effort to explain the Gospel to Asians of the Middle East in their terms. This is most apparent in Paul's letters to the Ephesians and the Colossians. It is of little wonder then that young Christians from Buddhist backgrounds favour these portions of Christian writings. They find them easier to understand. Therefore, in this model I have used insights gained from the study of Paul's letters to the Ephesians and the Colossians as basic guidelines.

When attempting to apply the Gospel to the context of an Asian Buddhist people group, it is important to remember that such an application involves changing the form of presentation only. The content of the biblical message is universal and must remain unchanged regardless of culture. Before a communicator tries to understand all aspects of the culture of a particular people group, he or she will have to study and thoroughly understand the essential biblical teaching concerning the Gospel of Jesus Christ. Only then will one be able to present the eternal truth in a way that is culturally acceptable to the hearers and meaningful to their hearts. Then the message will remain undistorted by non-essential cultural elements or by the idiosyncrasies of the messenger.

Explain the Common Worldview

We begin to share the good news of salvation through Jesus Christ by sharing a common perspective or worldview which we assume that the communicator and the receiver agree upon. We explain the elements of the three circles as follows:

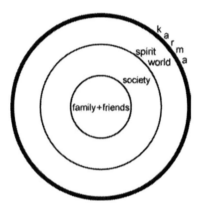

Figure 1: Our Common Worldview

The inner circle stands for a person's family and closest friends. Here are the closest possible relationships that offer the greatest possible security to any individual. The middle circle represents society with its hierarchical system of authority. On one hand this system can be exploited and on the other hand it also threatens to exploit. In Asian cultures the hierarchical structure of patron-client relationships in wider and closer circles is more prominent, in western societies it is less obvious, hidden under the guise of equality of human rights (Skinner and Kirsch 1975:93,199). This can result in a communication gap for westerners attempting to communicate to Buddhists in Asia. The outer circle stands for the spirit world which is very real to all societies on all levels and which subjects all of society to the power of spirits. Capital cities for instance are regarded as the abode of high-ranking gods and spirits as well and each city and town may have a special shrine for a dominating spiritual authority. This is in agreement with the biblical observation of Paul in Ephesians 2:2, where he regards all mankind under domination of the spirit of this world. Much of the western world has lost this perspective during the scientific age though there is a resurgence of this worldview in this age. In Buddhist societies the law of karma is regarded as governing this world as an all-encompassing force from which there is no escape or exemption. In non-Buddhist societies, the commonality with the endeavor to keep the law and so improve one's karma is the dependence upon personal efforts and achievement. In Buddhist doctrine there is no solution for the problem of guilt by forgiveness. From a biblical perspective all systems which are based on doctrines and supernatural beings outside of the compassion of God have a legalistic element inherent in them as a poor substitute for a forgiving personal relationship with God as Paul observed in Galatians 3:19. This brings about an urgent need of salvation by a forgiving, compassionate Savior, for people in Buddhist societies as well as for people in a post-Christian secular world.

Affirm Common Personal Values

Everyone is subject to certain laws and is responsible for one's actions. The principle of the law of karma applies to everyone in some way in this life and also after death. Everyone must adhere to basic precepts. Everyone consciously or unconsciously has the desire to know and enjoy the relationship with an ultimate reality (St. John 1996:177-183). The problem is that not everyone understands how to do this. Many long for harmony and security, yet they find themselves in a world of uncertainties, which includes suffering and the threat of many hells. Buddhism teaches that a person can avoid suffering by detaching oneself from the bonds of love, affection, and desire. Those who seriously practice this will become suspicious of deep personal relationships (Spiro 1970:63-65). However, there is no human existence outside of relationships. As Augustine said, there is a created vacuum within human nature, which only the Creator himself can fill (1957:89).

This desire for relationship is an open channel which communicators of the gospel can use in meeting a person's need. As people turn from insecurity to relationship with a heavenly Father who cares for them, they find that their most basic needs, including their deepest need for belonging, will be met. An accepting group of Christian brothers and sisters often helps to demonstrate the unselfish kind of love that God shows to people. Such fellowship is only possible through insight into the nature of the supreme God who loves sacrificially.

A high-ranking shaman in a Buddhist village once met a messenger of the Gospel and asked him, "Please pray for me. My spirits who served me all my life now want to kill me. I am in the last stage of diseases with multiple complications for which the doctors have no cure. Your spirit is more powerful and he can save me." The messenger had not even talked to him and was surprised about the insight of this man. After intensive prayer by many believers, the shaman was healed. After twelve more years he fully trusted in the great compassionate Savior. He faithfully served his people for many years, giving them the Word of God, even ruining his health cutting wood for his friends. His death left a shining example of the compassion of God that others now follow.

Explain the State of Humanity

Dependent upon the inquirer's interests, the communicator of the Gospel can elaborate on physical, intellectual, or emotional needs. In spite of much goodness that can be experienced in a lifetime, human life is often replete with worry, fear, insecurity, and confusion, even while one is seeking peace and joy. This coincides with the Buddhist teaching that human existence is characterized by ignorance and darkness. People may feel helpless in their self-centeredness. They cannot escape the darkness, bad karma and hell, which result from their egocentric lifestyle (Revelation 21:8). Life is meaningless for both Buddhist and those in secular western cultures. "There is nothing new under the sun, all life is vanity and meaningless!" was the observation of Solomon who lived about 3000 years ago (Ecclesiastes 1:2-9). These insights may have spread all over Asia and into the west from those days. The concept of striving for annihilation as a basic axiom to escape the meaninglessness of human existence, and suffering is a natural consequence of this philosophy of life. For Buddhists, eternal life could mean the biggest curse they can think of. It means an eternal perpetuation of their meaningless existence caused by the understanding of the law of karma and its consequent hells and rebirths. However, mankind naturally is looking for a way to fulfillment, freedom, and peace.

A western lady moved to an Asian monastery seeking karmic salvation through the observations of Buddhist rules. She was frustrated, however, by the fact that the other people in the monastery did not live a sacrificial lifestyle. To her, merit making meant sacrificial social activities. She wanted to motivate other nuns to get involved as nurses and social workers. She related to me her frustration about her efforts and the meaninglessness of her existence in the monastery. I indicated that the insight of the futility of life is one of the basic and most profound insights of Buddhism, and since she adheres to it, should be content with it. This insight however bothered her and resulted in her leaving the monastery and looking for fulfillment in her home culture, where she had seen more meaning in life. She saw that a compassionate sacrificial life style was a basic and even more fulfilling tenant held by people from her home environment that she could not find in an Asian Buddhist surrounding.

Empathize with Aspirations to Overcome Insecurities

A person's desire for freedom may find expression in doing the very things that their law forbids. When this leads to a vicious circle of guilt, shame, and desire for deliverance, this experience may be similar to that described by Paul, "The good I want to do I do not, and the evil which I do not want to do I do" (Romans 7:17). Dependence on spirits aggravates the sense of bondage and helplessness, but salvation through Jesus Christ offers deliverance. The inquirer may question with Paul, "Who will deliver me from this body of death?" (Romans 7:27). By identifying with his or her understanding of suffering, sin, and death as a consequence of sin, we show understanding for our common human predicament in this world.

When the communicator has been able to find agreement on these points he or she may continue with the example of a family. A child being born into any family receives the status of a son or daughter along with security and certain special privileges. Similarly, when a person enters the family of God, he or she experiences an inexplicable peace that cannot be easily shaken. Many even experience being ostracized or persecuted for their newly found faith, which they endure patiently. As a young child grows he or she will be more exposed to the world, to its wonders and dangers. He or she will learn about the do's and don'ts of society, to beware of evil people and the spirit world, and to behave wisely. Asian Buddhists try to appease the powers that are around in the world but at times are uncertain whether they have done the right offering at every important shrine. Westerners tend to be more confrontational in their communication to others and even to spiritual authorities, not reacting with appeasement but by personal effort to take control or confront and so manage lives and relationships according to their own values.

Introduce God as the Ultimate Reality

Introducing the concept of God as the common ground with Buddhists is not easy since Buddhism teaches reliance upon personal efforts alone. One may start with an agreement on a concept of an ultimate spiritual reality which lies beyond all visible or tangible existence leading gradually to a biblical concept of a triune God being the sum total of all perceivable goodness, purity and holiness.

The knowledge of a creator is at best vague in many Asian cultures. In South and South East Asia there is the knowledge of the concept of *Sekkya* or *Sattja* as a creator god, which is also found in Buddhist writings of some of these cultures. Prayers are offered to him for protection and success of any kind, though doing this is not regarded as a high level of Buddhist enlightenment. One can find a shrine of this deity among other gods and demigods at Buddhist temples. Sample prayers to this deity can be found at holy places and in the media. This is very similar to the situation in Athens with the shrine to the Unknown God among a pantheon of deities (Acts 17:23). Paul took this vague concept as common starting point for sharing the gospel to the Athenians.

From Genesis to Revelation we find evidence of a triune God: God the Father, God the Son, and God the Holy Spirit (Deuteronomy 6:4). We cannot adequately explain the Trinity because of our limited human minds, but we can attempt to illustrate it by a symbolic triangle. I have taken the illustration of the trinity by Sauer (1978:14) to highlight the three aspects of God as Father, Son and Holy Spirit in the shape of a triangle where the three angles are distinct and yet form a whole, (see Figure 2). The three angles represent three communication links between the Father, Son, and Holy Spirit. Genesis 1:2, 26, John 14-16, and Revelation 22 illustrate how the three personalities of the trinity communicate harmoniously and act in unison.

Figure 2: An Illustration of the Triune God

God is the supreme spirit. He is all knowing, beyond human comprehension. He is pure and holy, removed from mankind and yet faithful to his wayward creation by making himself known to them (Psalm 139). God is all-powerful. He is more powerful than any other human being, spirit or power since he is independent of them. He is and beyond the law of karma as the creator and Lord of the whole universe, unchanging though consistent with its basic meaning (Revelation 4:8-11). God is compassionate and merciful, ever caring for the welfare of humanity, like a partner in the most ideal relationship (Psalm 86:15; Luke 15:20).

Introduce the Compassionate Savior
In many Asian monasteries and at homes of scribes who copy these scriptures we can find Buddhist texts which mention the coming of a compassionate Savior. In Folk Buddhism and in intellectual Buddhism a vital expectation of *Maitreya*, or a coming Savior, is found all over Asia. Even the New Testament mentions that there would be many coming claiming deceitfully to be the Savior of mankind. The memory of his coming has been kept alive from the beginning of mankind over many generations through millennia in various forms, traditions as well as distortions. One can find allusions to this Savior in Asia ranging from a description of a most pure and holy being to a human creature with many faults (Sponberg and Hardacre 1988). We can take Genesis 3:15 as the first biblical reference to his coming. I intentionally present the concept of the Savior in a way which may appear to be vague. This is done in order to introduce a new way to share the gospel with those who also may have only a vague concept of the compassionate one themselves. The communicator thus identifies

with the listener rather than mentioning the name of Jesus prematurely.

This is in line with how Paul introduced Jesus Christ gradually to his hearers in Corinth (Acts 18:5). This is also in line with communicative styles in Asian cultures, which bring up the most important insight at a later stage in the discourse. Westerners tend to present the most important topic or theme first and then provide the details as arguments to prove their point. In the Buddhist context this is different. We could even say that it may be closer to God's way of communication to mankind, since he waited for centuries and millennia to unfold the full light of the gospel in history. Therefore, we also can afford to give a spark of insight to an important truth as a starting point and slowly elaborate to a full enlightenment of biblical truth.

Those best communicators of the gospel among Buddhists use this style of communication. The full revelation of love and power by the Lamb of God, who is the Savior of all peoples, and of his authority to usher in an era of peace for the whole world is only unfolded in the final stages of history, as described in the book of Revelation. Theravada Buddhists tend to ignore eschatological passages of their own scriptures and may deny the relevance of these predictions altogether since they seem to contradict the logic of the supremacy of the law of karma. The same tendency is also found with Jews who have their problems with interpreting the identity of the suffering and compassionate servant of God (Isaiah 53 and Psalm 22) as the promised Messiah.

Isaiah, who lived about 200 years before Gautama Buddha, promised a Savior and peacemaker who would bring a reign of peace. Isaiah's writings were known all over Asia since the Babylonian and Persian captivity (Isaiah 9:5). Other prophets predicted further details to this event. These scriptures were read and shared by Middle Eastern traders and migrant groups throughout Asia. It is not surprising that similar predictions are also found in Buddhist scriptures of various peoples in Asia. I personally know of the location of such scriptures. Five centuries after Gautama Buddha's death this Savior came to earth as he was promised. He prepared the way for all human beings to receive new spiritual life. His coming opened the way for humanity to be truly enlightened, delivered from evil and able to enjoy the peace and freedom which they were made for but could not achieve by their own efforts. He called himself, "the way" (John 11:35).

According to biblical records, this was in agreement with the eternal plan of the supreme God. He sent a part of himself as Lord of compassion and the Savior of humanity into this world. He became a child, born of the virgin Mary. As a human being he grew up, as all humans do, in a circle of family and friends. He healed the sick, cast out demons, taught twelve men as his disciples, and trained many other followers. The chief evil spirit, called *Mara* in many Asian languages, tempted him. He is also known as the angel of death, because he had power over death. This Savior, by his death on a cross and subsequent resurrection, overcame Mara's power (Hebrews 2:14). Through his tortured death on a cross he paid the penalty for all the bad karma of humankind.

In connection with introducing the Savior it is also necessary to refer to some other concepts, which may not be readily understood. The concept of punishment as consequence of sin is referred to in several languages of Asia with the same word, which originally meant only the act of sinning or breaking a law but developed into a comprehensive concept of punishment as well. In Burmese *apyit* means sin as well as punishment. The Palaungic word *abret* has the same meaning.

Buddhists do not easily understand the concept of substitutionary atonement or gaining merit for somebody else, however there are some local examples. Mothers can gain merit by having sons become monks. Thailand gained political and social deliverance by Queen Suriyothai who sacrificed herself for the nation. These are familiar examples of substitutionary merits for the salvation of others by Thai people. Similarly, on the basis of the immeasurable merits of the great compassionate one alone we can hope to receive salvation. He overcame all evil with compassion as he hung on the cross praying for his persecutors and his neighbors on the other crosses. By sacrificing himself for our sins as the only one who had no sin any human being can be saved and does not have to suffer the consequences of his or her karma (2 Corinthians 5:21). Anybody who takes refuge in the strength and power of these compassionate Savior's merits will receive those merits which he needs for his own salvation as well.

The message of the compassionate Savior Jesus Christ may be introduced in a cyclical fashion. Starting with his incarnation, one can tell about his overcoming the law of karma by his holy life, death, resurrection, ascension; readiness to help us, and his promise to return to earth in order to receive those who put their trust in him.

Explain the Cycle of a Believer's Identification with the Savior

When we have presented the worldview of God coming into our world in order to save us from the confines of karma, we can now explain what needs to be done in order to benefit from it. We point back to the world in which we live where the Savior has come and broken the barriers that confine us within the law of karma. As we follow him on the path of confidence and compassion, we too will experience salvation.

As gold is the most precious metal so these three steps are most sacred in importance. We may call them three golden steps leading to a new spiritual existence. They include discovering, believing, and receiving the reality of the supreme God.

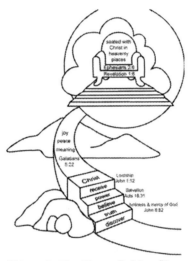

Figure 3: The Three Golden Steps

First we discover the truth as God has revealed it to us through scripture, testimony, and life of any messenger of this truth. As we learn about the life of the Savior we learn about the holiness and mercy of God. We see the spiritual reality of our demerits of neglecting basic precepts and not taking refuge in the ultimate reality. Ultimate spiritual reality can be discovered when a person grasps the truth about oneself, including one's shortcomings. He or she also needs to grasps the truth about God and his care for us when he sent the Savior. As we feel sorry for misdeeds and ask for forgiveness of our failures he takes them away along with all the bad karma, demerits or sins which we may have accumulated (John 8:32, 6:9, 1 John 1:9). The refusal to take refuge in the great compassionate Savior is defined by Jesus himself as the basic sin, which automatically excludes from salvation.

The second step is to believe in the power of God. This means we have authority to accept the merits of Jesus Christ, which are available for us by God's compassion or grace. "Behold the lamb of God which takes away the sins of the world." (John 1:29).

The third step is receiving Jesus Christ. This will release a believer inwardly from the power of evil and enable life to be lived in fellowship with the Savior. This also is the time when a believer accepts Jesus Christ as the guide in all aspects of life.

Deliverance from evil powers not only brings spiritual blessing and salvation to the individual but also to his or her whole family (Acts 16:31). God's power working through the Spirit of Jesus Christ in a believer paves the way so that people who are close to the inquirer can also come to know God and become enlightened. As the testimony and confession of the Samaritan women at the well-brought faith to the whole village (John 4), so also many Asians have been transformed through faith in the compassionate one and then testified to parents, children and friends with the same results.

God's power to deliver can be compared to the power of aerodynamics that overrules the power of gravity. An airplane may weigh several tons but when its engines start and its wings are set it lifts off into the skies as if there were no gravity to pull it down. The higher power of aerodynamics overrules the power of gravity and the plane soars upward. Passengers need not push or pull the plane; they have only to sit back and relax, trusting the captain and crew to take them to their destination. Similarly, we trust the greater power of God to give us new life. After being released from the fear of the consequences of bad karma by taking refuge in the merits of the Savior we are also released from the compulsion to sin which would otherwise spiral us downwards, even though we may be trying to do good.

When these three steps of discovering, believing, and receiving are taken by prayer the new heart becomes an inward reality, which will be felt in all areas of life. The result is a spiritual enlightenment and transformation, the beginning of a new life, which brings a person into a new and lasting relationship with the heart of a compassionate God, who cares for his creation like a parent for his sons and daughters.

Humanity's deepest need for meaning in life is met by this experience. The new relationship to God is compared to a child being adopted as a son or daughter into a new family (John 1:12). It is also compared to a bride accepting her bridegroom in marriage (Revelation 3:20). God intends for any human being to experience fulfillment in a way which was previously unknown, namely an increasingly intimate relationship between God and the one who has become his child. Those who realize that they would be totally lost without a relationship with the supreme God will place their complete trust in him by submitting to him and receiving Jesus Christ as their Lord and Savior. This step of faith is the ultimate reality of a new existence, or new birth (2 Corinthians 5:17).

The new birth can be illustrated by a comparison between the caterpillar and the butterfly. A caterpillar lives in a limited world. It is born and lives this stage of its life on the leaf of a tree but when it is transformed into a butterfly it ascends to the sky and feeds on the nectar of flowers. It experiences a new freedom and lives in dimensions previously unknown. Similarly, when we are born anew we experience a totally new life.

Help the Person to Accept Christ
If at this point a person is open to the truth which has been shared, he or she needs to actually open his or her heart to receive Christ. Praying a prayer of acceptance is most crucial. Such a prayer should include the following components:

1) Understanding and agreement with the truth of the Gospel message.

2) Expression that he or she believes in the power of Jesus to deliver from all sin.

3) Acceptance of Jesus Christ as Savior, and willingness to allow Jesus to guide from now on as a friend closer than a marriage partner (Revelation 3:20).

The person who wants to experience these three steps should express them in a prayer, possibly reading aloud. It is important that the prayer be voluntary and from the heart. The figure and prayer below can serve as a guide.

"Lord, I see your light and seek your compassion as the true and only answer to the negative effects of my karma, my demerits, and my sins. I trust your power to save me from all of my sins and any bondage of powers over my life and my family. I take refuge in you, Jesus Christ, and receive you as the compassionate Savior and Lord of my life. Thank you for making me your child and for coming into my life."

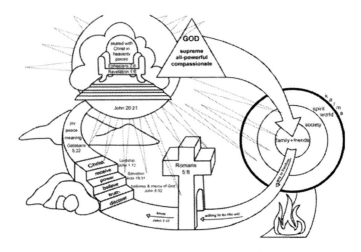

Figure 4: The Way To New Life

After the prayer the person needs to be assured that God has heard and answered. The communicator of the Gospel then can follow with a simple prayer of thanksgiving to God expressing gratitude for the privilege of that person now being a child of God.

Explain About the New Life Received

Once a person has prayed to receive Christ it is important to reassure new believers of their new status as a child of God. Assure of the privilege of living and reigning with Christ in a new spiritual realm (Ephesians 2:6, II Corinthians 5:17, I Peter 1:3). All of God's riches are now theirs (Ephesians 1:3, 14). Encourage young believers to deepen their new relationship with God as sons or daughters would relate to a loving father. Encourage them to relate to Jesus Christ as their Savior and to other believers as brothers and sisters (John1: 12; Revelation 3:20; Romans 5:1-5; Ephesians 3:15-17). As Christians enjoy new life they share with Christ a position of supernatural power, and reign with the King of Kings and Lord of Lords. It is like being a prince or princess who reigns with Christ throughout this life and eternity.

Along with the Father and the Son, the Holy Spirit also resides in the life of a believer making it possible to live a godly life. Through prayer and fellowship with Jesus Christ (John 15:5-7, 16:16-23), the Holy Spirit works to bless the family and friends of a believer (Acts 16:31). The Holy Spirit helps us to grow and produce God's fruit in our lives (Galatians 5:22). This can be illustrated by testimonies beginning with the example of the Philippian jailer (Acts 16:31). Being delivered from bondage to spiritual powers also brings with it inner security, contentment, and a growing ability to abstain from evil. It includes letting go of personal attachments to objects of spirit worship, including magic tools, charms, and mantras.

Following Christ the communicator should describe the role of the new believer as an agent of change in his environment and as a messenger of reconciliation (II Corinthians 5:20). Such a Christian, trusts in Christ for direction and help, and asks for his guidance in knowing how and when to get involved. Believers become a positive influence in their everyday world and draw others to Christ.

Susan (name changed) was a handicapped Buddhist teenager who sought healing by visiting many shrines. Nothing seemed to help. She was told that her condition was the result of her bad karma. No religious practice seemed to be able to cool her heart or give her inner peace. Once she confessed that her heart was burning as if she were already in hell. She heard the gospel and was curious to know God but was warned against following anything other than what was taught by her elders lest she endanger her life by offending the spirits. However, when she understood clearly that the compassionate One would be able to give her a cool heart she prayed to Him. She lost her fear of hell and spirits. Shortly afterward her parents and several of her friends also prayed to this Savior. The elders were infuriated and tried to force her back. When all else failed she was poisoned. While in pain she still cleaned the house and showed love in any way she could. Finally she lay down peacefully. She remembered the word of God to be faithful unto death so that she would receive the crown of life. People around her had never seen somebody dying in peace with a cool heart. All believed that they had to suffer many hells after death. They were greatly surprised about Susan's peaceful attitude and started seeking that same cool heart which they had seen in her. This was the beginning of a movement towards salvation among her people.

Anyone interested in sparking such a movement may try to use the outline of the model that I have presented in order to share this good news with those who may have a similar worldview. Groups of Asian young people have put this model into drama and found that many people, not only in Asian, but also in western cultures have responded and found a meaningful life through this message of the compassionate Savior.

10

TRANSFORMATIONAL MISSIONARY TRAINING FOR BUDDHIST CONTEXTS

David S. Lim

Since evangelical churches were made aware of the unreached people groups (UPGs) within nations by Dr. Ralph Winter in Lausanne '74 (that's more than thirty years ago), why have we hardly decreased the number of the unevangelized, including those in Buddhist societies, in the world today?[1] Can't we reach them more speedily and more effectively?

This paper ventures to answer two questions: (1) How can the Buddhist UPGs (from families to nations) be reached effectively? Our reply is that they can be *evangelized* rapidly through church planting movements (CPMs), and also discipled and *transformed* holistically through community development (CD)! This constitutes

---

[1]Barrett and Johnson 2004:25 shows that global Christianity (including 60% Roman Catholics) is losing by -.12% annually. 1.64 billion were unevangelized in 1970; still 1.74 billion (27.5% of world population) are unevangelized in mid-2004. And if present trends continue, 1.95 billion (24.5%) will still be unreached by 2025. Perhaps worse is the statistics that Christianity was 33% of the world's population in 1900, and it was still 33% as of 2000 - no net increase at all in our latest century!

the vision and curricular content of "Transformational Missionary Training" (TMT). Then also (2) How can missionaries be trained in doing such transformational ministry effectively? This work's latter half will describe what the TMT methodology looks like, as it is being implemented in the writer's institution called the Asian School for Development and Cross-cultural Studies (ASDECS), particularly as we have started to open a couple of extension training centers in Cambodia and soon also in Thailand.

TMT Vision and Curriculum

The first half of this paper presents the vision and the two curricular objectives of TMT:

Vision: Societal Transformation

In recent years, evangelicals have come to recognize a common objective for our mission: to "make disciples of nations" includes "teaching them to *obey all* that Christ has commanded us" (Mt. 28:18-20). "Transformation" is the favorite term that has surfaced to denote this goal in proclaiming this "whole gospel" of the kingdom of God. It means the restoration of "shalom" in the world through the establishment of Christ-centered communities of love, righteousness, justice and peace (Isa. 65:19-25; Rom. 12:1-15:13; cf. Rev. 21:24-26). It brings about harmony and reconciliation, whereby people are invited to repentance and faith in Jesus Christ, and then incorporated into faith-communities that seek to build right relationships with God, their neighbors, creation and their own selves (Mt. 22:37-39; 2 Cor. 10:5). Every person, community and people group will have been enabled to become what God intended each of them to be (Eph. 4:17-24; Col. 3:5-17).

The two concrete goals of "transformational mission" (TM) are saturation evangelism and community transformation. Whether the whole people group turns to Christ or not, we hope that the populace will have been *empowered* to become mature and responsible (not dependent) adults who can make dignified and wise decisions for their individual and communal life (including to be for or against Christ). They would be active participants (not passive spectators) in tackling issues that affect their lives and destinies in the light of God's Word.

Such lofty goals seem impossible, and indeed they are, humanly speaking. Yet the Bible reveals that our God is more than eager to have all peoples redeemed and transformed (1 Tim. 2:3-4; 2 Pet. 3:9; Lk. 15:3-7), and His Spirit is at work to make the "fields ripe unto harvest" (Jn. 16:7-11; cf. 4:34-38). In fact God will not end world history until this harvest is reaped (Mt. 24:14). God must have intended his mission to be achieved (and soon) in simple ways, though not without cost. Christ did not intend his Great Commission to take this long to only be half-fulfilled after almost 2,000 years since his salvific death on the cross! It seems clear to me that it is his Church that has failed to follow the Spirit's movement to send more laborers into the harvest (mainly due to inertia effected by its burdensome heavy church structures), and the few laborers have mainly failed to use the right strategies to hit this objective. May I suggest what the right methodology and strategy should be.

Objective #1: Church Planting Movements

In recent years, especially since 1999,[2] the missionary community has (re)discovered the "master plan of world evangelization."[4] The "secret formula" is CPM through "disciple-making" in small groups–often called "house-churches."[5] The goal is to do "rapid church multiplication," so that as many converts as possible are made to become quality witnesses and disciple-makers as soon as possible! Saturation evangelism even in hostile UPGs is possible, perhaps only through CPMs. And thank God, this has been done in China (mainly among "folk Buddhists"!), Cambodia, Mongolia, and many places, mostly in recent years![6]

The best CPM model seems to be the planting of "reproducible churches" with five characteristics marked by the acronym "P.O.U.C.H." Each church that was planted sought to plant another church within a year. The result? Within three years of implementing this type of "church multiplication" method, they had 55,000 believers (from an original group of about sixty) meeting in more than 550 cell or house churches, since many were able to reproduce within a few months! "P.O.U.C.H." include: (1) *Participative* meetings—the leader is a facilitator of discussion

---

[2] With thanks to the Southern Baptist International Mission Board that had David Garrison research and publish a book (1999), which was reproduced in USCWM's *Mission Frontiers* in April 2000 and expanded in 2004.

[4] Cf. Coleman 1964; Eims 1981. Also cf. Allen 1962, 1962a; Donovan 1978, Hunter 2000 and Lim 2004.

[5] This contrasts "church multiplication" (hence, *multi-church*) from "church growth" of *mega-churches*, cell-churches and even G-12; cf. Simson 2001; Petersen 1992; Neighbor 1990, Comiskey 1999, and Zdero 2004. Also cf. Snyder 1975; Boff 1986; Ringma 1992; Lim 2001, 2004.

[6] For a historical view, cf. Zdero 2004: 59-69. For its present global scope, cf. Garrison 2004: 35-168; and Zdero 2004: 69-76.

around God's Word, instead of being a lecturer or preacher; (2) *Obedience*—the goal of meetings is to make disciples, to teach one another to obey God's Word; (3) *Unpaid* lay leaders—they found that the most effective leaders were housewives who hardly finished Grade three! (4) *Cell or house churches*—multiplying small groups (of 10-20 adults) help keep personal relationships informal and intimate; and (5) *Houses* or venues that do not require rent or lot purchase (Garrison 2004:60-64). With almost no overhead costs, believers can start new churches among their friends and contacts through "natural relationships and simple witnessing for Christ in their kin or friends' facilities!

Yet the fastest so far is "Training for Trainers" (T4T) where a Chinese-American was able to disciple thirty believers in China to become witnesses and disciple-makers for Christ – in an amazing way! Within six months, they had more than 4,000 baptized members in 327 house-churches; in twelve months, more than 12,000 baptized members in 908 house-churches; in eighteen months, about 53,420 in 3,535 house-churches; and in twenty-four months, 104,542 in 9,320 house-churches! He began by just training them to compose and memorize their three-minute testimonies, and then each shares their testimony with five family members, friends, coworkers or neighbors! Those who respond positively were invited to a cell meeting which had a six-session curriculum: (1) assurance of salvation, (2) prayer, (3) daily devotions, (4) body-life in a house-church, (5) understanding God and His will, and (6) witnessing, which means learning to share their (memorized) testimonies to at least five people close to them (and start a new house-church with them) also! (Garrison 2004:286-291, 307-314).

These two CPM models approximate our Lord Jesus' strategy: To start his world transformation movement, he called twelve ordinary people (almost all rural folks!) and discipled them for a while (Mk. 3:13-15). Then he sent them out two by two (that's six pairs) to make twelve disciples each (Mt. 9:35-10:16). When he sent out disciples the second time, he did not commission the twelve, but the "seventy-two others" (Lk. 10:1, 17). These were sent out two by two also (that's thirty-six pairs) to make twelve disciples each, thereby making 432 new disciples in all. 1 Cor. 15:6 mentions that after the resurrection, our Lord appeared to more than 500 (432 + 72 + 11) brethren! If these 500 paired up, that's 250 making twelve new disciples each, they would be able to disciple exactly 3,000 new converts, which actually happened on the day of Pentecost. All converts were baptized *immediately*, since the apostles knew they would all be followed up and discipled in at least 250 house-churches in Jerusalem ("from house to house", cf. Ac. 2:41-47). No wonder their numbers increased *daily*!

To become a CPM expert, one just has to be a "disciple-maker" who has to learn only two basic skills: *friendship evangelism* and *leading cell groups*. (1) S/he learns how to share the Gospel and their personal testimony after establishing friendship with each of a few non-Christian relatives, friends, colleagues and even strangers. Converts and potential converts are then brought to her/his cell, or better, encouraged to start an evangelistic cell at their convenient place and time.[7]   And then (2) it becomes necessary to also learn

---

[7] Those who work among oral cultures should learn to do "chronological storying," cf. Gauran 1991. If there is no Bible in their native tongue, the native convert should be encouraged to lead the translation efforts, in close consultation with trained linguists and translators. Among non-literates, one can also use memorization, audio-visuals, songs and educated youth

how to lead small group discussions where one can facilitate a meeting in which all attendees can participate in setting their agenda and seeking the proper interpretation and application of God's Word for the issues relevant to their personal lives and social contexts (cf. 1 Cor. 14:26).

Thus the goal of transformation through saturation evangelism is made possible through a CPM! Reason and experience seem to indicate that such multiplication can happen only if the first converts are not brought in close contact with the traditional local churches – for obvious reasons: they will not only be exposing themselves to danger (being known as converts prematurely), but they will also become ineffective witnesses very soon, since they will be de-contextualized from their culture (into a Christian sub-culture) rapidly! (Garrison 2004: 194-196, 245-249). It seems best for new converts to form new churches.

Objective #2: Community Development
Yet to be really effective, especially to disciple and transform an entire family, clan or community, CPM should be combined with the community development (CD) strategy. The process involves not only approaching the people group *holistically*, but also doing so in as *contextual* and *empowering* way as possible, so as not to create dependency but rather to help the whole community grow together to its fullest potential![8]

By *holistic*, we mean that the point of entry and eventual development should cover the entire range of cultural and social life of the people group. Hence missionaries can enter through any

---

(Garrison 2004: 184-186).
[8] For secular models, cf. Andres 1988; Schumacher 1984. For Christian models, cf. Bobo 1986; Lim 1992; Linthicum 1991; Myers 1999; Samuel and Sugden 1999; Suderman 1999; Yamamori et al 1995 and 1998.

entry platform (read: area of expertise) that serves the community, either as professionals (like medical personnel, English or any teachers, managers, engineers, etc.), as businessmen (like setting up computer or language schools, travel agencies, beach resorts, etc.) or even as skilled workers (caregivers, drivers, seamen, domestic helpers, etc.)! The harvest can indeed be joined through any role, as long as the worker has CD perspective and skills!

By *contextual*, we mean that the needs or issues to be tackled are derived from the local situation of the target group itself. Every people and community has their own unique sets of problems and aspirations, thus rather than going among them with a pre-conceived message and a pre-packaged strategy, the missionary must be willing to learn from the populace, be appreciative of their culture (except perhaps the five percent that's sinful,[9] which has to be transformed!) and be flexible in his/her ways (1 Cor. 9:19-23).

And by *empowering*, we mean that the missionary should identify her/himself as a servant-leader and work *with* (not *for*) the people. The key is for one's ministry to have a clear commitment to encourage the local people themselves to be responsible for the welfare of their own people and community life. In the end, the people should be able to say, "we did it ourselves"!

In order to achieve all these, CD consists of only two very important community organizing skills: (1) *immersion*, which is to spend time with the people to learn about their culture, including their language, social structure, values, beliefs, leaders, etc.; it is best to learn basic field research techniques for this. And then (2) *core group formation*—upon working *with* the people to discern a local need or issue to tackle, the worker *facilitates* a process by

---

[9] It seems that the major *sins* are idolatry, individualism (pride), (personal) immorality and (social) injustice.

which a leadership core is formed to tackle the problem or attain their aspiration.[10] Local resources are tapped and maximized before any foreign help or funds are considered. Even before the successful completion of the program or project, the missionary may be able to leave when s/he sees that the people can already finish it on their own.

Through CPM, the ideal of an indigenous movement that is self-governing, self-supporting and self-propagating is already easily achieved. Even from the beginning, local leadership is developed and empowered to continue the multiplication of simple churches. Yet when CPM is combined with CD, the latter provides at least four more advantages: (1) it becomes possible to befriend and reach community leaders (the influencers!) from the start, thereby hastening the process of societal transformation! (2) it shows Christianity's relevance to any local need or issue; (3) it avoids creating dependency, since local leadership and resources are considered first and foremost! And (4) the programs and activities are contextualized and sustainable; thus the worker can leave as soon as the momentum is discernible! Such is the wonder of "transformational mission"(TM)! Should these CPM and CD skills not be the main emphases in the training of our missionaries, particularly those who are seeking to reach Buddhists? TM has already proven to be effective indeed in Cambodia and Sri Lanka, among others! (Sluka and Budiardjo 1995:47-78; Stephens 1995:103-115).

My view is that even if TM has already occurred in a people group, the church will still need to be constantly in a mission mode: each person and family has to be reached (can 100% conversion rate ever be reached?), and every child (new generation) has to be

---

[10] For more details, see Andres 1988: 5-23 and 35-43.

discipled. In the Old Testament, even if the whole of Israel was nominally "reached," God institutionalized "house-churches" (Dt. 6); celebrative worship in the temple was not weekly, but only three times a year (16:16).[11] Churches among nominally "reached" peoples should continue to use this "mission as transformation" paradigm lest they retrogress to become an UPG again, as is happening in most nominally Christian nations today!

TMT Methodology

This paper delineates the training methodology that will produce effective TM workers for ministry among UPGs, especially Buddhists. What is the best training paradigm by which we can train missionaries who will be able to bring about the transformation of Buddhist communities? Interestingly, proponents and practitioners of both TM approaches (CPM and CD) advocate the same training paradigm to educate and train workers with the attitudes, understanding and skills for TM. For TM to be truly *transformative*, just as the curriculum has to be holistic, contextual and empowering (see above), its methodology should be *simple, people-centered, practical, contextual* and *participatory*.

Simple
In order to attain both objectives of TMT, the methods have to be simple, so that even non-literates (which are the majority of UPGs) can do and replicate them. Our students should learn to define *basic Christianity* in *simple* forms that can be the basis for making contextual (read: multi-form) applications, even by the poor.

---

[11] Cf. Lim 2001 and Simson 2001.

All successful CPM models have developed simple MT strategies to train as many believers as possible (if possible, every believer) to evangelize, disciple and plant churches that plant churches. They include training in basic skills in friendship evangelism, leading small group discussions, transformational biblical hermeneutics and theologies, dynamics of social change,[12] learning styles of the poor, etc. all within the context of non-formal field ministry programs where the mentors are TM workers themselves. The simpler the TMT, the easier and faster the multiplication potential! No need to build buildings nor provide subsidies to train simple folks to do TM! The use of external funding have often led to the slowing down, if not the death, of CPMs![13]

For CD, *simplicity* in all aspects of ministry and training is also required in order to maximize people empowerment. Even among the poor, indigenous leadership for community transformation can be developed from the beginning! Then each ministry can be a rapid self-organized and self-sustaining movement that hardly needs external input and support. With simplicity in TMT, the missionary may be able to leave the TM soon; in fact, the sooner they leave, the better! (Garrison 2004:186-9; 193-4). Why? Because the new local believers will be able to do better, more contextualized, replication of TM among their people!

---

[12] TMT must develop non-violent means to challenge oppressive structures. The choice is not between the status quo and change; it is between violent and peaceful change. J. F. Kennedy said, "They who do not make peaceful change possible make violent change inevitable." We must seek new ways to resolve conflicts, injustice and underdevelopment.

[13] Garrison 2004: 249-255. It also refers to a quote of an American house-church network called Church Multiplication Associates: "We must raise leaders for the harvest from the harvest, and all the resources for an abundant harvest are in the harvest" (p. 164).

Relational

The second major mark of TMT is its people-centeredness and people-orientation. People need to see new ideas lived out in practice before they can accept them. Hence TMT requires this in two ways: the relationship of the teacher to the trainee as well as the training with regards to the approach of TM.

Firstly, following recognized sound educational principles, TMT requires that each teacher should be a role model of TM: as a CPM practitioner, a justice advocate and/or development agent working with a team of missionaries or coworkers. This may be more popularly called "discipling," and in this paper, TMT workers are best referred to as "disciple-makers."

"Values (and skills) are better caught than taught." Thus, while committed to the propagation of propositional truths, TM workers need to learn that their calling involves people. Truth is not disembodied: the gospel is truth incarnated in Christ, and the Bible teaches us to follow the example of Christ and "speak the truth *in love.*" The message and the messenger must become one as much as possible. And in embodying (and modeling) their teaching, the TM teachers should approach their students with love and respect. Hence the best way to teach and train others (in CPM and CD) is to relate with them as persons, as friends, in as close a personal relationship as possible.

Secondly, people-centeredness must be shown in the views and attitudes that are modeled before the trainees, particularly in relation to our target people. For instance, in TM our relationship is with Buddhists, not with Buddhism.

> It is the street-Buddhists who are the brothers and sisters
> whom I see, with whom I speak and with whom live. To
> love them *as they are* in all their complexity and not just
> to love anthropological, sociological, theological

'formulations' of brothers and sisters is the command of
God whom we have not seen (I John 4:20) (Koyama
1999:151).

TMT therefore emphasizes "discipling" one's trainees to focus
on developing close relationships with people: CPM calls this
"friendship evangelism" while CD calls this "immersion" or
"integration." Moreover, as we serve in a high-tech world, we have
to major in high touch work. To remain simple, we need to resist
the temptation to focus on high-tech, so as not to deflect from high
touch! Sadly many training programs have not been able to win
over this kind of temptation.

Practical

A close corollary to the relational nature of TMT is its being field-
based and action-oriented, founded on an intimate link between
reflection and practice, between classroom and fieldwork. It should
be conducted close to real life situations, identifying and organizing
learning resources that link the student with the actual milieu
through non-formal education and community participation.

Successful CPM have been able to develop on-the-job training
(OJT) programs, which train local leaders[14] and often with
emphasis on lay leaders, even new believers. Such "just-in-time
training" and mentoring programs aim to develop better equipped
(not better educated, which may come later) Christians who can
multiply churches that plant churches!(:180-1;189-91;229-231)[15]

---

[14] Hence, missionaries avoid becoming pastors or bringing in expatriate
pastors. A popular "discipling" model is to model, assist, watch and leave
(M.A.W.L.)! See Garrison 2004: 186-189 and 250-251.
[15] See also the "cascading model" of an Indian CPM (: 234-235). In a
Cambodian CPM, they say "Never do anything by yourself; always bring
a brother along with you so you can model and mentor as you go" (:187).

Of course, this entails a redefinition of what is leadership and leadership training: it is not the accumulation of more knowledge (one can be over-trained!), but the upgrading of actual ministry skills, which require (just enough) knowledge and wisdom (:242-3). OJT is also the training model of CD. Thus, in ASDECS we use traveling teachers and short-term modular courses even in our formal degree courses.

Moreover, this apprenticeship model may work very well in Asian Buddhist contexts. It fits the traditional training practice, perhaps of most civilizations except the post-Enlightenment western academic tradition, though it is changing rapidly into post-modern modes today, too! Buddhist novices and candidates for monkhood train even their children in practical ways, including going from house to house to solicit food, chant, and meditate.

Contextual

Following the incarnational pattern of God's redemptive action, TMT has to use the contextual approach to leadership training. Even modern education (including theological and missionary education) has become more and more decentralized through extension centers, correspondence courses, internet modules and various distance learning programs. Those in CD work have also been training among the poor contextually, using their local or "folk" communication media, like story-telling, poetry, drama, etc. This equips the poor to become "trainers of trainers" within their culture and communities, without having to "catch up" with "modern education."

In CPM training, contextualization is important and necessary because biblical values and standards have to be applied to particular issues in specific contexts. There seems to be a simple "weekly house-church meeting" programming model that fits contextual TM best and can be used universally even among illiterates. It automatically trains effective disciple-makers out of every believer for CPM through its free mixture of activities according to the needs and giftings of the participants, as set by the leaders in close consultation with all the members. Activities include: prayer and worship, Bible reflection, fellowship (try to include a simple/potluck meal together always!) and sharing, collection and stewardship, community service and missions support. Following 1 Cor. 14:26 pattern of meeting, all members have to come prepared to "disciple (or teach, encourage, confess sins, etc.) one another," as they participate in building their life together.

For Bible reflection, the leader facilitates discussion by choosing an appropriate Biblical text (or the like) and just asking two questions: (a) Which verse (or story) in the passage is most meaningful for you? Why? And (b) How can we apply what we have learned for the benefit of ourselves, our family, our fellow Christians and/or our community/workplace? For sharing time, they can answer any or all of these questions: What has God done for you lately? What has God been teaching you lately? What have you done for God lately? Once in a while, the group can choose to have guest speakers, excursions (watch a movie, eat out, sports, etc.) or joint meeting with other HCs. Emergency issues should usually take precedence over planned activities. Hence, between opening and closing prayers, each HC grows spiritually together (literally) "as the Spirit leads"!

This simple meeting format that emphasizes contextual application best fits TMT, and may be taught and modeled among the poor and illiterates. It has the other added value of our last TMT indicator: it is also participative!

Participative

Lastly, to be empowering and replicable, the best TMT must be also *participatory*. It is only through discussion types of meetings that all participants are naturally trained to become leaders, especially. servant-leaders for both CPM and CD. Since Paolo Freire's *Pedagogy of the Oppressed* (1970), many recent educators have come to understand that transformational education must be *dialogic* and therefore *participatory* through *democratic* processes (Ringma 1996:3-11). Otherwise it will fail to empower the people, particularly the poor (yet surely including the rich), to make decisions that truly will benefit them and their context.. People learn best through a series of question-and-answer experiences so that they can use their creative imagination to find better ways to develop a better future. A dialogic I-thou (personal) relationship as partners and co-learners is prerequisite to develop an *openness* to others and risk changing one's pre-understandings. This requires TMT advocates to be open-minded mentors and co-learners in community with their students (Ringma 1996:7-9).

To be truly transformative, TMT must also be "liberative," which means that students should he trained to take a "prophetic critical" stance. This is based on the theology of the reality of sin and the necessity of repentance (Greek: *metanoia*): everything, except God and His word (read: the gospel) which are absolute, are to be relativized. Nothing on earth (not even any form of Christianity) should be absolutized, given the tendency of humans and their societies to fall into sin (Ringma 1996:7-9). Hence, TMT should develop critical awareness which raises new social consciousness. In a situation of sin, poverty and injustice, the consciousness of people is submerged in a reality simply adjusting itself to natural and/or supernatural forces. Liberation happens only when they become aware that they are active subjects of their history and culture, through an educational process that seeks to produce a critical mind, especially in light of the gospel.

For CPM, even in contexts used to rote learning, critical thinking can be introduced and promoted naturally though collective exercises in "real life" case studies by listening to one another's views as they reflect on God's word together in an atmosphere of mutual respect. In areas where religious intolerance, discrimination and even persecution prevails, TM workers need to model the use of participative strategies that uphold human dignity and freedom. This may include skills to build communities of peace and develop sustainable socio-economic programs that fit the local market and global realities. And evangelizing in the context of pluralism requires humility, especially since most of us will bear witness from the margins of Buddhist societies. TM workers need to learn to invite without arrogance, propose without trying to impose. They must allow the strength of the other's arguments and admit the limits of their own knowledge. All knowledge and truth belong to God, not to us, and God has not revealed everything.

Further, TMT must aim at critical discernment that results not just in personal transformation, but also in social transformation. This also means taking the side of the poor. The rich benefit from the status quo, thus are normally conservative if not reactionary. It is the poor who are pressed by survival needs to seek transformation. Sadly, most of our training structures have quite an *elitist* framework, that their education will "trickle down" to the grassroots. Thereby they fail to think on how their theological and missionary education can be relevant and beneficial (in short, transformational!) to the poor.[16] Only when our churches (and

---

[16] Failing to be pro-poor, our schools have produced leaders who are at

seminaries) becomes truly the "churches (and seminaries) of the poor" can we start to truly train TM workers for the UPGs.[17]

Perhaps the ultimate test is whether our MT is ready to critique and transform ecclesiastical structures: What kind of churches are we going to plant and multiply? Are we going to perpetuate the non-liberative Christendom system which has kept the poor poor and the laity disempowered to do transformation in the world? Are we ready to teach our students how to transform our churches into "networks of *cell groups*" (Roman Catholic "Basic Ecclesial Communities" (BEC) and Protestant "house churches"),[18] where each Christian grows spiritually in their respective cells (each serving as a small discipler-maker training center), where each mature Christian can lead his/her own cell, preferably one in his/her place of *residence* (during the weekend) and another in his/her place of *work/study* (on a weekday),[19] and where each cell discerns who are the TM workers worth supporting to become "clergy," some to serve as *coordinators* (or pastors) of local networks of cells, while others as *missionaries* to start "cell networks" elsewhere in the world.

---

best reformist, become bureaucrats or even entrepreneurs who are unable to critique our defective culture (i.e., colonial, paternalistic, patronage-based) so as develop alternative transformative structures that liberate.

[17] On the methodological ingredients for TMT, cf. Craig 1996: 37-52. On some social agenda items for empowering TMT, see Carr 1994: 45-67.

[18] Note that though the NT churches had their problems, they were able to impact their communities and the Empire within a generation, even if they were truly "churches of the poor and oppressed," not unlike what's happening in China, India and other Third World nations today.

[19] Modern life has added this new dimension of 8-5 world, thus the need for "office cells," to locate the church *in* the streets, offices and boardrooms of the nations.

Are we ready to adopt this participatory and liberative philosophy of education for TMT? May we dare to come up with radical answers to both truth and structural questions, resulting in individual and social change. Then the next issue is whether we have the moral courage to live out the implications of the answers that we discover. TMT should help liberate us from fear, so we can obey God's call, no matter how radical, in light of our Christian conscience and commitments.

Conclusion

So what kind of study programs should we develop to achieve the above TMT paradigm, perhaps with the best use of the least possible resources? May I suggest that it should be in the form of non-formal "discipler-maker training programs" rather than academic degree programs. What I mean is that we set up small "discipler-maker[20] training centers" that develop the TMs that we envision—without pulling them out of the marketplace and without the need for much external funding. The key concept is to disciple an expanding core group of leaders, who will work inter- or cross-disciplinarily to impact key structures among the unreached (Wanak 1994:69-97. Seminaries should become major training centers to develop servant-leaders who can transform their church networks into such disciple-making centers.

---

[20] Though often used interchangeably with "disciple" and "discipleship," "disciple-maker" is used here to emphasize the qualitative maturity and the quantitative reproducing capacity of the TM worker to make disciples who will disciple others (cf. 2 Tim. 2:2).

These centers shall recruit and develop teams of "faculty" who can mentor others and develop resources for TM, through non-formal short-term *seminars* which may offer "certificates of participation." These would best be monitored and nurtured in (decentralized) "fellowship" structures, each being self-governing, self-sustaining and self-expanding, yet inter-linked with the other disciplines through some coordinating centers.

This training paradigm calls us to follow the way of the cross. Our human instinct and desire is to follow the tempting way of the world, to form power structures to promote, project and propagate our ideals, even our way of the cross ideals. But this runs counter (actually contradicts) our understanding of the way of Jesus and the apostles.[21] We are to take captive all earthly philosophies and ideologies to submit to Christ through spiritual weapons (i.e., prayerful acts born out of sacrificial love, cf. 2 Cor. 10:3-5).

To be consistent with this educational paradigm, we may have to constantly remain a "mustard seed conspiracy"[22] which develop "soft structures" to use the humblest and simplest possible means in the most loving (read: empowering) and the least domineering (read: powerful) way possible to bring out the best from the bottom up (i.e., democratically) and not from the top down (read: autocratically), serving alongside *with* (not *for*) the people. It seems that the Quakers were the most consistent in following this mustard seed strategy. They provided the leadership in social movements for slavery's abolition, women's rights, temperance, peace and

---

[21] The most developed training program was that of Paul renting a hall for public lectures in Ephesus, which contributed to the total evangelization of Asia Minor within 3 years, cf. Acts 19:1-10; 20:17-35.

[22] Evangelical seminary graduates should be familiar with the writings of E. Trueblood, T. Sine, W. Stringfellow, D. Kraybill, J. Ellul, H. Yoder, and Os Guinness.

American Indian rights; and presently in some major transnational social movement organizations (Greenpeace, Oxfam, Amnesty International and others). Ane they were able to propagate effectively without much structural visibility, with hardly any public structures except their meeting halls, and just with seminars among ordinary people led by small teams of committed disciples! How I wish that they laid equal emphasis on CPM also!

This contrasts with the past elitist (read: imperialist) models of Roman Catholic, Anglican, Presbyterian and Methodist missions which set out to transform (read: civilize) societies with Christian universities (which have fast become secularized, and rightly so!). After pouring so much Christian resources, their impact (especially in the "mission field") has been minimal – having won some youth (rarely the intelligent nor the nationalistic ones!), they succeeded in turning off their families, clans and even whole peoples against Christianity! This aggressive approach is being replicated today by many evangelical groups which are trying to set up mega-churches with their mega-projects, like Christian cathedrals, Christian universities, Christian tri-media, Christian hospitals, even Christian sports centers, especially to propagate their outmoded narrow interpretation of scriptures. Yet the more fervently they do these, the more marginalized they become, creating a subculture that is irrelevant and unintelligible to the unreached. We've also discovered that worldliness (unspiritual spirituality) is very much present and alive even in these "holy" churches and Christian institutions!

So it seems best to pause a while from going into more sophisticated training programs that will force us to develop faculties and build facilities (especially libraries), which are already available in our universities and seminaries (Protestant and

Catholic). This will require not just a lot of overhead to develop and maintain, but also demand a lot of unnecessary duplication which the universities and seminaries are already providing. Our methodology must fit our mission to reach the unreached, and give enlightened and effective witness in our pluralistic world today.

Now that we have the strategy for rapid and effective evangelization of UPGs, the problem remaining is its implementation. It may seem too radical for most of our churches and even many missions today. It requires a major paradigm shift: not just in our vision and objective (to multiply house-churches rather than build mega-churches), but also in our methodology (to simply do disciple-making for CPM, not just plant a church) and strategy (to reach entire peoples holistically and not just win a few individuals at a time for CD). This may be our best chance to positively fast-track the effective evangelization and transformation of entire people groups, including Buddhist ones, in our generation!

The call is to just go back to biblical basics and strategic simplicity! China's house-churches are already trying to send 100,000 such missionaries with this mission and TMT paradigm in their Back to Jerusalem movement (Hattaway 2003). We hope the Filipino missions movement will be able to mobilize 200,000 to do this type of mission and TMT by 2010, too. And this is what ASDECS and our training staff (through our simple formal and non-formal training programs) are committed to do in TMT among Buddhist peoples and beyond. The harvest of Buddhists and other peoples is ripe and still plentiful. May multitudes of effective disciple-makers be raised for TMT soon, so that "...the end will come" (cf. Matt. 24:14). *Maranatha*!

REFERENCES

Chapter 1

Bivin, David and Roy Blizzard. 1994. *Understanding the Difficult Words of Jesus: New Insights From a Hebraic Perspective.* Dayton, OH: Center for Judaic-Christian Studies.

Branden, Nathaniel. 1985. *Honoring the Self.* Los Angeles, CA: Bantam.

Gilbert, Roberta M. 1991. *Extraordinary Relationships: A New Way of Thinking About Human Interaction.* Minneapolis: MN: Chronimed Publishing.

Kaiser, Walter C. 1981. Toward An Exegetical Theology: *Biblical Exegesis for Preaching and Teaching.* Grand Rapids, MI: Baker.

Keirsey, David and Marilyn Bate. 1978. *Please Understand Me: Character and Temperament Types.* Del Mar, CA: Prometheus Nemesis Books.

Komin, Suntaree. 1991. *Psychology of the Thai People: Values and Behavior Pattern.* Bangkok: National Institute of Development Administration.

Kort, Wesley A. 1985. *Story, Text, and Scripture: Literary Interests in Biblical Narrative.* Pennsylvania, PA: Pennsylvania State University Press.

Lewis, Ralph L. and Greg Lewis. 1985. *Inductive Preaching: Helping People Listen.* Westchester, IL: Crossway Books.

Mejudhon, Ubolwan. 1994. "*The Way of Meekness: Being Thai and Christian in the Thai Way.*" D. Miss Dissertation. Wilmore, KY: Asbury Theological Seminary.

_____. 2002. "*Evangelism in the New Millennium: An Integrated Model of Theology, Anthropology and Religious Studies.*" Bangkok, Thailand: SEANET.

Mosley, Ron Joshua. 1996. *Joshua: A Guide to the Real Jesus and the Original Church.*

_____. 1981. *A History of Christian Theology.* Philadelphia, PA: The Westminster Press.

_____. 2002. "*Hans Frei and the Screening of Biblical Narrative.*" Religion Online.

The Lausanne Theology and Education Group. 1978. *"The Willowbank Report: Report of a Consultation on Gospel and Culture"* Willowbank, Bermuda.

The Lockman Foundation. 1964. *New American Standard Bible*. U.S.A: The Lockman Foundation.

Rollins, Wayne G. 1981. *Jung and the Bible*. Atlanta, GA: John Knox.

Schreiter, Robert J. 1981. *Constructing Local Theologies*. Maryknoll, NY: Orbis Books.

Snow, Eric. 2002. *"Narrative Theology"* Religion Online.

Thompson, David I. 1982. *Bible Studies that Work*. Grand Rapids, MI: Francis Asbury Press.

Triana, Robert A. 1981. *Methodical Bible Study*. Grand Rapids, MI: Francis Asbury Press.

Warne, Clifford. 1971. *The Magic of Story-Telling*. Sydney, ANZEA.

Wilson, Marvin R. 1985. *Our Father Abraham: Jewish Roots of the Christian Faith*. Grand Rapids, MI: Eerdmans.

Young, Brad H. 1995. *Jesus, the Jewish Theologian*. Peabody, MT: Hendrickson Publishers, Inc.

Chapter 2

Burnett, David. 1990. *Clash of Worlds*. Crowborough: MARC.

_____. 1996. *The Spirit of Buddhism*. Crowborough: Monarch.

Cole, W. Owen. 1994. *Six World Faith*. London: Cassell.

Dalai Lama, *The Good Heart: A Buddhist Perspective on the Teachings of Jesus*.

Dharmasiri, Gunapala. 1988. *A Buddhist Critique of the Christian Concept of God*. Antioch: Golden Leaves.

Gethin, Rupert. 1988. *The Foundations of Buddhism*. New York: OPUS.

Goonewarde, Anil D. 1996. "Buddhism." In *Six World Faiths*. W. Owen Cole. ed. London: Cassell.

Griffiths, Paul J. 1994. *Christianity Through Non-Christian Eyes*. Maryknoll: Orbis.

Gross, Rita and Terry Muck. 2000. *Buddhists Talk About Jesus and Christians talk about the Buddha*. New York: Continuum.

Hanh, Thich Nhat. 1997. *Living Buddha, Living Christ*. New York: Riverhead Books.

Hoekema, A. A. 1986. *Created in God's Image*. Grand Rapids, MI: Eerdmans.

Johnstone, Patrick. 2001. *Operation World.* Cumbria: Paternoster.
Kidner, Derek. 1967. *Genesis.* London: Tyndale Press.
Lim, David and Steve Spaulding, eds. 2003. *Sharing Jesus in the Buddhist World.* Pasadena, CA: William Carey Library.
Netland, Harold. 1991. *Dissonant Voices: Religious Pluralism and the Question of Truth.* Grand Rapids, MI: Eerdmans.
_____. 2001. *Encountering Religious Pluralism: The Challenge to Christian Faith and Mission.* Downers Grove, IL: IVP.
St. Ruth, Diana. *Buddhism in Britain.* http://www.bbc.co.uk/religion/religions/buddhism/features/buddhism_in_britain/index.shtml.
Stott, John. 1975. *The Christian Mission in the World.* Downers Grove, IL: IVP.
Vroom, Hendrik. 1996. *No Other Gods: Christian Belief in Dialogue with Buddhism, Hinduism and Islam.* Grand Rapids, MI: Eerdmans.
Waltke, Bruce. 2001. *Genesis: A Commentary.* Grand Rapids, MI: Zondervan.
Williams, Paul. 2000. *Buddhist Thought: A Complete Introduction to the Indian Tradition.* London: Routledge.
_____. 2002. *The Unexpected Ways: On Converting from Buddhism to Catholicism* Edinburgh: T and T Clark.
Wolfe, Regina W. and Christine E. Gudorf, eds. 2001. *Ethics and World Religions: Cross Cultural Case Studies.* Maryknoll, NY: Orbis Books.
Wright, Christopher. 1995. *Walking in the Ways of the Lord: The Ethical Authority of the Old Testament.* Downers Grove, IL: IVP.
http://www.gospelcom.net/apologeticsindex/rnb/archives/00001079.html
"The Direction of Buddhism in America Today," http://www.urbandharma.org/udharma5/tension2.html

Chapter 3
Alexander, J.A. 1963. *A Commentary on the Acts of the Apostles Volume 2*, Edinburgh: The Banner of Truth Trust.
Blaiklock, E.M. 1959. *Acts: The Acts of the Apostles: A Historical Commentary.* Grand Rapids, MI: Eerdmans.

Bock, D. 1993. "Athenians who have Never Heard." In *Through No Fault of Their Own? The Fate of Those Who Have Never Heard.* William B. Crocket and James G. Sigountos, eds. Pp. 118ff. Grand Rapids, MI: Baker.

Boice, J.M. 1997. *Acts: An Expositional Commentary.* Grand Rapids, MI: Baker Books.

Bruce, F.F. 1998. Acts: *New International Commentary on the New Testament.* Grand Rapids, MI: Eerdmans.

Clarke, A.D. and B. W. Winter. 1991. *One God One Lord in a World of Religious Pluralism.* Cambridge: Tyndale House.

Conybeare, W.J. and J.S. Howson. 1949. *The Life and Epistles of Paul.* Grand Rapids, MI: Eerdmans.

Conzelmann, H. 1966. "The Address of Paul" in *Studies in Luke.* Nashville,TN: Abingdon Press.

Cotterell, P. 1993. *Mission and Meaninglessness.* London: SPCK.

Deissmann, A. 1926. *Paul.* London: Hodder and Stoughton.

Demarest, Bruce A. 1992. *One God, One Lord.* Grand Rapids, MI: Baker.

De Silva, Lynn. 1974. *Buddhism: Beliefs and Practices in Sri Lanka.* Colombo: The Wesley Press.

Dharmaraj, J.S. 1993. *Colonialism and Christian Mission: Post Colonial Reflection,* Delhi: ISPCK.

Dibelius, M. 1956. "Paulon the Areopagus." In *Studies in the Acts of the Apostles.* London: SCM Press.

Dunn, J.D.G. 1996. *Acts: Epworth Commentaries.* Peterborough: Epworth Press.

Fernando, Ajith. 1998. *Acts: The NIV Application Commentary.* Grand Rapids, MI: Zondervan.

Gartner, B. 1955. *The Areopagus Speech and Natural Revelation.* Uppsala: Gleerup.

Gogerly, D. J. 1831. *Missionary Letter.* London: Archives.

Goldingay, J.E. and C.J.H. Wright. 1991. "Yahweh our God, Yahweh One." In *One God One Lord in a World of Religious Pluralism.* D. Clarke and B. Winter, eds. Cambridge: Tyndale House.

Gombrich, R. and G. Obeyesekere, 1988. *Buddhism Transformed: Religious Change in Sri Lanka.* Princeton: Princeton University Press.

Gombrich, R. "The consecration of a Buddhist image." *Journal of Asian Studies.* 26/1 (1966): 23-36.

Grayston, Kenneth. 1966. *Theology as Exploration.* London.

Grimm, C.L.W. and J.H. Thayer. 1889. *A Greek-English Lexicon of the New Testament*. Edinburgh.

Haenchen, E. 1971. *The Acts of the Apostles: A Commentary*. Philadelphia. PA: Westminster Press.

Henry, C.F.H. 1991. "Is it Fair?" In *Through No Fault of their Own*. William V. Crockett and James G. Sigountos, eds. Pp. 284. Grand Rapids, MI: Baker Books House.

Ilangasinha, H.B.M. 1992. *Buddhism in Medieval Sri Lanka*. South Asia Books.

Jayatilleke, K.N. 2000. *The Message of the Buddha*. Kandy: Buddhist Publication Society.

Keener, C.S. 1993. *The IVP Bible Background Commentary*. Downer's Grove, IL: Intervarsity Press.

Kittle, G. and G. Friedrich, ed. 1965 *Theological Dictionary of the New Testament Volume 3*. Grand Rapids, MI: Eerdmans.

Larkin, William J. 1995. *Acts*. Downers Grove, IL: InterVarsity Press.

Longenecker. R.N. 1992. *Acts: The Expositor's Bible Commentary Volume 9*. Grand Rapids, MI: Zondervan.

Marshall, I. Howard. 1988. *Acts: Tyndale New Testament Commentary*. Leicester: Inter-Varsity Press.

Nyanatiloka, M. 1964. *Karma and Rebirth*. Kandy: Buddhist Publication Society.

Neil, W. 1973. *Acts: New Century Bible*. London: Marshall, Morgan and Scott.

Panikkar, R. 1964. *The Unknown Christ of Hinduism*. Darton: Longman and Todd.

Polhill, John B. 1992. *Acts: The New American Commentary*. Nashville, TN: Broadman and Holman.

Rahula, W. 1959. *What the Buddha Taught*. New York: Grove Press.

Renehan, R. 1979. "Acts 17:28" In *Greek, Roman and Byzantine Studies*, 20.

Richardson, D. 1984. *Eternity in Their Hearts*. Ventura: Regal Books.

Small, W.J.T. 1971. *A History of the Methodist Church in Ceylon*. Colombo: Wesley Press.

Sproul, R.C. 1982. *Reason to Believe*. Grand Rapids, MI: Zondervan.

Stob, R. 1950. *Christianity and Classical Civilization*. Grand Rapids, MI: Eerdmans.

Stonehouse, N.B. 1957. *Paul Before the Areopagus and Other New Testament Studies*. Grand Rapids, MI: Eerdmans.

Stott, John R.W. 1994. *The Message of Acts: The Bible Speaks Today*. Leicester: Inter-Varsity Press.

Talbert, C.H. 1984. *Acts: Knox Preaching Guides*. Atlanta, GA: John Knox Press.

Toussaint, S.D. 1983. *Acts: The Bible Knowledge Commentary New Testament*. Wheaton, IL: Victor Books.

Weerasingha, Tissa. 1989. *The Cross and the Bo Tree*. Taichung, Taiwan: Asia Theological Association.

Wijebandara, C. 1993. *Early Buddhism: Its Religious and Intellectual Milieu*. Sri Lanka: Postgraduate Institute of Pali and Buddhist Studies, University of Kelaniya.

Williams, D.J. 1985. *Acts: A Good News Commentary*. San Francisco: Harper and Row.

Wright, C. 1994. "The Unique Christ in the Plurality of Religions" In *The Unique Christ in our Pluralistic World*. B.J. Nicholl, ed. Grand Rapids, MI: Baker.

Wycherley, R.E. 1968. "St. Paul at Athens" *Journal of Theological Studies*.

Chapter 4

Braswell, George W., Jr. 1994. *Understanding World Religions*. Nashville, TN: Broadman and Homan Publishers.

Davis, John R. 1998. *Poles Apart; Contextualizing the Gospel in Asia*. Bangalore: Asia Theological Association.

Dryness, William A. 1990. *Learning About Theology from the Third World*. Grand Rapids, MI: Zondervan.

Harvey, Peter. 1990. *An Introduction to Buddhism: Teachings, History and Practices*. Cambridge: Cambridge University Press.

Holmes, David. 1997. *The Heart of Theravada Buddhism: The Noble Eightfold Path*. Bangkok: International Commercial Company (ICC) Publishing and Communications.

Hong-Shik Shin. 1990. *The Thought and Life of Hinayana Buddhism*. Bangkok: Kanok Bannasan (OMF Publishers).

Igleheart, Glenn. 1985. *Interfaith Witnessing; A Guide for Southern Baptists*. Richmond, VA:Foreign Mission Board.

Khantipalo, Bhikkhu. 1989. *Buddhism Explained, An Introduction to the Teaching of Lord Buddha.* Chiang Mai: Silkworm Books.

Lohitkun, Teeraparb. 1995. *Tai in Southeast Asia.* Bangkok: Manager Publishing.

Marshall, David. 1996. *How Jesus Fulfills the Chinese Culture.* Seattle, WA: Kuai Mu Press.

Niles, D. T. 1967. *Buddhism and the Claims of Christ; The Christian Dogmas.* Richmond, VA: John Knox Press.

Piper, John. 1993. *Let the Nations Be Glad! The Supremacy of God in Missions.* Grand Rapids, MI: Baker Books.

Raguin, Yves, S.J. 1997. *Transplanting the Lotus* "Areopagus: A Living Encounter With Today's Religious World" Winter/Spring 1997(9)4.

Richardson, Don. 1981. *Eternity in Their Hearts.* Ventura, CA: Regal Books.

Tannenbaum, Nicola Beth. 1995. *Who Can Compete Against the World? Power-Protection and Buddhism in Shan Worldview.* Ann Arbor, MI: Association for Asian Studies.

Willard, Dallas. 1998. *The Divine Conspiracy; Rediscovering our Hidden Life in God.* San Francisco: Harper Collins.

_____. 2002. *Renovation of the Heart; Putting on the Character of Christ.* Colorado Springs, CO; NavPress.

Yos Santasombat. 2001. *Lak Chang; A Reconstruction of Tai Identity in Daikong.* Canberra: Pandanus Books.

Chapter 5

Aikman, David. 2003. *Jesus In Beijing: How Christianity is Transforming China and Changing the Balance of Power. Washington, D.C.:* Regnery Publishing.

Bailey, Stephen. 2002. "*Communication Strategies for Christian Witness Among the Lowland Lao Informed By Worldview Themes in Khwan Rituals.*" Doctoral Dissertation. Pasadena, CA: Fuller Theological Seminary.

_____. 2003. "Communication Strategies for Christian Witness Among the Lao." In *Sharing Jesus in the Buddhist World.* David Lim and Steve Spaulding, eds. Pasadena, CA: William Carey Library.

Barrett, David B., George T. Kurian and Todd M. Johnson, eds. 2001. *World Christian Encyclopedia: A Comprehensive Survey of Churches and Religions in the Modern World.* New York: Oxford University Press.

Jenkins, Philip. 2002. *The New Christendom.* Oxford University Press.

Kraft, Charles. 1999. "Contextualization in Three Dimensions." Inaugural Lecture, Chair of Global Mission. October 20. Fuller Theological Seminary.

Ladwig, Patrice. 2003. "Death Rituals Among the Lao: An Ethnological Analysis." *Tai Culture* 15(1).

Lefferts, H. Leedom, Jr., 1999. "Women's Power and Theravada Buddhism." In *Laos: Culture and Society.* Grant Evans, ed. Chiang Mai, Thailand: Silkworm Books.

Mulder, Niels. 1979. "The Concepts of Power and Moral Goodness in the Contemporary Thai Worldview." *Journal of the Siam Society* 67(1).

Reynolds, Frank E.. 1978. "Ritual and Social Hierarchy: An Aspect of Traditional Religion in Buddhist Laos." In *Religion and Legitimation of Power in Thailand, Laos, and Burma.* Bardwell L. Smith, ed. Chambersburg, PA: ANIMA Books.

Sanneh, Lamin. 2003. *Whose Religion is Christianity? The Gospel Beyond the West.* Grand Rapids, MI: Eerdmans.

_____. 1996. *Translating the Message: The Missionary Impact on Culture.* New York: Orbis Books.

Tambiah, Stanley J. 1970. *Buddhism and the Spirit Cults in Northeast Thailand.* Cambridge: Cambridge University Press.

Chapter 6

Anderson, C. A. 1964. *A Dictionary of the Social Sciences.* New York: The Free Press.

Carrithers, M. 1992. *Why Humans Have Cultures: Explaining Anthropology and Social Diversity.* Oxford: Oxford University Press.

DeNeui, Paul H. 2003. "Contextualizing With Thai Folk Buddhists." In *Sharing Jesus in the Buddhist World.* David Lim and Steve Spaulding, eds. Pasadena, CA: William Carey Library.

Hofstede, G. 1982. *Culture's Consequences: International Differences in Work-Related Values.* Abridged ed. Beverly Hills, CA: Sage.

Johnson, Alan. R. 2004. *Structural and Ministry Philosophy Issues in Church Planting Among Buddhist Peoples.* Paper presented at the SEANET Missiological Forum, Chiang Mai, Thailand.

Mejudhon, Nanthachai. 1997. *Meekness: A New Approach to Christian Witness to the Thai People.* Unpublished D. Miss., Asbury, KY: Asbury Theological Seminary.

Mejudhon, Ubolwan. 2003. "An Integrated Model of Evangelism to Buddhists Using Theology, Anthropology, and Religious Studies." In *Sharing Jesus in the Buddhist World.* David Lim and Steve Spaulding, eds. Pasadena, CA: William Carey Library.

Mulder, Niels 1997. *Thai Images: The Culture of the Public World.* Bangkok, Thailand: Silkworm Books.

Chapter 7

Berentsen, Jan-Martin. 1985. "Ancestor Worship in Missiological Perspective," In *Christian Alternatives to Ancestor Practices.* Bong Rin Ro, ed. Taichung, Taiwan: Asia Theological Association.

Bowers, Russell H. 2003. *Folk Buddhism in Southeast Asia.* Cambodia: Training of Timothys.

Grunlan, Stephen A. and Marvin K. Mayers. 1979. *Cultural Anthropology: A Christian Perspective.* Grand Rapids, MI: Zondervan,

Henry, Rodney L. 1986. *Filipino Spirit World.* Manila, Philippines: OMF Literature Inc.

Hung, Daniel. 1983. "M Blockage: Ancestor Worship," *EMQ.* 19(1). Hwang, Bernard. 1977. Ancestor Cult Today," *Missiology* V(3).

Hickey, Gerald. 1964. *Village in Viet Nam.* New Haven, CT: Yale University Press.

Hiebert, Paul G. 1985. *Anthropological Insights for Missionaries.* Grand Rapids MI: Baker Book House.

_____. 1993. "Popular Religions," *Toward the Twenty-first Century in Christian Mission,* Grand Rapids MI: Eerdmans.

Kraft, Charles H. 1991. *Christianity in Culture.* Maryknoll, NY: Orbis.

Liao, David C. E. 1972. *The Unresponsive: Resistant or Neglected?* Chicago, IL: Moody Press.

Liaw, Stephen. 1983. "Ancestor Worship in Taiwan and Evangelism of the Chinese." In *Christian Alternatives to Ancestor Practices.* Bong Rin Ro, ed. Taichung, Taiwan: ATA.

Lowe, Chuck. 2001. *Honoring God and Family: A Christian Response to Idol Food in Chinese Popular Religion.* Wheaton IL: EMIS.

Maguire, Jack. 2001. *Essential Buddhism: A Complete Guide to Beliefs and Practices.* New York: Pocket Books.

Nyanasamvara, Somdet Phra. n.d. *Forty-Five Years of the Buddha (Book One).* Thailand: The Buddhist University.

Peiris, Ralph. 1956. *Sinhalese Social Organization.* Colombo: Ceylon University Press.

Reimer, Reginald E. 1975. "The Religious Dimension of the Vietnamese Cult of the Ancestors." *Missiology.* III (2).

Ro, Bong Rin, ed. 1985. *Christian Alternatives to Ancestor Practices.* Taichung, Taiwan: Asia Theological Association.

Samagalski, Alan. 1984. *China – A Travel Survival Kit.* Hong Kong: Lonely Planet Publications.

Shibata, Chizuo. 1985. "Some Problematic Aspects of Japanese Ancestor Worship," In *Christian Alternatives to Ancestor Practices.* Bong Rin Ro, ed. Taichung, Taiwan: ATA.

Tan, Kim-Sai. 1985. "Christian Alternatives to Ancestor Worship in Malaysia." In *Christian Alternatives to Ancestor Practices.* Bong Rin Ro, ed. Taichung, Taiwan: ATA.

Taylor, John V. 1963. *The Primal Vision.* London: SCM Press.

Taylor, Robert B. 1973. *Introduction to Cultural Anthropology.* Boston: Allyn and Bacon Inc.

Tylor, Edward B. 1889. *Primitive Cultures.* New York: Henry Holt and Company.

Van Engen, Charles E. 1998. "Reflecting Theologically about the Resistant." In *Reaching the Resistant: Barriers and Bridges for Mission.* Pasadena, CA: William Carey Library.

Weerasingha, Tissa. 1989. *The Cross and the Bo Tree.* Taichung, Taiwan: Asia Theological Association.

Wei, Yuan-Kwei. 1985. "Historical Analysis of Ancestor Worship in Ancient China." In *Christian Alternatives to Ancestor Practices.* Bong Rin Ro, ed. Taichung, Taiwan: ATA.

Chapter 8

Abeyasinghe, Tikiri. 1966. *Portuguese Rule in Ceylon*. Colombo: Lake House.

Ariyapala, M.B. 1968. *Society in Medieval Ceylon*. Colombo: Dept. of Cultural Affairs.

Baldaeus, Philip. 1996. *Description of the Great Island and Most Famous Isle of Ceylon*. New Delhi: Asian Educational Services.

Bechert, Heinz and Richard Gombrich. 1991. *The World of Buddhism*. London: Thames and Hudson.

Berwick, T. 1870. *Judicial Report: Kandy Administration Report*. Colombo: Government Press.

Cordiner, James. 1807. *A Description of Ceylon*. London: Longman, Hurst, Rees, and Orme.

Darling, Evangeline. 1991. *Story of a Christian Mission*. Dehiwela: Sri Devi Printers.

Davy, John. 1987. *An Account of the Interior of Ceylon and of its Inhabitants with Travels in that Island*, first printed 1821, Dehiwela: Tisara.

De Silva, K.M. 1959. *University of Ceylon: History of Ceylon*, vol. 3. Colombo: Ceylon University Press.

D'Oyly, John. 1938. *Letters to Ceylon 1814-1824*. London: Heffer and Sons Limited.

De Queyroz, Fernao. 1982. *The Temporal and Spiritual Conquest of Ceylon*. India: Asian Educational Services.

Disanayake, J.B. 1999. *Gamaka Suvanda Siv Siya Gav Aseya*. Colombo: Lakehouse.

Ellawala, H. 1962. *Purana Lanakave Samaja Itihasaya*. Colombo: Cultural Department.

Gombrich, Richard, ed. 1991. *The World of Buddhism*. Delhi: Motilal Banarsidas.

Gombrich, Richard and Gananatha Obeyesekere. 1990. *Buddhism Transformed*. Delhi: Motalal Banarsidass.

Harvey, Peter. 2004. *An Introduction to Buddhism*. Cambridge: University Press.

Kumaa, Hemantha. 2001. *Pavula ha Vivahaya*. Mulleriyava, Wiejesooriya: Book Centrem.

Herath, H.M.D.R. December 24, 2004. "The Practicality of Kandyan Wedding Rituals" (Sinhala) *Lakbima*.

Hinnells, John R., ed. 1995. *A New Dictionary of Religions.*
      Oxford: Blackwell.
Humphreys, Christmas. 1984. *A Popular Dictionary of Buddhism.*
      London: Buddhist Society.
Knox, Robert. 1681. *Historical Relation of the Island of Ceylon.*
      London: R. Chiswell.
Leach, Edmund. 1982. *Social Anthropology.* London: Fontana Books.
Liyangamege, Amaradasa. 1968. *The Decline of Polonnaruwa and
      the Rise of Dambadeniay.* Colombo: Government Press.
Malalgoda, Kitsiri. 1976. *Buddhism in Sinhalese Society, 1750-
      1900.* Berkeley, CA: University of California Press.
Obeyesekere, Gananath. 1963. "The Great Tradition and the Little
      in the Perspective of Sinhalese Buddhism." *Journal of Royal
      Asiatic Society.* XXII(2).
Olcott, Henry Steel. 1942. *Buddhist Catechism.* Reprinted. Kessinger Pub.
Parker, H. 1982. *Village Falk Tales of Ceylon.* Dehiwela: Tisara Press.
Peiris, Ralph. 1956. *Sinhalaese Social Organization: The Kandyan Period.*
      Colombo: University of Ceylon Press.
Pieris, P.E., ed. 1910. *History of Ceylon with a Summary of de Barros and
      de Couto, Antinio Bacarro and the Documentos Remittidos with
      Paranagi Hatana and Kustantinu Hatana.* Colombo: Government
      Press.
Percival, Robert. 1803. *An Account of the Island of Ceylon.* India:
      Asian Educational Services.
Ray, H.C., ed. 1959. *University of Ceylon, History of Ceylon,* vol. 1, part
      1. Colombo: University Press.
Ribeiro, Juao. 1685. *Fatalidado Historica da Ilha de Ceilao.* Asian
      Educational Services (English).
Senaratna, P.M. 1999. *Srilankakave Vivaha Caritra,* Colombo: Gunasena.
Spiro, Milford E. 1971. *Buddhism and Society: A Great Tradition and its
      Burmese Vicissitudes,* London: George Allen and Unwin Ltd.
Sri Lanka National Archives. 1968. Document no. 5/63/1/45/68.
Suravira, A.V., ed. 1976. *Rajavaliya.* Colombo: Lake House.
Wickremesinghe, K.D.P. 2002. *The Biography of the Buddha,*
      Colombo: PLW Company.
Wijetunga, Harischandra. 1984. *Practical Sinhalese Dictionary,*
      Colombo: Cultural Department.
Walshe, M.O.C. 1986. *Buddhism and Sex.* Buddhist Publication Society.
Wright, Arnold. 1907. Twentieth Century Impressions of Ceylon.

Chapter 9

The Holy Bible. 1984. New International Version. Grand Rapids, MI: Zondervan Publishers.

St. Augustine, Augustinus. 1957. *Die Wolke der Zeugen (The Cloud of Witnesses).* Verlag, Germany: Johannes Stauda.

Mulder, Niels. 1978. *Everyday Life in Thailand: An Interpretation.* Bangkok Thailand: Ruen Kaew Press.

St. John, Marden. 1996. *Self-Understanding of Thai: Targeting a Message So it Hits the Mark!* (Self-published).

Sauer, Erich. 1978. *From Eternity to Eternity.* Exeter, Great Britain: Paternoster Press. 2nd ed.

Skinner, G.William and Kirsch, A. Thomas, ed. 1975. *Change and Persistence in Thai Society.* Ithaca, NY: Cornell University Press.

Spiro, Melford E. 1970. *Buddhism and Society: A Great Tradition and Its Burmese Vicissitudes.* New York: Harper Paperbacks.

Sponberg, Alan and Helen Hardacre, eds. 1988. *Maitreya, The Future Buddha.* Cambridge, NY: Cambridge University Press.

Tambiah, S.J. 1975. *Buddhism and the Spirit Cults in North-East Thailand.* Cambridge, NY: Cambridge University Press.

Chapter 10

Allen, Roland. 1962. *Missionary Methods: St. Paul's or Ours?* Grand Rapids, MI: Eerdmans.

———. 1962a. *The Spontaneous Expansion of the Church.* Grand Rapids, MI: Eerdmans.

Andres, Tomas. 1988. *Community Development: A Manual.* Quezon City: New Day Publishers.

Barrett, David and Johnson, Todd. 2004. "Status of Global Mission, 2004, in Context of 20th and 21st Centuries," *International Bulletin of Missionary Research* 28.1 (January 2004):25.

Bobo, Kimberly. 1986. *Lives Matter: A Handbook for Christian Organizing.* Kansas City, MO: Sheed and Ward.

Boff, Leonardo. 1986. *Ecclesiogenesis.* Maryknoll, NY: Orbis.

Carr, Neville. 1994. "Evaluating Theological Education: Ten Biblical Criteria,",In *Directions in Theological Education.* L. Wanak, ed. Manila: PABATS.

Coleman, Robert. 1964. *The Master Plan of Evangelism.* Old Tappan, NJ: Revell.

Comiskey, Joel. 1999. *Groups of 12*. Houston: Touch Publications.

Craig, Jenny. 1996. "The Relevance of a Liberation Theology Hermeneutic for Filipino Theology," *Phronesis* 3(1).

Donovan, Vincent. 1978. *Christianity Rediscovered*. London: SCM.

Eims, Leroy. 1981.*The Lost Art of Disciple Making*. Colorado Springs, CO: NavPress.

Escobar, Samuel. 2000."Evangelical Missiology: Peering into the Future at the 21st Century." In *Global Missiology for the 21st Century: The Iguassu Dialogue*. W. Taylor, ed. Grand Rapids, MI: Baker.

Garrison, David. 1999. *Church Planting Movements*. International Mission Board of the Southern Baptist Convention. Richmond, VA: Office of Overseas Operations.

_____. 2004. *Church Planting Movements*. Midlothian,VA: WIGTake Resources.

Gauran, Johani. 1991. *The Witnessing Kit*. Makati City: Church Strengthening Ministry.

Hattaway, Paul, et al. 2003. *Back to Jerusalem*. Carlisle: Piquant

Hunter, George III. 2000. *The Celtic Way of Evangelism*. Nashville, TN: Abingdon.

Koyama, Kosuke. 1999. *Waterbuffalo Theology (25th Anniv. Ed.)*. Maryknoll, New York: Orbis.

Lim, David. 1987. *The Servant Nature of the Church in the Pauline Corpus*. Ph.D. Diss. Pasadena, CA: Fuller Theological Seminary.

_____. 1992. *Transforming Communities*. Manila: OMF Literature.

_____. 2001. "Why Local Churches Hinder Real Church Growth." Quezon City: CMI-Phil.

_____. 2003. "Towards a Radical Contextualization Paradigm in Evangelizing Buddhists." In *Sharing Jesus in the Buddhist World*. David Lim and Steve Spaulding, eds. Pp. 71-94. Pasadena, CA: William Carey Library.

_____. 2004. "Mobilizing Churches for Evangelism and Missions," 2004. Paper presented to Focus Group #10 of Lausanne Congress 2004; *Journal of Asian Mission* 6:1.

Linthicum, Robert. 1991. *Empowering the Poor*. Monrovia, CA: MARC.

Mendoza, Ernesto. 1999. *Radical and Evangelical: Portrait of a Filipino Christian*. Quezon City: New Day Publishers.

Montgomery, Jim. 2001. *I'm Gonna Let It Shine!* Pasadena, CA: W. Carey Library.

Myers, Bryant. 1999. *Walking with the Poor*. Maryknoll, NY: Orbis.

Neighbor, Ralph, Jr. 1990. *Where Do We Go from Here?* Houston, TX:Touch Publications.

Petersen, Jim. 1992. *Church Without Walls.* Colorado Springs, CO: NavPress.

Ringma, Charles. 1992. *Catch the Wind.* Manila: OMF Lit.

_____. 1996. "Adult Christian Education and Theological Hermeneutics," *Phronesis* 3:1 (1996).

Samuel, V. and C. Sugden. 1999. *Mission as Transformation.* Oxford: Regnum.

Schumacher, E. F. 1984. *Small is Beautiful.* London: Abacus.

Simson, Wolfgang. 2001. *Houses That Change the World.* Carlisle: Paternoster.

Sluka, M. and T. Budiardjo. 1995. "A Church Emerging in Rural Cambodia." In *Serving with the Poor in Asia.* Ted Yamamori, B. Myers and D. Conner, eds. Monrovia, CA: MARC.

Snyder, Howard. 1975. *The Problem of Wineskins.* Downers Grove, IL: IVP.

Stephens, George. 1995. "Living a New Reality in Kandy, Sri Lanka." In *Serving with the Poor in Asia.* Ted Yamamori, B. Myers and D. Conner, eds. Monrovia, CA: MARC.

Suderman, Robert. 1999. *Calloused Hands, Courageous Souls: Holistic Spirituality of Development and Mission.* Monrovia, CA: MARC.

Wanak, Lee. 1994. "Church and School in Symbiotic Relationship: Toward a Theology of Specialized Institutions." In *Directions in Theological Education.* Manila: PABATS.

Yamamori, Ted, B. Myers and D. Conner, eds. 1995. *Serving with the Poor in Asia.* Monrovia, CA: MARC.

_____, _____, and K. Luscombe, eds. 1998. *Serving with the Urban Poor.* Monrovia, CA: MARC.

Zdero, Rad. 2004. *The Global House Church Movement.* Pasadena, CA: William Carey Library.

INDEX